C000195707

"*A wonderfully lucid and fascinating book of the Las Vegas
scene during the mobster days and the transition to corporate
ownership of the casinos. A fascinating book of stories, facts, and
illustrations of one of the most interesting cities in the world.
Andy's personality shows though in his fluid writing style.
A most enjoyable must read book.*"

—"BR" Bob L. Riley, Aerospace Engineer, poker player,
author many aerospace and fighter technical papers,
AGARD World paper 1979, John Player British Engineer of the
year 1985, NAA F/A-18 E/F Aircraft Collier Trophy Award 1999.

"*Very enjoyable and interesting read. I want a copy of the
completed book. Thanks for sharing the Intro. My opinion: Anyone
with a gambling/Vegas background will be interested in this book.*"

—Al Rainosek, Ph.D

ALSO BY ANDREW J. MᶜLEAN

Trump Strategies For Real Estate:
Billionaire Lessons For the Small Investor,
with lead author George H. Ross. 2005

Investing in Real Estate,
with Gary Eldred, 6th edition

Casino Player's Handbook: The Ultimate Guide
to Where and How to Play in America's Casinos

The RV Book: The Ultimate Guide
to Selecting and Operating a Recreational Vehicle

The Complete Guide to Real Estate Loans

Making Money in Foreclosures: How to Invest Profitably
in Distressed Real Estate

The Las Vegas Chronicles

THE INSIDE STORY OF SIN CITY, CELEBRITIES, SPECIAL PLAYERS AND FASCINATING CASINO OWNERS

ANDREW J. McLEAN

SCOTLINE
SL
PRESS

D'Iberville, Mississippi

Publisher's Cataloging-in-Publication
(Provided by Quality Books, Inc.)
McLean, Andrew James.
Las Vegas chronicles : the inside story of mob
activity, memorable celebrities, special players, and
fascinating casino owners / Andrew James McLean.
p. cm.
Includes bibliographical references and index.
"Featuring the saga of Billy Wilkerson, the
man who invented Las Vegas."
ISBN-13: 978-0-9658499-5-1
ISBN-10: 0-9658499-5-3
Library of Congress Control Number: 2011910104

1. Las Vegas (Nev.)--History--Anecdotes. 2. Las
Vegas (Nev.)--Biography--Anecdotes. 3. Las Vegas (Nev.)
--Social life and customs--Anecdotes. 4. Celebrities--
Nevada--Las Vegas--Biography--Anecdotes. 5. Organized
crime--Nevada--Las Vegas--History--Anecdotes.
6. Wilkerson, Billy, 1890-1962. I. Title.

F849.L35M35 2011 979.3'135
QBI11-600030

Library of Congress Cataloging-in-Publication Data:
McLean, Andrew J., 1944 –
The las vegas chronicles: The inside story of mob activity, memorable celebrities, special players, and fascinating casino owners / Andrew James McLean.

Includes bibliographical references and index.

Scotline Press, LLC
D'lberville, Mississippi
For information on other books by Andrew J. McLean,
visit his website at: www.AndrewJamesMcLean.com

Celebrity charcoal portraits by David Tomasovsky, Gulfport, MS.
Cover and interior design by Concierge Marketing, Inc.

Printed in the United States of America
10   9   8   7   6   5   4   3   2   1

ACKNOWLEDGMENTS

Part of the enjoyment of writing a book like this is to thank everyone who gave of their time and memories. Special thanks to Jenny Rouse for being my copy editor, and Chris Roerden for the final line edit. Also, appreciation to Michael Groetsch, Bruce Davis and George Thatcher for their helpful input.

CONTENTS

FOREWORD

I first met Andrew McLean in a poker game at the Grand Casino in Biloxi, Mississippi during the summer of 1998. After learning that we were both authors (Andy has authored 10 published books to my 2) and has common interests that include poker and redheads (our soul-mates), we were destined to become close friends. Even the fury of Hurricane Katrina that destroyed our homelands—Biloxi and New Orleans — could not destroy our friendship. We have and will always be committed to sharing stories that make others think and sometimes smile.

As an avid poker player, Andy is the only friend I have that can simultaneously discuss No-Limit Texas Hold'em and the intricacies of book publishing within the same sentence. In that respect, he discusses both topics with the passion that it takes to be a good writer. Andy's ability as a prolific storyteller comes through in *The Las Vegas Chronicles* in a way that only he can tell.

When Andy first asked me to write his Foreword, I hesitated to take on another project. After agreeing to review his opening chapter, I found time to read it while eating lunch in a small New Orleans restaurant. It was at that moment that I realized that Andy had written a winner. Although I am someone whose attention span is limited in duration, I became enthralled in his work. It brought me back to a place and time so filled with suspense and intrigue that I read his 31 page opening before finishing desert. Andy's saga of Billy Wilkerson, the man who invented Las Vegas, and his unlikely Mob-associated partner, Bugsy Siegel, certainly warrants the attention of Hollywood producers.

Andy's prior books cover an eclectic range of topics that includes finance, real estate and the casino industry. His most notable work, a bestseller in four languages, is *Investing In Real Estate* currently in its sixth edition. His more recent book *Trump Strategies for Real Estate*, also a bestseller and co-authored with George H. Ross, Donald Trump's right-hand man, provides Andy with a fan base that's thirsty for more. Although the *Las Vegas Chronicles* is a deviation from his past writings, it is perhaps his best. His 19 years working in the casino industry has provided him with the insight necessary in understanding how "Sin City" earned its name and reputation.

His fabulous book *The Las Vegas Chronicles* proves that "What Happens in Vegas" doesn't necessarily stay in Las Vegas. It only stays hidden until a prolific writer like Andy McLean digs it up from the shadows of the graveyard.

— Michael J. Groetsch
Author of *He Promised He'd Stop*
and *The Battering Syndrome*

Chapter 1
BILLY WILKERSON—THE MAN WHO INVENTED LAS VEGAS

*"I got it. I got it. It came to me like a vision. Like a religious
epiphany. I am talking about the single biggest idea ever had...
What do people fantasize about? Sex, romance, money, adventure.
I'm building a monument to all of it! I've found the answer to the
dreams of America. I'm talking about a hotel. I'm talking about a
place where gambling is allowed, where everything is allowed. The
whole territory is wide open. I'm talking about where everything
is allowed. I'm talking about a place, an oasis, a city. I'm talking
about Las Vegas, Nevada!"*[1]

—Ben Siegel,
as portrayed by Warren Beatty in the 1991 film *Bugsy*

*B*lending fact with a large helping of fiction, the producers of the film Bugsy would have you believe mobster "Bugsy" Siegel dreamt up the famed Flamingo Hotel. From there, it's easy to see how an eccentric killer could be endowed in legend as the creator of the modern city of Las Vegas.

The movie's closing credits gave further credence to this deeply rooted legend by claiming the events portrayed were based in fact. In reality, Bugsy—with financial assistance from Meyer Lansky's East Coast Mob—took over the famed casino resort long after construction began. The only legend Siegel built was his reputation as a psychotic killer, responsible for at least 25 murders.

If not Bugsy Siegel, who did create the famed Flamingo Hotel? This is the hotel that evolved into the fabulous Las Vegas Strip, the gaming and entertainment capital of the world?

Contrary to the fictionalized film version, the man behind the Flamingo Hotel was a successful nightclub owner and acclaimed publisher of the *Hollywood Reporter*. William R. "Billy" Wilkerson earned his notoriety and much of his wealth from the five famous nightclubs he built along Hollywood's glamorous Sunset Strip during the 1930s and early 1940s.

Wilkerson's experience as a shrewd nightclub owner together with his love of gambling inevitably led him to Las Vegas, where he bought the 33-acre site on which the Flamingo stands today. Using his own money, he designed and built the initial stages of the famed resort.

With some inaccuracies, the film *Bugsy* depicts the decades of intrigue surrounding mob activity in the operation of Las Vegas casinos. The city's forefathers and current resort owners weren't about to correct the fallacies because the Bugsy Siegel legend brought considerable notoriety to Las Vegas, attracting the press and the public in droves. In reality, the only thing Siegel ever built was his reputation as a psychotic killer, responsible for at least 25 murders.

Billy Wilkerson

After the Flamingo's completion, other entrepreneurs emulated Wilkerson's palatial resort idea, building luxurious casino hotels nearby, including the Desert Inn and the Sands. Almost overnight, Las Vegas seemed transformed from a sandy, remote whistle stop to a neon-lit metropolis featuring some of the largest and most luxurious casino-resort hotels on the planet.

True, Bugsy and the "boys" muscled in on the resort casino with suitcases full of cash during the Flamingo's latter phase of construction. But the original concept of the resort and its creation was entirely Wilkerson's. In time, the gambling-addicted Hollywood publisher was justly credited with also inventing the Las Vegas Strip.

Ben Siegel, on the other hand, would surely be bugged about the name of a film describing his life as a ruthless mobster, even though he'd be elated to know he'd passed the screen test and gone on to make the Hollywood big screen.

MYTHS ARE CREATED
WHEN THE TRUTH IS FORGOTTEN

In *The Man Who Invented Las Vegas*, Billy Wilkerson's son, W. R. Wilkerson III, recalled the children's game of Telephone in which one person whispers a single word in the first child's ear with instructions to pass it on. One by one, the youngsters whisper the word around the group until it reaches the last child, who announces the secret "The word was never the same. At some point it became convoluted," Wilkerson's son wrote. "Myths are created in the same fashion. They spring to life the moment the truth is forgotten. They are further distorted by the permutations of the Telephone Game of History. As myths are passed on by word of mouth, they become universally accepted as truth. Myths also tend to elbow aside rightful claimants who remain silent."[2]

Billy Wilkerson was a rightful claimant to the Flamingo's role in Las Vegas fame, but he chose to remain silent. The Flamingo debacle turned out to be a very disappointing episode in his life. Wanting nothing more to do with the undertaking, following Siegel's death he never did take credit as the hotel's founder. After Billy was legally released from the project in 1947, he distanced himself from the Flamingo, almost never speaking of it. The lore of Las Vegas, of course, fulfilled his wishes by crediting the Flamingo's creation to his former pupil and archenemy.

Truth be known, the Flamingo was a huge flop when it opened in 1946—many years after the successful debuts of the western-themed El Rancho Vegas in 1941, the Pair-O-Dice Club in 1931 (which later became the Last Frontier), and a few sawdust joints that existed along downtown's Fremont Street.

For the captivating true story of the legendary Flamingo Hotel and how the fabulous Las Vegas Strip evolved from its creation, let's turn to Billy Wilkerson's life story.

BILLY WILKERSON'S EARLY LIFE

Born in September 1890 in Nashville, Tennessee, Wilkerson developed an early interest in the medical field. After his family relocated to Philadelphia, Pennsylvania, he began studying medicine until his father, a renowned gambler, died unexpectedly and left behind a huge mountain of debt. Wilkerson was forced to give up his medical training and find employment to support himself and his mother.

A short time later, in a stroke of luck for Wilkerson, a friend from medical school placed a World Series wager and won. "The prize" A small Nickelodeon in Fort Lee, New Jersey, which Wilkerson agreed to manage in exchange for a share of the profits. Visions of a medical career faded into memory as Wilkerson discovered his penchant for the fledgling movie industry. Between 1918 and 1929, he held a variety of movie-related jobs from the production of one-reelers to sales. During this period he also served as District Manager for Universal Pictures, which led him to abandon the East Coast for Southern California, the heart of the movie industry. There, he turned his earlier investment in a New York trade paper into the first daily trade paper for the movie industry.

WILKERSON
MOVES TO HOLLYWOOD

Intending to leave New York City and begin a new life in California, Billy Wilkerson, in October 1929 at the age of thirty nine, sold his interest in his daily trade paper for $20,000. Unfortunately, he met a stockbroker, took his advice, and in one day invested the entire proceeds, plus a $25,000 loan, in the stock market. That ill-fated day was Black Tuesday, the day the stock market crashed and set off the Great Depression. Almost penniless, and in debt as his father had been, Wilkerson left New York City the same afternoon, and with his wife and daughter, motored cross-country to make their home in Hollywood.

Less than a year later and with the help of investors who believed in his trade paper idea, Wilkerson realized his dream with publication of his first edition of the *Hollywood Reporter*. The magazine "reported on movies, studios, and personalities in an outrageously candid style." By 1936, the controversial magazine had become very successful and was fondly thought of as the industry bible. Even President Franklin D. Roosevelt had the paper airmailed daily to his desk at the White House."

Wilkerson set his sight beyond that of a prominent magazine publisher—he wanted to be a nightclub proprietor as well. A shrewd businessman, he was aware of two compelling reasons to start new ventures in Hollywood at the onset of the Great Depression. One was his belief that existing establishments for local night life were "ordinary." He envisioned extraordinary nightclubs that offered class, sophistication, and ambiance. His second reason lay in his knowledge that entertainment people from Beverly Hills had money—lots of it—despite the difficult economic times.

Inspiration for his Hollywood ventures came from his New York speakeasy triumphs during Prohibition's 1920s and from his many trips to Europe, where he was fond of spending time in Parisian cafés and nightclubs. Wilkerson's vision of Parisian-styled nightspots became the model for a chain of very profitable Southern California cafés and nightclubs.

Ciro's Menu

Though the movie industry dominated Hollywood, the Sunset Strip became the town's glamorous social hub where the stars went to be seen. Wilkerson's enterprises at this time included Ciro's, Café Trocadero, Sunset House, LaRue, and L'Aiglon. These nightspots made him America's most successful nightclub owner and restaurateur.

A COMPULSION TO GAMBLE

Wilkerson suffered from an obsessive compulsive disorder that manifested itself in many ways, including an addiction to gambling. Despite having lost everything on Black Tuesday, within six months of arriving in California he bet and lost over one million dollars. From craps to poker to horse races, no sum was too large or too small to wager. This compulsive nature—a trait evident in his father—affected every facet of Wilkerson's life, including his smoking three packs of cigarettes and drinking more than a dozen Coca-Colas a day. Most remarkable though, not unlike his father before him, Wilkerson's most compulsive behavior was gambling—he loved playing craps, poker, and the horses—and regularly risked vast sums of money. After relocating to California, he gambled away close to $1 million, and came close to bankruptcy.

His son noted in *The Man Who Invented Las Vegas*, "From the moment Wilkerson awoke in the morning he thought of nothing else but gambling. He planned his entire day around the gaming tables and race courses. Usually, he would work in the morning and head out for the track in the afternoon. He paid regular visits to Santa Anita or Hollywood Park. He kept a pair of dice in his coat pocket, and a deck of playing cards was never far from reach. At restaurants he would roll the dice on tabletops to determine who picked up the check. Even in his restaurants guests paid if they lost."[3]

During the early 1930s, Wilkerson regularly played poker at a weekly high stakes game in the Hollywood homes of movie moguls Samuel Goldwyn and Joe Schenck. These legendary games required a minimum buy-in of $20,000, and Wilkerson frequently lost.

Until the late 1930s, Southern California was wide open to gambling and prostitution, but when authorities outlawed these activities, compulsive gamblers like Wilkerson traveled out of state to seek legal gambling. Consequently, Las Vegas became a favorite gambling setting for Wilkerson. He often chartered a plane in the morning from Los Angeles Municipal Airport to Alamo Airport today McCarran International. A short cab ride later he'd be playing at the El Rancho Vegas or downtown's El Cortez. Typically, he played a few hours at the tables, winning or losing ten to twenty thousand dollars before returning to Hollywood.

Distressed at the extent of his losses over the years, and his inability to control his gambling habits, Wilkerson confided in his friend, movie mogul Joe Schenck. Schenck offered a piece of advice that changed Wilkerson's life. "Billy, you need to be on the other side of the table if you're going to endure those kinds of losses.... Build a casino. Own the house." Wilkerson realized Schenck had something, and thanked him for the insight.

INSPIRATION TO BUILD THE FLAMINGO

In 1944, with Schenck's advice in mind, the beleaguered Hollywood publisher decided to take a more serious look at Las Vegas. Until then, he thought the place served only diehard gamblers like himself, and lacked the glamour and atmosphere he enjoyed in European venues. The few so-called sawdust joints operating downtown in those days were a far cry from today's casinos. They were saloons that offered a few casino games, such as two or three blackjack tables and perhaps one roulette table.

Though Wilkerson disliked the desert, the town's remote location nevertheless helped induce the troubled gambler into believing Las Vegas could become an ideal site for gambling. Supporting his opportunistic vision was his recognition that a huge market for Las Vegas lay untouched in Hollywood—an expensive bottle of champagne waiting to be uncorked.

Wilkerson's first business venture in Vegas came in December 1944 when he arranged to lease the El Rancho Vegas for six months at $50,000. He soon realized that building in Nevada required a more impressive attraction than the modest western-themed El Rancho. More than simply a casino and a hotel, he needed something grander in scope—to lure the rich movie people from Beverly Hills to the barren desert—something more glamorous than his Hollywood nightclubs. He needed a special resort-hotel. A month later, Wilkerson spotted a for sale sign along Highway 91 a few miles south of downtown. (Years later this would evolve into the Fabulous Las Vegas Strip.) The thirty three-acre site belonged to Margaret Folsom, who had bought the land for $7,500 only a few months earlier from one of Las Vegas's first settlers, Charles "Pops" Squires. Mr. Squires reportedly purchased the parcel years past for $8.75 an acre.

Despite his hopeless addiction to gambling, Wilkerson remained a shrewd businessman. To avoid inflating the selling price that might result from rumors of a high roller's interest in Las Vegas property, he hired his attorney, Greg Bautzer, to negotiate on his behalf. Within a day, Bautzer managed to nail down a purchase price of $84,000, buying Folsom's property in his name and waiting nearly a year before registering the deed.

From the beginning, the Hollywood publisher envisioned his future resort as a gambling paradise that would house all his passions under one roof. Furthermore, it had to be unique and outshine the "pedestrian" competition in town. He pictured a desert oasis not only for gamblers, but also for visitors who wanted to relax, who would enjoy a luxurious resort featuring fine dining, floor shows with top-name entertainers, and a variety of outdoor activities.

To put this revelation on paper, in February 1945 he met with architect George Russell and decorator Tom Douglas at his Hollywood office, where he outlined his idea for a central "hub," with the casino as the focal point of a massive complex. Surrounding the casino on the 33-acre property, he wanted to build an indoor shopping mall, glamorous showroom, upscale nightclub, a bar-lounge, several fine restaurants, a café, luxury hotel, and a spa with steam rooms and gym. Outdoor recreation would include a large swimming pool, private bungalows, and handball and tennis courts. Additional features to enhance the sprawling resort included a nine-hole golf course along with a riding stable and a shooting range.

Summing up his casino hub concept, Wilkerson explained his overriding goal to his architect and decorator: to make losing money as simple and as painless as possible for the gambler. His vision was to create an ultra-gambling resort that let players find a total escape in which to "indulge their passion in palatial luxury."

The focus of the complex was the casino—the bread and butter of the expansive facility. Wilkerson wanted a design that funneled hotel guests through the casino at every cross point. No windows, no wall clocks. All overhead lighting dim, ensuring that time would pass unnoticed. These elements, he argued, would cloak the true time of day and allow nothing visible to interfere with the total gambling experience.

Wilkerson introduced other radical changes that altered casino design in Las Vegas for years to come. Before 1945, casino game tables had hard edges and typically lacked comfortable seating. Wilkerson believed gaming should be a pleasurable experience, so he ordered rounded edges and cushioned leather padding on all game tables. He also complemented each game with comfortable stools and chairs. His most notable innovation included "air conditioning," which made the Flamingo the first hotel in America with indoor cooling.

Next he faced the task of choosing a suitable name and logo for his planned casino-resort. Wilkerson usually named his projects long before they were completed. As evidenced by the names of his stylish Hollywood nightclubs he gained inspiration on his many travels. In the case of his Las Vegas casino he turned to his love of birds, particularly the beautiful long-legged pink variety he'd encountered during a trip to Florida. To develop an appropriate logo he turned to Hollywood graphic artist Bert Worth.

ENTER GUS GREENBAUM AND MOE SEDWAY

Wilkerson had gained a lot of business expertise running the *Hollywood Reporter* and his various upscale nightspots. Despite his success in those endeavors, he knew managing an immense casino complex was an entirely different undertaking. Although a gambler by nature, he understood little about the inner workings of a gambling establishment. In his determination to create a successful high-class casino, he knew he needed professionals with experience in casino management.

Wilkerson turned for help to Gus Greenbaum and Moe Sedway, owners of the El Cortez Casino, who had developed a good reputation for operating table games. In the mid 1940s, Las Vegas casino owners typically farmed out gaming operations to independent contractors adept in certain functions. For a silent partnership and a percentage of the gaming profits, these two men agreed to manage Wilkerson's Flamingo casino and be completely responsible for every phase of its operation. In addition, they agreed to help procure all required gaming licenses.

At first glance the arrangement appeared to be a great partnership. Although Greenbaum and Sedway lacked Wilkerson's panache for developing a glamorous business, they knew everything there was to know about the successful operation of a casino.

Up to now, Wilkerson had invested $300,000 of his own money in the project. His gambling losses and debts to Moe Sedway totaled $400,000, meaning he was still $400,000 short of the money needed to finish building the Flamingo. With characteristic confidence, he decided to make up the difference at Sedway's El Cortez, risking $200,000 in April 1945, only to lose it all.

Nevertheless, in November 1945, contractors broke ground on the Flamingo. Within six weeks, with nearly a third of the resort's construction complete, Wilkerson ran into more troubles. The project's construction budget had ballooned to just under $1.2 million—a $400,000 shortfall that Wilkerson did not have.

Adding to his problem was the post-war economy. The period immediately following the end of World War II witnessed a scarcity in building materials and inflated prices which invariably exceeded Wilkerson's original construction budget. To make up for the deficit, he once again tried his luck at the gaming tables. Taking $150,000 of the remaining construction funds, he confidently risked it at the gaming tables. Once again he lost everything.

Casino developers such as Wilkerson lacked the financial resources in the 1940s available to them today, because in those days banks refused to lend money to build casinos. Once Wilkerson's compulsive gambling sapped his bankroll, he needed the type of construction funding only The Mob could provide. These were the days before Valley Bank expedited loans from the Teamsters Pension Fund, before Wall Street and corporate America solicited the public to purchase gaming stock, and before Michael Milken created junk-bond financing, which in 1989 financed construction of the Mirage. Before these investment sources existed, there was only the Mafia with its suitcases full of illicit cash.

With most of his construction funding gone, the part-time publisher became desperate. He tried to convince several Hollywood studio heads to donate materials from their back lots, but to no avail. What little he did receive barely helped in the overall construction effort.

By January of 1946, Wilkerson's cash amounted to less than $50,000. No one would lend him money. Construction of his dream resort ground to a standstill. Distraught, and with no one to turn to, he paid everyone at the construction site in cash and virtually abandoned the unfinished Flamingo.

A month passed. The shell of a partially constructed Flamingo rested in the arid desert—its steel girders standing erect like a flesh-picked skeleton in the midst of a 33-acre western ghost town. With the Hollywood publisher at the end of his financial rope, Moe Sedway brought Wilkerson's idle project to the attention of East Coast Mob boss Meyer Lansky. Sedway saw the financially troubled Flamingo as a marvelous opportunity for his syndicate pals to expand their Las Vegas operations.

Meyer Lansky

At first, Lansky failed to share Sedway's optimism about Las Vegas. Lansky believed the Flamingo's setting—a remote site where summer temperatures soared to well over 100° F – was too inhospitable to attract crowds of high rollers. The New Yorker's skepticism began to fade when Sedway described in vivid detail Wilkerson's dream of a lavish air-conditioned resort. As Lansky visualized how huge sums of money could be earned in air-cooled comfort, he decided to finance the Flamingo's completion.

The scheme was carefully thought out and set in motion. Someone unknown to Wilkerson would make him an offer he couldn't refuse. That February, Wilkerson and the builder,

Bud Raulston, were touring the building site when a well-dressed middle-aged businessman drove onto the site. He got out of the car, approached the two men, and introduced himself as G. Harry Rothberg from New York City. Rothberg said he represented an East Coast investment firm, knew the project was having financial problems, and wanted to invest in the Flamingo. Moreover, he wanted to be helpful. His firm was capable of funding the necessary money to complete the project.

Rothberg proposed to provide $1 million up front and leave Wilkerson with a one-third ownership share. All others would be silent partners. The contractual agreement gave Wilkerson creative freedom and stipulated that when the Flamingo opened, not later than March 1, 1947, Wilkerson would become sole general manager. In exchange for financing, Wilkerson would hold a one-third share in the project. It would also be spelled out in a contractual agreement that he would make all creative decisions. Moreover, when the Flamingo became operational (no later than March 1, 1947), Wilkerson would be its sole general manager: all others would be silent partners.

Wilkerson thanked Rothberg for the offer and told him he would give it serious consideration. At this point Wilkerson felt he was out of options. He'd already thought of abandoning the project altogether. He had no problem with the idea of investors, especially silent ones who took a piece of the action without getting involved with operations. Overall, Wilkerson found the offer acceptable, except for one aspect. When they met a second time a few days later, he negotiated for an additional contractual condition—title to the land would be held exclusively in his name. Rothberg agreed, and by March 1946 a contract was signed between Rothberg and Wilkerson. Soon after, $1 million was made available and construction resumed on the Flamingo.

Within a month, three men drove onto the construction site in a fancy, late-model car. Wilkerson immediately recognized two of the men: Gus Greenbaum and Moe Sedway, the silent partners who had agreed to run the casino. They brought with them a well-dressed man who boldly introduced himself as the publisher's new partner in the Flamingo. The audacious individual was none other than Meyer Lansky's mob enforcer, the notorious Ben Siegel.

THE SIEGEL/WILKERSON PARTNERSHIP

Meyer Lansky's choice of Ben Siegel to oversee his Las Vegas interests seemed a natural liaison. Wilkerson already knew Siegel—they lived near each other in Beverly Hills. In the beginning the partnership went smoothly. The two worked together out of Wilkerson's office. The usually aggressive and brash gangster became remarkably useful, followed Wilkerson's guidance, and learned as much as he could from the ground up about building a multi-faceted resort. Siegel was particularly helpful at gathering black market building materials through his underworld connections in California. But things soon went awry. For whatever reason, Siegel, the gangster with a hair-trigger temper, started acting like his old self, playing the role of big shot. Instead of the pupil following the tutelage of Wilkerson, Siegel began making decisions without consulting Wilkerson. His behavior seemed filled with paranoia and resentment, as when he changed the architectural plans and informed the construction workers that Wilkerson had promoted him to boss. Taking credit for Wilkerson's ideas, Siegel went so far as to claim that the Flamingo was his own idea. Although he apologized whenever Wilkerson grew angry, Siegel kept demanding more involvement in the project.

Wilkerson compromised by allowing Siegel to oversee the hotel, while Wilkerson retained the upper hand with everything else. But things became further disorganized when Siegel asked to have his own architect and builder. The result was total mayhem, as two distinct management spheres functioned within one complex and with no communication between them. Matters came to a head when Siegel's unbridled greed and extravagance overspent the budget allotted. He went to Wilkerson for more money, but that was denied.

In May 1946, Siegel decided the original agreement between Wilkerson and Rothberg had been a mistake. Instead, Siegel wanted sole operational control of the Flamingo. To buy out Wilkerson's creative input, Siegel offered Wilkerson five percent more stock participation and formed a new corporation, naming himself as president and taking control of all operations. Now Siegel was the largest principal stockholder, all other partners, including Wilkerson became mere shareholders. From then on, the Flamingo functioned as a Mob-run operation, with Siegel at the helm taking credit for Wilkerson's vision.

Siegel wasted no time putting his own plans into action. Never again would he consult with Wilkerson. He fired all of Wilkerson's on-site affiliates and staff. The original architect and decorator were replaced by Del Webb and Richard Stadelman, and responsibility for interior decorations given to the gangster's girlfriend, the notorious Virginia Hill.

However, a few strings were still left untied by the self-appointed president of the Flamingo. Most crucial was ownership of the 33-acre parcel of land. According to the original contract with Rothberg, Wilkerson was one-third owner of the project and sole owner of the land. Siegel was not satisfied, as he wanted control of the land too. He offered Wilkerson an additional five percent shareholder stake in exchange for title to the land. They negotiated, and Wilkerson granted land ownership to Siegel for ten percent more in stock. As a result, in August 1946, Wilkerson held a 48 percent share in the Flamingo Corporation, making him its largest single shareholder.

THE ILL-FATED STOCKHOLDER MEETING

In December 1946, Wilkerson received a phone call from the Director of the FBI, J. Edgar Hoover, warning him about Ben Siegel. Unfortunately, the call came too late. Wilkerson had too much involved in the Flamingo to remove himself without endangering his investment. To protect himself and his interests, Wilkerson decided to make the best of a very bad situation. He hired a press agent, and the two began developing a significant publicity campaign to make sure the outside world became aware of the Flamingo. The campaign would focus on the property's gala opening in December 1946, and on the hotel's extravagant cost, which Wilkerson placed at $5 million. In that way Wilkerson would alert The Mob to Siegel's over-spending and possible skimming. In the midst of the publicity campaign,

Siegel held a stockholder's meeting at the unfinished hotel. Present at the meeting were Wilkerson's attorney Greg Bautzer, along with Gus Greenbaum and Moe Sedway. Representing Ben Siegel were Louis Wiener, his legal counsel, and Clifford Jones, at the time Lieutenant Governor of the State of Nevada.

At the meeting, Siegel proceeded in true Mob fashion, demanding Wilkerson hand over his ownership shares free and clear. After learning Siegel had oversold shares of Flamingo stock, thereby driving down the price, Wilkerson's attorney refused. Siegel flew into one of his psychotic rages and threatened to kill Wilkerson.

Prior to this meeting, Wilkerson had ignored the gangster's nasty occupation and killer reputation. Now, however, Siegel's true persona came to haunt him, and Wilkerson feared for his life. From that point on all communication between Siegel and Wilkerson took place via their attorneys. To further ensure his safety Wilkerson took the first flight to New York, where he boarded a ship bound for France. From the port of Le Havre he drove to Paris and booked a room in an upscale hotel under an assumed name. Only a trusted few knew of his whereabouts. Wilkerson planned to wait it out until Siegel's partners learned of his extravagant spending and his overselling of Flamingo stock. Wilkerson expected them to eventually fire Siegel, leading to a change in management, and Wilkerson would be reinstated as creative director. He would finally be able to complete his dream resort.

THE FLAMINGO OPENS

The gala opening of the Flamingo on December 26 was a star-studded affair. Band leader Xavier Cugat provided the music. Celebrity guests included Rose Marie, George Jessel, George Raft, Joan Crawford, Clark Gable, and Lana Turner. Jimmy Durante headlined the entertainment. The splashy opening unfortunately bombed due to poor timing. The day after Christmas is typically a very slow day for Las Vegas, and it rained that day. The other problem was the hotel's still unfinished construction left the guests with nowhere to stay.

When Meyer Lansky learned of the Flamingo's weak opening, he convinced the other syndicate bosses to give Siegel more time to operate the resort. By January 1947, however, the lack of business forced Siegel to close the Flamingo until construction on the hotel could be completed. Through all this, Wilkerson had held onto his hope that the Flamingo's Mob investors would eventually refuse to allow the hotel's ownership to remain in the hands of a psychopath. Yet once the Flamingo closed, Wilkerson realized he needed to get out from under, so he offered to sell his share for $2 million, with a stipulation absolving him of further obligations and responsibility—including financial.

Despite construction on the hotel still unfinished, the Flamingo re-opened in March 1947 to a different result. Within two months the resort earned a $250,000 profit, allowing Lansky to point out to the boys that his lifelong friend Ben Siegel was, after all, correct in his belief about Las Vegas.

On March 19 both Siegel and Rothberg signed a legal document that totally absolved Wilkerson from any wrongdoing in the

Flamingo Corporation. He was to receive partial payment of $300,000 in early May, with the balance due in ninety days. Within a week of the signing, the publisher received a frightening phone call from an anonymous woman. Frantic, she told Wilkerson her recently paroled husband had been contracted to kill him. Wilkerson must have taken the warning seriously because he immediately headed back to Paris. Soon, his daily Trade View column for the *Reporter* was by-lined from the French capital.

While in Paris, Wilkerson received a call from his manager, George Kennedy, telling him of a message from an unknown person who said Wilkerson needed to stay in Paris "until this is over." Kennedy claimed to have no knowledge of the meaning or origin of the strange message. Less than a month later, on the morning of June 21, Wilkerson bought his newspaper, sat down at a sidewalk café, and ordered a Coke. When he unfolded the paper, he saw the article telling of Ben Siegel's death. Immediately he returned to his hotel to pack his bags, and within 48 hours Wilkerson flew back to Los Angeles.

LATER LIFE

Billy Wilkerson's addictions included workaholism, and its ramifications affected his personal life leading to five divorces. Yet it was his sixth wife, Beatrice Noble, as well as fatherhood that inspired him to quit the habits that had besieged him all his life. In his sixth decade, with the birth of his son in October 1951, he finally quit gambling and settled down, enjoying a stable and happy family relationship.

After the Flamingo debacle, Billy Wilkerson continued to head the *Hollywood Reporter* and write his daily Trade View column until his death in September 1962. He was 71.

Chapter 2

THE INSIDE STORY OF MOB ACTIVITY IN LAS VEGAS

To inflict more suffering into their victims and to be sure they would become infected, some gunmen etched grooves into the bullet heads then rubbed garlic into the grooves—or so legend has it.
—David Tomasovsky,
ex-lawman and contributing artist.

Wilkerson's archenemy Ben Siegel met a different end. Inevitably, the mobster's troubled control of the Flamingo, cost overruns, clumsy management of the project, and drastic changes to the original architectural plans cost Siegel his life.

MOB TIES

Mobsters of every stripe came to Las Vegas trying to emulate the success of the Flamingo resort: ex-bootleggers, hoods, thieves, loan sharks, and killers—Las Vegas's founding fathers. Their influence lasted almost 50 years, and their impact on those formative years will forever be ingrained in the lore of the city.

Others are scarcely remembered, such as two mobsters who dared to rob the Flamingo in 1951, Tony Trombino and Tony Brancato—known as the "Dumb Tonys," so-named for foolishly robbing a Mob-run casino. Within a year, both were assassinated. The crime remained unsolved until 1977 when Hollywood gangster Jimmy "the Weasel" Fratiano turned state's evidence and admitted to the killing.

After the double assassinations, no one robbed The Fabulous Flamingo again. The Mob, just like legitimate business men, knew the value of advertising. Other memorable Vegas mobsters with provocative nicknames included two of the city's most notorious: Benjamin "Bugsy" Siegel and Tony "the Ant" Spilotro. Neither man liked his moniker: Siegel earned his early growing up in New York City. When angered or thwarted he was said to "go buggy." He preferred to be called Ben. Spilotro's nickname was adopted by the media after FBI agent William F. Roemer Jr. referred to him as "a little pissant." Unable to publish the term, the media simply used the expression "Ant."

During its heyday from about 1950 to the early 1980s, The Mob controlled almost every sizable casino resort along the fabulous Las Vegas Strip, stealing untold millions in cash from casino count rooms.

Among the early casino operators of Las Vegas, one particularly colorful man was Tony Cornero. Like many other young men in Prohibition era America, he made big money as an illegal bootlegger. Cornero, along with his two brothers, built the first casino resort situated away from downtown Las Vegas. In between his Vegas ventures, Cornero operated two gambling ships anchored three miles off the California coast in international waters, just out of reach of state authorities. Later, Tony Cornero became responsible for creating the infamous Stardust Hotel and Casino, but just before its opening he mysteriously died.

Soon after gambling was legalized in Nevada in 1931, other racket bosses and bootleggers like Tony Cornero flocked into the state seeking refuge from the law. Historian Alan Balboni wrote, "Providing liquor and gambling to Americans in the 1920s and 1930s was a somewhat dangerous enterprise, yet one that provided opportunities for wealth and power for those willing to take the risk. Rare indeed was a Las Vegas Strip founding father in the two decades after World War II who had not been involved in manufacturing or distributing liquor in the 1920s."[4]

Nevertheless, mob activity in Las Vegas, though present, was virtually undiscovered, especially by the public at large. That is until a timely event occurred in 1950.

KEFAUVER HEARINGS

In 1950 for the first time, Americans focused on the Mafia and organized crime. Estes Kefauver, the Democratic Senator from Tennessee, chaired hearings of the Special Committee to Investigate Crime in Interstate Commerce, popularly known as the Kefauver Committee. The televised hearings included testimony from the likes of Frank Costello, Tony Accardo, Meyer Lansky, Mickey Cohen, and Willie Moretti, all taking the Fifth Amendment, unwilling to incriminate themselves over their shady business dealings.

To a man they denied ties to the Mafia, La Cosa Nostra, the Chicago Outfit, or the East Coast Mob—which the committee labeled organized crime. Under oath, some claimed never to have heard of the Mafia. Others ventured to say that they may have read about the Mafia once or twice in newspapers. As the hearings progressed, Senator Kefauver enlightened them and his 30 million television viewers.

"The Mafia is a shadowy international organization that lurks behind much of America's organized criminal activity," Kefauver said. "It is an organization about which none of its members, on fear of death, will talk. In fact, some of the witnesses called before us, who we had good reason to believe could tell us about the Mafia, sought to dismiss it as a sort of fairy tale, or legend that children hear in Sicily, where the Mafia originated. The Mafia, however, is no fairy tale. It is ominously real, and it has scarred the face of America with almost every conceivable type of criminal violence, including murder, traffic in narcotics, smuggling, extortion, white slavery, kidnapping, and labor racketeering."[5]

WHY THE MOB CAME TO LAS VEGAS

Why did these unsavory underworld characters want to come to Las Vegas? The attraction of Vegas is related to several events that coincided at that particular time in history. Between 1920 and 1933, America was in the midst of the Prohibition era brought on by a misguided law called the Volstead Act, which made it illegal to produce, distribute, and consume alcohol throughout most of America. Combined with the

Great Depression, which began in October 1929 and lasted 11 years, Prohibition's effects were devastating to both America's economy and the world's economy.

Prior to abatement of Prohibition, bootleggers made a fortune supplying illicit booze to a thirsty America. "The racketeers were the dispensers of dreams and escape—in the form of alcohol, gambling, money, drugs and sex—and, by the early Thirties, they had enormous wealth and influence," wrote Richard Hammer in his *Playboy's Illustrated History of Organized Crime*.

With the repeal of Prohibition in 1933, most of the rumrunners were suddenly out of business. They had to do something with the huge profits they made during Prohibition. It seemed only natural for these gangsters, flush with an abundance of cash, to invest their ill-gotten gains in the only state in America where gambling was legal.

Las Vegas was not their first choice. When mobsters first came to Nevada they were drawn to Reno. They could see it was a thriving city, a good place to do business. But their applications to build or buy out existing casinos were turned down. The city fathers wanted nothing to do with gangsters. Unable to conduct business there, they came south to Las Vegas.

Before the Gaming Control Board was created by the state in 1955, acquiring a gaming license in Las Vegas was a simple process. Gaming had been under the jurisdiction of the county sheriff's department and the Nevada Tax Commission. In fact, prior to the Kefauver Hearings, new buyers of an existing casino could be "grandfathered" into being approved for ownership, which meant they would not have to apply for a new license. Instead, new owners could take over the existing gaming license with no questions asked. From 1931 to the mid-sixties Las Vegas was a wide-open city—open to mobsters, to gamblers, to hookers, and to money launderers. Vegas was wide-open in another sense—free of regulation. The lack of cameras on either casino floors or counting rooms facilitated skimming, the practice of withdrawing a share of the income for management and for investors—who were mostly Mob bosses—and thereby lower the total income reported to the IRS. The absence of limits on cash transactions and minimal reporting requirements made Vegas a haven for money laundering. Casinos were virtual forests where, as Meyer Lansky once observed, "You simply shook the trees and watched thousand-dollar bills fall like leaves."

MOE SEDWAY
AND THE TRANSAMERICA WIRE SERVICE

One of the first racketeers who wanted a legitimate business in Las Vegas was Moe Sedway. In 1937, Sedway, a trusted lifelong crony of Ben Siegel, was sent from Chicago to set up the Transamerica wire service in Nevada. This wire service, essential to Las Vegas bookmakers, was controlled by the Chicago Outfit's Al Capone. Without it, they could be driven into bankruptcy by past-posting bettors—betting after races were decided. The Mob knew that if they could control the wire service, they could also control the bookies. When the state of Nevada legalized sports betting in 1941, Sedway, with the help of his pal Ben Siegel, began forcing The Mob's wire service into each Las Vegas casino.

In the early days of legalized gambling, everyone involved with gaming control knew problems would eventually arise. The *Las*

Vegas Review-Journal quotes Robbins Cahill, former Secretary of the Nevada Tax Commission, as saying, "You didn't get church bishops and solid, upright, outstanding citizens who were in the social register that wanted to go into the gaming business. They were people who were gamblers. And because Nevada was the only state where it was allowed legally, they, of course, had to get their experience in places where it was illegal."[6]

WILBUR CLARK'S DESERT INN

In 1947, Wilbur Clark began construction on the Desert Inn. But three years later when he ran into financial trouble, Clark made the mistake of borrowing from the Cleveland Mob's Moe Dalitz. At the completion of construction Clark ended up owning only six percent of the resort.

Within months of the Desert Inn's opening, a Senate hearing on organized crime in America was ordered. The Kefauver Hearings projected a bad image for Las Vegas, yet had a positive effect on Nevada by sparking the creation of the respected State Gaming Control Board in 1955.

THE DUNES:
A QUINTESSENTIAL MOB OPERATION

The story of the Dunes is another example of a classic Mob operation. Down through the years the resort changed hands from one group of mobsters to another. Owner of record Joe Sullivan, together with his silent partner, New England crime boss Raymond Patriarca, opened the doors in May 1955. For its grand opening, Frank Sinatra wore a turban and rode an elephant into the lobby. Despite the fanfare, the Dunes struggled because of its location away from the most popular casinos in what was then south Las Vegas (now the busy intersection of Las Vegas Boulevard and Flamingo Road).

Rescue came in the form of a lease agreement with the owners of the Sands, which included bookmaker Sandy Waterman, Cleveland gambler Carl Cohen, Sands Manager Charles Turner, and former Mob enforcer Charles "Toolie" Kandell. Unable to turn the Dunes into a success, the group later sold the resort to Major Riddle and Bill Miller, businessmen with underworld ties.

In 1962 Riddle sold 15 percent of the Dunes to George Duckworth and Midwest bookmakers Charles "Kewpie" Rich and Sid Wyman. That change in ownership, as cited by John L. Smith in *Sharks in the Desert*, was the beginning of profitability for the Dunes.[7] Rich and Wyman developed close ties with the East Coast Mob and—through Julius "Big Julie" Weintraub—with the New York diamond merchants. This collaboration gave birth to an advertising angle that eventually became a staple in the casino industry: the Las Vegas junket, offering free flights, food, and lodging to induce visitors to spend their money on the pleasures of gambling. An additional amenity enticing visitors to the Dunes included the new Miracle Mile golf course. Innovative marketing of the Dunes brought in thousands of players and millions of dollars to Las Vegas casinos.

Julie Weintraub, in his role as collector of the markers owed to the Dunes, was nearly killed when he tried to collect from the wrong people. He was found in the parking lot at New York's

Kennedy airport severely beaten. When questioned by Senator Kefauver, although Julie didn't even speak Italian, he observed the Mafia code of *omertà* and maintained silence about the members of the Columbo Crime Family-his attackers.

Big Julie's junkets brought in players and dollars. Casino management's skimming practices ensured that most of those dollars landed in the pockets of the Mob and out of the coffers of Uncle Sam. Bundles of untaxed $100 bills crossed the country via courier from Las Vegas to the casino's secret owners.

By 1975, the Dunes succumbed to yet another transfer of ownership. Still under the thumb of the Chicago Outfit, the Dunes' new owners included Morris Shenker, attorney to Teamster boss Jimmy Hoffa and a friend of Outfit underboss Joseph "Joey the Clown" Lombardo. Given the lack of regulation even into the 1970's, Shenker had no trouble securing a casino license.

Under Shenker's ownership, the Dunes' clientele included mobsters from cities across the country: Kansas City's Nick Civella, Anthony Giodano from Shenker's hometown of St. Louis, and "Matty the Horse" Iannelo, a member of New York's Genovese family. One Genovese mobster, Tony Spolotro, took over management of the poker room at the Dunes, apparently without objection from Shenker.

After Shenker, the sequence of ownership moved to John Anderson, a gambler and wealthy farmer from California who profited handsomely from selling the Dunes to Japanese billionaire Masao Nangaku for the hugely inflated price of $155 million. The Mob took the naïve Japanese businessman to the cleaners, and he ended up selling the hotel to Steve Wynn's Mirage Resorts for $75 million, less than half his original purchase price. Unfortunately for Nangaku, he fared no better in his home country, where he later lost everything in the crash of the Tokyo real estate market.[8]

The final owner of the Dunes was Steve Wynn, a legitimate businessman and well-known resort developer in Las Vegas. Wynn reached the big-time with his purchase and renovation of the Golden Nugget, then went on to build the Mirage, with its indoor forest and outdoor volcano, and its sister resort next door, Treasure Island. After Wynn purchased the Dunes, he promptly tore it down, imploding the hotel in a display of explosions and fireworks. The grand show served as a symbol to residents of Las Vegas that their city had moved out from under the control of organized crime.

THE MOBBED-UP STARDUST

During its controversial history, the Stardust underwent several changes in ownership—unusual in that the property was very profitable. Originally named the Starlite, the resort was conceived and built by Tony Cornero, who mysteriously died shooting dice at the Desert Inn before construction was completed. Moe Dalitz and his affiliates supervised the completion of the casino, and renamed it the Stardust.

In *Sharks in the Desert*, John L. Smith wrote, "By 1961, Stardust's management included Credit Manager Hyman Goldbaum, a career criminal with seven known aliases, 14 criminal convictions including an assault conviction, and a three-year prison sentence for income tax evasion. Casino Manager and five-percent owner Johnny Drew was a veteran associate of

Al Capone, and was once fined for running a crooked dice game at an Elks convention, and general manager Morris Kleinman had served three years for tax evasion."[9]

In 1968, billionaire Howard Hughes made an offer of $30.5 million to purchase the Stardust, but the deal was not sanctioned by the Securities and Exchange Commission on the grounds that his acquisition of any more Las Vegas casinos (he already owned six) might violate the Sherman Antitrust Act.

By the 1970s, the Argent Corporation, owner of record of the Stardust, reportedly had siphoned off between $7 million and $15 million using rigged scales. The skimming operation was eventually discovered by the FBI. In 1984 the Nevada Gaming Commission levied a $3 million fine against the Stardust for skimming, which to date was the highest fine ever issued by the Commission.

Long-standing suspicions about the Stardust's hidden ownership were put to rest when the Boyd Group, a reputable, locally based gaming company, bought the casino in 1985. The Stardust had been a virtual gold mine to the Chicago Outfit, because the money skimmed was huge. When the squeaky-clean Boyd group purchased the Stardust, its enormous profits with every dollar of the gross receipts recorded, surprised the new owners. FBI agent-turned-author William F. Roemer Jr. an expert on mob activity in Las Vegas, wrote, "The amount of skim had been so heavy that the profit and loss statement did not present a true picture of the gold mine that the Stardust was."

TONY CORNERO, THE "ADMIRAL"

Against the backdrop of Prohibition and the Great Depression, Tony Cornero's storied life of running gambling ships and operating Las Vegas casinos was as vibrant as a modern-day soap opera.

Anthony "Tony" Cornero made his name and most of his money during the mid 1930s and 1940s bootlegging and running two illegal gambling ships off southern California. His alias was Tony Stralla, with nicknames "Tony the Hat," and the "Admiral."

Tony Cornero

Cornero's varied criminal career began soon after he and his family immigrated to America from northern Italy. At age 16 he was arrested for robbery and sentenced to 10 months in reform school. During the next 10 years he established a lengthy criminal record, including three counts of attempted murder and two counts of bootlegging. In the early 1920s, when Cornero was not incarcerated, he made a living driving a taxi in San Francisco. In 1923, with Prohibition the law of the land, Cornero became a rumrunner, supplying much of southern California's underground nightclubs and high-class clientele with illicit booze. Like today's drug runners who smuggle their contraband onto Florida beaches using high speed "cigar boats," Cornero smuggled Canadian whiskey and Mexican and Caribbean rum onto Southern California beaches using shrimp boats capable of outrunning the U.S. Coast Guard's antiquated and undermanned vessels. Cornero's skills as a bootlegger made him a millionaire by the age of 25.

One fateful night in 1926, authorities caught up with Cornero returning from Mexico with an estimated 1,000 cases of rum. He was arrested and sentenced to two years' imprisonment, but while in transit to prison by rail, Cornero escaped and jumped off the train. From there the fugitive managed to elude his captors and eventually boarded a ship for Vancouver, British Columbia. When he reached Europe, Cornero remained in hiding until 1929, when he returned to Los Angeles and turned himself in to authorities.

Cornero served his two years in prison, and soon after his release in 1931 he reestablished himself in Culver City, California, as a big-time bootlegger producing up to 5,000 gallons of booze daily. With the repeal of Prohibition in 1933, Cornero and his two brothers, Louis and Frank, moved to Las Vegas intending to establish a legitimate casino.

CORNERO'S GREEN MEADOWS VENTURE

After moving to Las Vegas, Tony Cornero and his brothers purchased a 30-acre site along Fremont Street near the intersection of East Charleston, a location farther east than the established sawdust joints downtown. There, the Corneros created the upscale "Green Meadows." Compared to the existing downtown casinos such as the El Cortez and Apache Hotel, the Meadows was considered a most impressive facility.

Virtually all of the downtown so-called "pedestrian" joints attracted people dressed in jeans and boots. However, photographs taken at the Meadows' grand opening show many guests from Las Vegas's professional and business elite dressed in suits and evening attire.

Charles "Lucky" Luciano

Although the hotel had only 30 sleeping rooms, they were "all with bath," as the local newspaper pointed out, with hot water available at all hours. The hotel's public relations person planted the news article to emphasize that the Meadows had electric lights. Jack Laughlin, producer of such well-known stage shows as "No, No, Nanette" was hired to create the "Meadows Revue."

Another draw at the Meadows was the Cornero brothers' bootlegged Canadian whiskey, unavailable to patrons of competing casinos, who managed to imbibe the inferior "bathtub" booze made in nearby North Las Vegas and Lincoln County.

When the Meadows began making big money, Tony Cornero started investing in other local casinos. His newfound success soon lured unwanted attention from the wrong people. East Coast syndicate leaders Charlie "Lucky" Luciano and Meyer Lansky tried to muscle in on the Meadows' gaming profits. Cornero's refusal to comply led to the breakout of a gang war. It ended rather quickly when his enemies torched and burned the

Meadows in May 1932, and Cornero simply gave up. Disappointed, the former rumrunner-turned-casino-entrepreneur sold his Las Vegas interests and moved back to Los Angeles.

CASINOS AFLOAT

In 1938 Tony Cornero decided to operate shipboard gambling in international waters, where he figured to avoid interference from the law. He purchased two large ships and transformed them into luxurious floating casinos. His premiere cruise ship, the SS Rex, could accommodate 2,000 gamblers in addition to 350 crew including gourmet chefs. Its first-class dining room offered French cuisine exclusively, a complete orchestra, tuxedo-clad croupiers, waiters, waitresses, and armed security guards. Most patrons who came aboard were wealthy southern Californians from Long Beach and Santa Monica. They arrived via 25-cent water taxies beyond the "three mile limit," where the gambling ships were anchored. Both of Cornero's floating casinos reportedly earned a staggering profit of $300,000 a night.

Cornero's nefarious prosperity set off outrage and condemnation from California authorities. The newly appointed district attorney, Earl Warren, ordered a series of raids intended to shut down gambling ships outside California waters.

For nearly eight years Cornero battled with state authorities over their jurisdiction and the legality of their entering international waters. One such raid occurred in May 1946, after Earl Warren became governor of California. Authorities refigured the starting point of the three-mile limit, thereby bringing the gambling ships under California jurisdiction.

Police boarded several Coast Guard cutters and motored out to the gambling ships to shut them down and arrest Cornero. When the cutters arrived, Cornero had a surprise for the police who tried to board. He ordered the ship's fire hoses turned on them, reportedly yelling at the boarders that they were committing piracy on the high seas. The confrontation lasted three days before Cornero surrendered. The Coast Guard confiscated the SS Rex, and soon after, Cornero closed down his other gambling ship, the SS Tango.

In his next venture Tony Cornero tried to establish illegal land-based casinos in Los Angeles, but was thwarted by the West Coast Mob's emissary, Mickey Cohen, who warned Cornero to stay out of his territory. Taking the notorious gangster's warning seriously, Cornero returned to Las Vegas.

ATTEMPTED MURDER AND STARDUST MEMORIES

In Las Vegas, Cornero made a deal to lease the Apache Hotel and name it the Rex. At first the Las Vegas City Council voted in favor of Cornero's gaming license, despite knowing of his criminal background, his history with the Meadows, and his gambling ships off the California coast. Several months later the Council reconsidered the issue and revoked his gaming license, closing the Rex.

Again, Tony Cornero moved back to Los Angeles and began making plans to build a casino south of San Diego, in Mexico's Baja California. On February 9, 1948, after returning from Mexico, an event happened he never could have anticipated.

Two Mexicans appeared mysteriously at Cornero's home in Beverly Hills. One held a carton, the other knocked on the door. When Cornero opened the door, the man holding the carton said, "Here, Cornero, this is for you," pulled out a handgun, and shot him four times in the stomach. "It was a clear message from the casino owners of Las Vegas. Expertise about running casinos should not be shared with our neighbors to the South, who had the intention of taking business away from Las Vegas," wrote Steve Fischer in *When the Mob Ran Vegas*.

Critically wounded, Cornero underwent surgery that night and survived, returning once again to Las Vegas. The year was 1955. He decided to build another hotel casino much larger than the Green Meadows, on the old Los Angeles Highway (State Highway 91), nicknamed "the Strip." He purchased a 40-acre site on the west side just south of Sahara Avenue and considered calling the project the Starlite Hotel and Casino.

To raise money to build the plushest hotel on the old Los Angeles Highway, Cornero began selling shares of stock in his Starlite project. Like most underworld men of the time, he didn't worry about the finer points of federal or state law. Nor was he prudent with his bookkeeping. He was known to keep records of investments in his head or on matchbook covers he carried in his pocket. Conceivably, $20,000 would earn the investor four percent of net profits from the keno parlor, or three percent of the profits from the showroom. Even though Cornero kept careless records, over the years he developed a reputation as a very productive earner.

Meanwhile, construction began on the Starlite. Not until later that year after the casino complex was half built, did Cornero make application to the Nevada Gaming Commission for a gaming license. They turned him down.

Not to be denied, Cornero approached his friend Milton B. "Farmer" Page and inquired if he would "front" for the Starlite. Page accepted, on condition that he would be in charge of running it. While all this was taking place, construction of the casino complex progressed, the price of building materials soared, and Cornero ran out of construction funds.

Like Billy Wilkerson before him, Cornero envisioned Las Vegas much as it would become in later years, with spacious casinos replacing the sawdust-floored dives that sported two or three tables. Toward that end, he planned the Starlite as more than a casino—he planned a grand resort to attract the wealthy clientele who once frequented his offshore gambling ships. Mirroring his strategy of providing convenient boat transportation from the shores of California to his floating casinos, Cornero built a landing strip in Vegas for small aircraft to ferry wealthy gamblers to his resort.

Rather than halt construction on the Starlite when he ran out of money, Cornero approached Moe Dalitz and his partner in New York, Meyer Lansky. Offering the Stardust as collateral, Cornero obtained $1.25 million in the first of at least three loans. As the Starlite neared completion, he called a meeting of his investors for July 31, 1955, to explain the need for another infusion of $800,000 to stock the resort with food, liquor, and enough cash on-hand for all the casino cages.

Alas, Tony Cornero died the day of that meeting, July 31, 1955, never to see the Starlite completed. Eventually new management renamed it the Stardust Resort and Casino, and when it opened in 1958 it was the largest hotel in the world, eventually becoming a colossal success that endured 48 years. During its colorful history, the "mobbed up" Stardust was a major source of intrigue for the film *Casino*.

In the 1970s, the FBI exposed the Stardust's owner, "Argent Corporation," in the largest skimming operation ever reported. Between $7 and $15 million had been siphoned off using rigged scales to underestimate weighed coins taken from slot machines.

The FBI's investigation into the Stardust's skimming operations resulted, in 1984, in the highest fine ever issued by Nevada's Gaming Commission, $3 million. The Chicago Outfit sold the resort the following year to a locally owned legitimate, respected gaming company, the Boyd Group. The Boyd family was surprised when an accurate accounting of the casino's receipts showed enormous profits.

In *The Enforcer*, one of several books written by an ex-FBI senior agent in the Bureau's Chicago organized-crime squad, author William F. Roemer Jr. wrote: "The amount of skim had been so heavy, that the profit and loss statement did not present a true picture of the gold mine the Stardust was."[10] When Boyd Gaming closed the doors on this infamous resort in November 2006, anticipating replacing it with a more modern complex of resort hotels and convention facilities, the final chapter of this storied resort casino was written.

SUSPICIOUS END FOR THE ADMIRAL

When Tony Cornero died the same day of his investors' meeting, he was shooting dice on the casino floor of Moe Dalitz's

Desert Inn. According to witnesses, all of a sudden Cornero grabbed his stomach and dropped dead. Although no autopsy was performed, the official coroner's report determined that he died of natural causes. Nevertheless, rumors flew that his drink had been poisoned. Mysteriously, his body was removed from the casino floor before the Sheriff's Department or the coroner was contacted. Something else was suspicious too—the glass Cornero had been drinking from was conveniently removed and washed. The police never had the opportunity to examine it.

The day after Cornero's passing, Las Vegas newspapers carried front-page stories about his life and death. *Review-Journal* reporter Bob Holdorf best captured the circumstances of his death:

Tony died the way he had lived.

He died at a gambling table.

Probably, the diminutive gambler was happy as hell when he felt the surging heat whip across his chest, and blot out the world.

What other way was there for him to go?

In a bed? Never!

In a gun battle? They tried that!

In an ambush? They tried that, too!

Tony went the way any tough gambling hombre wants to get it. Fast and painless! The pain that hit Tony Cornero Stralla lasted something less than 10 seconds and then it was all over.

He had crapped out.[11]

After Cornero's death, Moe Dalitz and his mob pals supervised the completion of a slightly less luxurious Stardust than Cornero had pictured.

MOE DALITZ: A LAS VEGAS LEGEND

Perhaps no mobster in the history of America became more revered for his contributions to legitimate society than Moe Dalitz, known as the Godfather of Las Vegas. In December 1899, Morris Barney Dalitz was born into a working class family in Boston. When he was still a young boy the family moved to Michigan, where his father opened the Varsity Laundry in Ann Arbor to serve University of Michigan students. Moe—as he was known to his friends—apparently inherited his entrepreneurial bent from his father. Barely into his twenties, he was using his father's laundry trucks to smuggle booze from Detroit to Cleveland. Already well known for his bootlegging and racketeering activities throughout the Midwest, the young opportunist ran roadside gambling joints from Michigan to Ohio and Kentucky. Passage of the

Moe Dalitz

Volstead Act on October 28, 1919, outlawing alcohol production, distribution, and consumption, had handed Moe the business opportunity of a lifetime.

The millions that Dalitz reaped from his illegitimate enterprises he shrewdly invested in legitimate businesses in the Midwest and eventually in Las Vegas, providing himself with an aura of respectability. Unlike the Prohibition-era bootleggers who flocked to Las Vegas and continued to operate in the shadowy underworld, Dalitz shook off his early-won infamy and made an outward transition from Mafioso to philanthropist and legitimate citizen. His net worth mushroomed to over $100 million, which he shared with his associates, many of whom became millionaires as real estate developers.

Although in later years Jimmy Hoffa, president of the Teamster's Union, furnished millions of dollars in loans to Las Vegas casino operators, including Moe Dalitz, in the early years it was union organizing that brought the two men together. An interesting conflict developed between the two when the future Teamster president tried to unionize Dalitz's laundry workers. Dalitz hired Mafia enforcers to head off the union organizers.

EARLY MOB TIES

Moe Dalitz started out with the notorious Purple Gang in Detroit, but he also belonged to the equally nefarious Mayfield Road Gang, according to law enforcement agencies in Cleveland. Years later during the 1951 Kefauver hearings, testimony from a Cleveland police officer identified Moe Dalitz as part of the gangster element that gave rise to organized crime in that Ohio city. "Ruthless beatings, unsolved murders and shakedowns, threats and bribery came to this community as a result of gangsters' rise to power," said the officer of Dalitz's early "business" methods. By the 1930s, Dalitz had a very impressive list of legitimate businesses, holding ownership interest in a variety of companies: The Michigan Industrial Laundry in Detroit, Pioneer Linen Supply, Milco Sales, Dalitz Realty, Berdene Realty, and the Detroit Steel Company in Cleveland.

Unlike ordinary peddlers of illicit rum and bathtub gin, who battled for territories on the Cleveland streets in so-called Whiskey Wars, Dalitz ferried Canadian whiskey in trucks floating on barges across Lake Erie. He developed a clever method of using a floating buoy to mark the contraband, all of which could be thrown overboard and sunk to the bottom if he encountered police. Then, after the authorities left the area, Dalitz could retrieve the contraband that had been marked by the buoy. While the common bootleggers of the Prohibition era wound up either dead or imprisoned Dalitz came away unscathed.

With the repeal of Prohibition in 1933, Dalitz already had a string of illicit casinos operating, including the Pettibone Club, the Jungle Inn, the Mound Club, the Lookout House, and the Beverly Hills Club. He was also known to have a partnership with the Maceo Syndicate, which ran Galveston and supplied liquor from Canada and Mexico.

Dalitz once joked to a friend, "How was I to know those gambling joints were illegal? There were so many judges and politicians in them I figured they had to be all right."

Dalitz was patriotic too, and served honorably in the U.S. Army during the early 1940s, earning the rank of captain. After the end of World War II, he found life at home in the Midwest difficult. America had changed since the so-called roaring twenties and early 1930s, when drinking alcohol and gambling in an underground speakeasy, though illegal, wasn't considered a social scourge. Postwar, nonetheless, all that changed. Law enforcement and high-ranking politicians cracked down hard on illegal gambling.

DALITZ BUYS INTO LAS VEGAS

By the late 1940s, Meyer Lansky, one of the lead architects of modern organized crime, had invested millions in Cuban casinos. To the Feds, Dalitz played an integral role inside Lansky's powerful organization, though he dabbled only in Cuban casinos. Dalitz was more impressed with Nevada's bright future, so he moved to Las Vegas, a vibrant city within the only state in the continental USA where gambling had been legalized. There he found his oasis, where gifted men with special gaming skills were respected and could thrive in a non-hostile environment.

Moe's first business acquisition in Las Vegas, the still unfinished Desert Inn (DI), opened in 1950. Wilbur Clark had begun building the resort, but much like Billy Wilkerson before him, Clark unfortunately ran out of money before completing construction. Dalitz led a group of financial backers from Cleveland, including Sam Tucker, Thomas McGinty, and Morris Kleinman, to fund the last phases of the resort's construction. When the DI finally opened, Clark was the designated front man and public face of the resort, while Dalitz remained in the background as the principal owner.

Within a year of the DI's opening, Senator Estes Kefauver initiated hearings on gambling and organized crime in America. Dalitz was called to testify, and more than held his own.

In one exchange, Kefauver questioned Dalitz about the source of funding for Las Vegas investments: "...You did get yourself a pretty good little nest-egg out of rum running, didn't you?"

Dalitz replied, "Well, I didn't inherit any money, Senator... If you people wouldn't have drunk it, I wouldn't have bootlegged it."[12]

THE NEED FOR SELF-PRESERVATION

Like his long-time friend Meyer Lansky, Moe Dalitz understood, that volatile men were not accustomed to reasoning together; that in order to survive a united front was needed. The best method to ensure cohesion among them was to blend. Thus, partnerships were formed when Mafia-made men married off their sons and daughters into rival clans in the cause of self-preservation. Likewise, in Las Vegas, Dalitz became the chief arbiter for the men who owned Las Vegas.

An interesting example of conflict resolution among the mobster casino owners in Las Vegas occurred during construction of the Stardust (nee Starlite)—by far the largest resort of its day. Moe Dalitz feared the Stardust would provide too much competition. With the threat of a Mob war looming, Dalitz called for a meeting among the big casino operators, most of whom flew in from out of town, including Dalitz's men Morris Kleinman and Longy Zwillman. Meyer Lansky chaired the meeting. The outcome was a negotiated settlement in which each of the owners received an interest in each other's hotels. As a bonus, lawyers arranged the agreement to prevent the government from knowing who owned what.

Dalitz and other mob leaders made one other important policy decision. They came to the conclusion that doing business profitably in Las Vegas required certain rules. Business could not be conducted the old fashioned way. During Prohibition, territories were divided among gangs with the help of machine guns and dynamite. Violence wouldn't work in a city that had come to thrive on gambling tourists. If the mob was to flourish, the dapper gaming aficionados in their high desert refuge had to get along, maintain a low profile, and stay out of the spotlight. Gang war and bloodshed were taboo, to keep Las Vegas from being labeled as nothing more than a killing field and a city of nefarious gambling joints.

As a counter move, the syndicate bosses mandated that contract murders must be performed outside of Nevada, thereby avoiding heat from law enforcement. When the decision was made to eliminate the Flamingo's Ben Siegel in June 1947 and the Riviera's Gus Greenbaum in December 1958, the killings occurred elsewhere.

Dalitz's concept of cohesion among owners became obsolete when the Chicago Outfit sent Anthony Spilotro, the "enforcer," to Las Vegas to reassert its authoritarian rule over the street rackets. Within weeks, five dead bodies turned up in the desert—beginning the bloody era in Sin City. That kind of action was precisely what the founding fathers had feared. High-profile violence inevitably led to exposure of the casino skim and the fall from grace of the traditional mob in casino front offices.

Later in his life, Moe Dalitz was responsible for building a championship golf course surrounded by multi-million-dollar homes, with the picturesque Desert Inn at the forefront. According to a Dalitz protégé Irwin Molasky, "Moe was an innovative thinker." It was Moe's idea to give his hotel guests something extra—so he conceived building a golf course in the midst of mansion-like homes, all in the shadow of the beautiful Desert Inn. Moe was the innovator behind bringing the Tournament of Champions PGA Tour event to Las Vegas, giving the city a shot in the arm from beneficial publicity. By using Wilbur Clark's affable image and by inserting the necessary money into the project, Moe Dalitz created the classiest gaming palace in the budding casino-resort community.

After the death of Tony Cornero in 1955, Dalitz helped supervise completion of the Stardust Resort & Casino. Then, in 1958, funded by millions in Teamsters loans with additional backing from Louis Jacobs' Emprise Corp., Dalitz and his affiliates took over the Stardust from a crew led by Jake "The Barber" Factor. These skilled, experienced gamers converted the Stardust into a huge winner by expanding the hotel and gaming area, and introducing the Parisian-style floor show, the *Lido de Paris*. This change paved the way for many firsts in Las Vegas, including the first extravagant topless revue in a casino resort, and later the renowned illusionists Siegfried & Roy.

Dalitz ran the Desert Inn until 1967, when he sold it to billionaire tycoon Howard Hughes. That sale marked the beginning of Hughes's famous $300 million spending spree, which ultimately made him the biggest casino operator in Nevada. For Dalitz, the sale of the Desert Inn was an opportunity to get the authorities off his back.

By this time a whole line of posh casino imitators had built lavish resorts along the Las Vegas Strip, including Caesars Palace, the Sands, the Dunes, Aladdin, and Tropicana.

So-called Sin City was emerging from its mob image, even though plenty of shady characters remained on the casino floor. Hughes, a novice casino operator when he purchased the Desert Inn, neglected to weed out the bandits stationed at craps table three. Though the table was listed as closed on the daily work sheet, the floor bosses and dealers reportedly spent months taking home the cash box and dividing it up!

DALITZ'S LATER YEARS

Long after the sale of the Desert Inn, Moe worked out of the Paradise Development office on Maryland Parkway across the street from Sunrise Hospital, the medical facility he was largely responsible for financing and building.

On a televised A & E story about the mob in Las Vegas, Ed Becker reported that Sunrise Hospital had been used covertly as a conduit for the casino skim. Allegedly, hospital patients were bandaged from head to toe with the casino skim tucked under their dressings, then sent off to Chicago or other suspicious Midwest locales.

Over the years critics came and went. Meanwhile, Dalitz continued amassing his financial empire and dutifully paying his taxes. He endured nearly a lifetime of criminal activity allegations, yet was indicted only twice—once in Buffalo in 1930, and once 35 years later in Los Angeles for tax evasion. Both charges were dismissed.

Dalitz shied away from interviews, which typically led back to his bootlegger days in the Midwest. Those who knew the man leading a secret life claimed, "he was not without a sense of humor and his own sense of image-making."

Dalitz once told a local reporter for the *Las Vegas Review-Journal*, "When I left home it was during Prohibition in Ann Arbor, Michigan, and I went into the liquor business while it was illegal. Then when the repeal came along, we went into the casino business in Kentucky and Ohio, where it was illegal. I learned everything I know there."[13]

Over the years, Moe impressed Las Vegas business leaders with his business acumen and success. On the other hand, those who engaged in the evils of Las Vegas gambling, such as authors Ed Reid and Ovid Demaris, were less impressed, evidenced by their 1963 book, *The Green Felt Jungle*. Their conclusion—that "he was a little mobster from Cleveland,"—was similar to the opinion of law enforcement excerpted from a chapter criticizing Dalitz for his racketeering days and notorious ties to known mobsters. The authors wrote that Dalitz "was still a hoodlum in conscience and mind, but his heart has weakened."[14]

The seasoned Moe Dalitz was more complex than people realized. At a time when most gaming executives were busy serving their self interests, Dalitz found time to help other Las Vegans. His influence with Jimmy Hoffa, for example, secured Teamster loans for more than casinos. Even though his initial ties with the Teamster boss were less than friendly, Dalitz later showed he had clout with Hoffa by securing in 1959, a $1 million low-interest Teamster loan to build Sunrise Hospital.

Other examples of clout came in the form of loans to construct a golf course and shopping malls at a time when most lending institutions shunned Las Vegas entrepreneurs.

Marydean Martin, a Las Vegas advertising executive and friend of Dalitz, once said, "Moe was always such a gentleman. He gave back to the community. When the Maude Frazier Building (at UNLV) was built, it had no furniture. He bought all the furniture and didn't want anybody to know about it. He was that kind of person. Moe almost never complained, but he was feeling down. He said, 'I'll bet your grandpa drank whiskey,' and I said that he did. 'I'm the guy who made the whiskey, and I'm considered the bad guy. When does the time ever come that you're forgiven?'

"I said, 'I don't know.' It was one of the very few times he ever said anything about it."[15]

Dalitz regularly donated to the Las Vegas Public Library system as well as other community organizations. He took pride in helping performers such as Frank Sinatra get their first breaks in show business. During his later years, Moe Dalitz counted among his frequent visitors such well-known personalities as Senate Majority Leader Harry Reid, Barbara Walters, Frank Sinatra, Suzanne Somers, Wayne Newton, and Buddy Hackett.

Because Las Vegas was an "open city" in Mob Syndicate terms, no single crime family owned the city; it was open for business to all the crime families. With their early financing of the Desert Inn, the Cleveland Mob got an early foothold in the Las Vegas casino business, which gave Moe Dalitz a head start in building his fortune. Despite his investments in legitimate businesses, his high-profile philanthropy, and his standing in Las Vegas society, the FBI believed—according to James Neff in his acclaimed *Mobbed Up*—that Moe Dalitz never relinquished his ties to The Mob.

By the late 1970s a pillar of Las Vegas casino society, Dalitz became the subject of a *Penthouse* magazine article, "La Costa: The Hundred-Million-Dollar Resort with Criminal Clientele." The article reported on the development of a San Diego spa, Rancho La Costa, funded by the Teamsters. The article named names, characterizing the spa as in effect run by criminals for the pleasure of a criminal clientele. Moe Dalitz and his co-investors, including Irwin Molasky, Merv Adelson, and Allard Roen, filed a defamation suit. They lost initially, then settled on repeal with a letter of clarification.

In 1976, Dalitz was named Humanitarian of the Year by the American Cancer Research Center and Hospital. Six years later he received the Torch of Liberty Award from the Anti-Defamation League of B'nai B'rith. Most notably, in 1979 he set up the Moe Dalitz Charitable Remainder Unitrust, a million-dollar fund to be divided upon his death. Because the last casino he built was the Sundance in downtown Las Vegas, later renamed the Fitzgerald, no fewer than 14 nonprofit organizations shared $1.3 million when he passed away at age 90.

He is remembered as a philanthropist and tireless worker who helped mold Las Vegas into a modern city.

BENJAMIN "BUGSY" SIEGEL

No one personified the mob in Las Vegas more than Benjamin

Bugsy Siegel

Siegel, the psychotic hoodlum given the moniker "Bugsy." A notoriously successful gangster, unfortunately for him he turned out to be a terrible builder and businessman. In Vegas lore he will forever be remembered by his connections to the renowned Flamingo Hotel and his outrageous girlfriend Virginia Hill.

Although Billy Wilkerson's dream of owning a luxurious Las Vegas casino became a fleeting memory, for the gangster Benjamin "Bugsy" Siegel that casino was the inevitable cause of his gruesome demise. His syndicate-style execution gave notice that no one—not even a lifelong pal of Meyer Lansky—can steal from his mob affiliates and get away with it. Siegel's gruesome murder not only made headlines worldwide, it linked the dashing psychopath forever with the fortunes of Las Vegas.

As time marches on, continued persistence of the myth that the Flamingo was Ben Siegel's idea tells you something about how legends are made. Genuine history buffs know the true founder of the Flamingo was Billy Wilkerson—though Siegel and the mob did wrestle controlling ownership from Wilkerson in the winter of 1946. Over the years Siegel was credited for everything from putting the glamour into today's fabulous Strip resorts to inventing Las Vegas itself. Nevertheless, few appreciate just how big a gangster he truly was.

EARLY YEARS

No one knows exactly where and when Ben Siegel began killing. Given his sociopathic behavior, many experts believe he may have started his murderous ways in his early teens. By the time he moved from New York to Las Vegas, Siegel was believed responsible for at least 25 murders.

Born Benjamin Siegelbaum in Brooklyn, New York, in 1905, he began his life of crime as a young boy. At first it was simple theft; then he and an accomplice, a young Moe Sedway, graduated to shaking down pushcart merchants on Manhattan's lower east side. After shortening his name to Siegel, he devised a protection racket whereby vulnerable street peddlers were forced to pay a dollar a day to avoid their merchandise being incinerated.

While still a teenager, Siegel joined up with Meyer Lansky—a friendship that developed into the gang that founded the notorious syndicate Murder Incorporated. Early on, the two men were known for their viciousness even while their operation concentrated primarily on car theft, gambling, and extortion. Eventually they graduated to a string of killings on behalf of the New York bootlegging community to which they now belonged. At the age of 23, Siegel married his high school sweetheart, Esta, the sister of another Mob hit man, Whitey Krakower. Siegel and Esta had two daughters, though the marriage ended in divorce as a result of Siegel's notorious womanizing.

Through Lansky, Siegel met and became friends with Charles "Lucky" Luciano, who later established the National Syndicate, the governing body of the country's five organized crime families. A year later, Siegel and Lansky began building ties to Charles Luciano and Frank Costello, future bosses of the Genovese crime family. Siegel and Lansky also became aligned with Frank Costello, future boss of the Genovese crime family, and Albert "Mad Hatter" Anastasia, Luciano's right hand man. In 1931 Siegel, Anastasia, Joe Adonis, and Vito Genovese formed the team that assassinated Mob boss Joe Masseria, paving the way for Luciano's rise to the top of the Syndicate. By then, Siegel and Lansky were firmly planted in the booze smuggling business.

Ten years later, following Prohibition, Siegel and Lansky switched from bootlegging to racketeering, including gambling, bookmaking, and running numbers. Siegel established himself in a suite at the Waldorf Astoria, where he lived in high style surrounded by bodyguards. He also traveled in a bullet-proof limousine.

SIEGEL'S FASCINATION WITH HOLLYWOOD

A number of published sources list Ben Siegel as one of the most feared and respected members of the East Coast Syndicate. Siegel not only evolved into a big-time earner for his syndicate pals but also became a very wealthy man in his own right.

In 1937 the Mob sent Ben Siegel West to oversee their national race and wire service for bookies. Some say that while there he wanted to become an actor. In any case he became fascinated with Hollywood and loved to hobnob with Hollywood stars, including Jean Harlow and George Raft. In Hollywood, Siegel led two lives—seducing starlets and running with the Hollywood crowd. At the same time, he was expanding his underworld activities, which included extorting money from gangster Tony Cornero's offshore gambling enterprises, muscling in on the businesses of nearby race tracks and dog tracks, investing in prostitution rings, and trafficking in illegal drugs from Mexico. Hardly an illegal activity existed in the American southwest that didn't involve Ben Siegel.

He took an interest in Las Vegas and began buying into small casinos, moving up to the Golden Nugget and New Frontier, while his friend Lansky concentrated on the El Cortez. Siegel's biggest moneymaker, however, was the wire service, a revenue stream that reportedly produced $25,000 a month.

Eventually, Siegel recruited Los Angeles gang boss Mickey Cohen as his lieutenant and moved Esta and their two daughters, Barbara and Millicent, to California. FBI reports noted that Siegel claimed on his tax return to earn his living through legal gambling at the Santa Anita race track.

SIEGEL ACQUITTED
IN GREENBERG MURDER TRIAL

In November 1939, Siegel was tried for the murder of Harry Greenberg, who had become a police informant. He was eventually acquitted of the charge, but all the publicity surrounding Siegel's trial affected his reputation. He especially hated the nickname "Bugsy," which the press popularized during the trial. The name, a synonym for crazy, originated from his youth on the streets of Brooklyn, where he was known for his crazy rages and psychopathic behavior. No one who valued his life used the nickname to Siegel's face.

Stories of Siegel's violence and intimidation were commonplace in Las Vegas. Once a tourist failed to refer to the boss by his proper name and instead addressed him as Bugsy. Siegel beat the tourist bloody with his ever-present 38 revolver. In another incident, Siegel forced hotel publicist Abe Schiller to crawl on his hands and knees around the pool after Schiller referred to the gangster's past and raised a question about the Bugsy nickname.

Those close to Ben Siegel knew that he craved legitimacy and respectability. Those qualities, however, always seemed beyond his reach. But everything changed in the spring of 1946. The Mob placed Siegel in charge of overseeing their interest in Billy Wilkerson's Flamingo—giving him a second opportunity to reinvent himself.

Originally, Meyer Lansky had sent Moe Sedway and Ben Siegel to Las Vegas in 1946 to look into expanding operations in the high-desert town. But nothing about the location attracted Siegel, who left Sedway in charge and took off for Hollywood. Years later, at Lansky's insistence, Siegel consented to being the watchdog of The Mob's interest in the Flamingo.

SIEGEL'S TAKEOVER OF THE FLAMINGO

In the period following the end of World War II, the scarcity of building materials caused the project to run over budget. It incurred other problems when Siegel got involved in making a lot of "interesting" changes in the project's building plans:

changes that conflicted with blueprints Wilkerson, the man in charge at the time, had already approved.

Siegel's design changes to the Flamingo were not only extravagant but also ludicrous, providing each room with its own sewer system at a cost of over a million dollars. That change required the purchase of new toilets ($50,000) and a new boiler (an additional $113,000). A change in kitchen design costing $29,000 could be considered relatively modest on the scale at which Siegel operated.

As if these cost overruns weren't bad enough, Siegel's lack of oversight resulted in substantial thefts of building materials and supplies. Many of the pilfered supplies were sold back to the project the following day. The World War II shortage of steel and other crucial building supplies drove cost overruns even higher. By the time of the Flamingo's completion in 1947, the one-million-dollar proposed cost had escalated to $6 million, a phenomenal overrun of $5 million. These extravagant, exorbitant costs testified to Siegel's troubled mind. The four-story Flamingo was built like a fortified vault, with reinforced concrete walls poured around heavy-duty steel stolen from naval shipyards. Siegel's roof-top suite was built with trap doors and escape hatches; one reportedly led to a getaway car in his private garage. "There were gun portals and hallways leading to nowhere." By the time the Flamingo finally opened its doors, it was virtually "a physical manifestation of Siegel's inherent fears," cited the *Las Vegas Review-Journal*.

The first sign of trouble for Siegel came in November of 1946, when The Mob issued an ultimatum: provide an accounting of expenditures or forfeit funding. Producing some kind of budget for the boys was the last thing Siegel wanted to do. Alas, how does one justify spending $6 million for a project originally budgeted at $1 million —perhaps $1.5 million, tops?

When Siegel realized he could be in serious danger, he tried to raise money by selling nonexistent stock in the Flamingo. Then he hurried to finish construction by doubling his on-site work force, believing the project could be completed in half the time. The mobster-turned-inept-project manager paid overtime and double-time. He even offered bonuses tied to performance deadlines, hoping to increase productivity.

A second money-raising scheme involved moving the opening up from the original date of March 1, 1947, to December 26, 1946, in hopes of earning enough money from casino profits to cover construction costs and begin paying dividends to investors.

The Flamingo's opening turned out to be a huge flop. After two weeks in operation the gaming tables were $275,000 in the red. As a result Siegel finally shut down the entire complex in late January. Meanwhile, Meyer Lansky persuaded the boys back in New York to grant a reprieve, which gave an extension to his lifelong pal. With Siegel getting yet another chance, he reopened the Flamingo in March as originally planned and made an effort to turn things around.

Meanwhile, the dons back east grew impatient for a more immediate return on their investment. The situation got worse when Lansky learned that Siegel's girlfriend, Virginia Hill, had access to the Flamingo building fund and frequently flew to Switzerland to make large cash deposits into a numbered Swiss bank account.

SIEGEL'S DEMISE

On the night of June 20, 1947, two men sat quietly in Virginia Hill's Beverly Hills mansion on North Linden Drive. One of them, Ben Siegel, was reading the *Los Angeles Times*; the other was his associate, syndicate conduit Allen Smiley. Siegel's girlfriend had flown to Europe a few days earlier. Suddenly, an unknown assailant fired nine shots through a window with a .30-caliber M1 carbine. Four shots entered Siegel's body, killing him almost instantly—two shots to the head, and two through the lungs. Smiley was never harmed in the assault. No suspects were ever charged in the murder, and the crime remains officially unsolved.

The Los Angeles Coroner's Report stated that Siegel's death was caused by cerebral hemorrhage. Remarkably, though, the pressure created by a bullet's striking and passing through Siegel's skull blew his left eye out of its socket. According to author Anthony Bruno, "Siegel was actually not shot exactly through the eye (the eyeball would have been destroyed if this had been the case), the bullet-through-the-eye style of killing, nevertheless became popular in Mafia lore and in movies, and was called the 'Moe Greene special' after the character Moe Greene—based on Siegel—who was killed in this manner in *The Godfather*."[16]

Siegel's high Hollywood profile undoubtedly became an embarrassment to the boys back east. He was frequently seen with such major silver screen stars as Cary Grant and everyone's favorite gangster portrayer, George Raft.

The order to kill Siegel came down because he'd committed more than one major sin. He'd lost money for The Mob, stolen money from The Mob, and brought publicity to The Mob, whose members preferred to keep a low profile. His murder showcased Las Vegas as the Mecca of underworld gambling. To paraphrase Wallace Turner's book *Gambler's Money*, the Mob arrived in Vegas and the Mob stayed.

George Raft once said of his pal, "He was a frustrated actor and secretly wanted a movie career, but he never quite had nerve enough to ask for a part in one of my pictures."[17]

But others knew Bugsy as an intense individual who harbored a charitable streak. He was a soft touch for the Damon Runyon Cancer Fund. His employees at the Flamingo thought well of him. He was good to them, and a lot of tears were shed when he was killed.

Still others knew Siegel as a textbook paranoid, always on edge, who, according to Don Garvin, the Flamingo's chief engineer, insisted on changing the locks of his room at the Flamingo every other week. Unable to trust Garvin to the task, Siegel and his then girlfriend Virginia Hill would watch from the hallway as the locksmith worked. Yet no amount of caution prevented the boys from disciplining one of their own. In the end, Ben Siegel emerged as an immortal Las Vegas legend, even though he neither invented Las Vegas nor originated the idea for the Flamingo.

In December 1993, the original Flamingo Hotel structure was torn down and the hotel's garden was built on the site. In the garden is a bronze plague set in front of the wedding chapel dedicated to Benjamin "Bugsy" Siegel. At the time the Bugsy Siegel Memorial was the only place in Las Vegas that formally acknowledged the Mob.

WHEREABOUTS OF VIRGINIA HILL

Minutes after Ben Siegel's death, Gus Greenbaum and an associate showed up at the Flamingo and informed Miss Hill of her lover's demise, telling her they were taking over the Flamingo.

Soon after, Hill flew back to Europe, where she lived her remaining years. Whether she returned the embezzled $2 million to Meyer Lansky is unclear, although the film *Bugsy* makes it appear she did. Actually, she most likely did give back the stolen money. If she hadn't the mob would surely not have allowed her to live.

During the final years of her life, separated from her husband, Virginia Hill was reported to be financially supported by her only child, Peter Hauser, who worked as a restaurant waiter. That Miss Hill needed financial support gives even more credence to the theory that she returned the embezzled $2 million to Lansky.

EARLY LIFE

Born in 1916 in Alabama, Virginia Hill—aka "the Flamingo," so-named for her long legs—was already a beauty in the 1930s when she moved to Marietta, Georgia, with her mother and two brothers. She left home at 17 and moved to Chicago, taking a job as a dancer at the World's Fair and working as a waitress on the side. At the restaurant she met the first mobster in her life—Joseph Epstein, Al Capone's accountant. Soon the two were sleeping together and working together in his bookmaking business. While in Chicago, she became the mistress of one gangster after another, all members of the Capone outfit, including Frank Nitti, Joe Adonis, Charles Fischetti, Frank Costello, and Major Riddle. The sassy sharp-tongued Georgia peach managed to keep her status on the A-list of underworld women while she stood toe-to-toe with many of Capone's cronies, and eventually Ben Siegel.

Hill's relationships with the Chicago Outfit were short-lived. She set her sights on Hollywood and left for Los Angeles, intending to use her Mob connections to become a star of the silver screen. Instead, the long-legged beauty met and fell in love with Ben Siegel.

Virginia Hill and Ben Siegel became acquainted through Joe Adonis in 1937 at a restaurant in New York City. Only a one-night stand, but they rekindled their relationship later at a party in New York in 1939. After that the pair became inseparable. They fell in love, and as their relationship evolved, they fought as hard as they loved. Both were known for having a short fuse.

Virginia Hill

Remarkably, Hill was one of the few people who dared stand up to Siegel when he went berserk.

Yet even before Hill met Siegel, she was one of the select few women entrusted with Mafia secrets. She was allegedly a courier for the Chicago Outfit, a charge she denied during the 1950-51 Kefauver Hearings.

During those hearings, Charles W. Tobey, the Senator from New

Hampshire, became curious about the reason so many men had given Virginia Hill so much money. He made the mistake of asking about her income. He had information there were a doctor in Chicago, Joe Epstein from the Capone mob, two gangsters from New York, Joey Adonis and Ben Siegel, a millionaire in Mexico, and a New York concert violinist—all giving her money over the years, for no apparent reason.

According to author Steve Fischer from *When the Mob Ran Vegas*, the official testimony, the Q and A with Miss Hill went like this:

> **SENATOR TOBEY:** Why would Joe Epstein give you all that money, Miss Hill?
>
> **WITNESS:** You really want to know?
>
> **SENATOR TOBEY:** Yes, I really want to know.
>
> **WITNESS:** Then I'll tell you why. Because I'm the best cocksucker in town!

According to observers, Hill's crude reply left the entire committee speechless and shocked television viewers across the country.

> **SENATOR KEFAUVER:** Order! I demand order!

> —Excerpt from Virginia Hill's testimony before
> the Senate Special Committee to Investigate
> Organized Crime in Interstate Gambling

Bea Sedway, the wife of Moe Sedway and a friend of both Hill and Siegel, said that when it came to informing on the mob, "She was smart and she knew how to keep her mouth shut."

Fifteen years after she testified in front of the Kefauver Committee, in March 1966, Virginia Hill died at the age of 49 of an apparent overdose of sleeping pills in Koppl, near Salzburg, Austria. Her body was found near an uninhabited area near a bridge spanning a small stream called the Alterbach.

Historians offer two competing theories about the death of Virginia Hill. The first that she was depressed about her life circumstances and no longer at the top of her game, so she swallowed a bottle of sleeping pills, walked outdoors, and lay down in the cold to die. The second involves a visit paid to Hill two days before her death by her former paramour, Mob hit man Joe Adonis. According to this theory, either the Mob finally caught up with her and meted out justice for her role in helping Siegel steal their money, or they killed her because she tried to shake down Adonis for money by threatening to tell the world what she knew about Mob activities.

GUS GREENBAUM: SYNDICATE ACCOUNTANT EXTRAORDINAIRE

Unlike tough guy Bugsy Siegel, who wasn't very good at handling money, Gus Greenbaum had a reputation as an efficient money manager and resort operator. An associate of Meyer Lansky, Greenbaum was a noted syndicate accountant for Las Vegas casino operations. Perhaps he's best known in Las

Vegas for bringing success to the fledgling Flamingo Hotel after Bugsy's death.

Born in 1894, Greenbaum joined Lansky's organization on New York's Lower East Side in the mid 1910s. In 1928 during Prohibition, Greenbaum began working with the Chicago Outfit, managing the Southwest division of the Transamerica Race Wire Service. Shortly after World War II, he was sent to Las Vegas to join Moe Sedway and Morris Rosen and get a handle on the Syndicate's gambling operations. Partnered with Sedway, Greenbaum ran the El Cortez until 1945, when Billy Wilkerson hired him to manage casino operations for the Flamingo Hotel.

From December 1946 until his death in June 1947, Bugsy Siegel was in charge of construction and creative control of the Flamingo. Immediately after Siegel's murder, Greenbaum took over, and within several months turned around the struggling resort and made it profitable. Eventually, he gained control of several other Syndicate casinos and their bookmaking operations.

Greenbaum had planned to retire to Arizona, and reportedly rejected offers to run the Riviera at the behest of mob boss Tony Accardo. Soon, Greenbaum was persuaded to change his mind— he accepted the job of managing the Riviera after his sister-in-law was murdered in her sleep.

Shortly after Greenbaum became the Riviera's general manager, his excessive gambling, womanizing, and drug use got him into embezzling from casino cash boxes. When his stealing was discovered by Syndicate bosses, in December 1958 Greenbaum and his wife, Bess, were found dead in their Arizona home, their throats slashed.

In the film *The Godfather*, Greenbaum's name is blended with Moe Sedway's for the fictional character Moe Greene.

JOHN "MARSHALL" CAIFANO

First the murder of Bugsy then of sticky-fingered Gus Greenbaum and two innocent relations, his sister-in-law and his wife, Bess. Apparently the dons back east who ruled the men of Las Vegas had problems finding the right person to look after their lucrative operations. Nevertheless, the boys had plenty of applicants interested in being overseers of mob-controlled casinos. Among them was John Caifano from Chicago. His extensive police rap sheet included convictions for burglary, extortion, larceny, and interstate fraud. Both he and Frankie Carbo were suspects in Bugsy Siegel's demise, both having been in the Beverly Hills area that June night in 1947. Both were acquainted with Allen Smiley, the man sitting next to Siegel when he was killed.

Born Marchello Giuseppe Caifano in Sicily in 1911, he immigrated to New York City and later moved to Chicago, where he became a high-ranking member of the Chicago Outfit. Moving again in 1951 to Las Vegas, Caifano changed his name to John Marshall when he was made overseer of mob-controlled casinos. It was reported that in exchange for the "Don" chair of Las Vegas, Caifano's beautiful blond-haired wife, Darlene, was traded to the Godfather of the Chicago Mob, San Giancana, a childhood pal of Caifano's. Caifano had been the go-to-guy for Chicago mobsters Tony Accardo and his underboss Sam Giancana. Caifano was fascinated with car bombs, such as the one that blew Willie Bioff to bits and pieces November 1955 when the Outfit snitch turned the key to the ignition of his pickup truck. Neither was Caifano a novice at killing with a knife up close, a technique equally capable of sending a message to anyone who divulged too much information about the Outfit.

Years earlier, in 1943, Caifano was suspected in the torture and arson murder in Chicago of the speakeasy waitress Estelle Carey. The Outfit suspected Carey's boyfriend was cooperating in a police investigation, so she was ice-picked to death. To complete the message she was also set afire.

Johnny Tocco knew Caifano first-hand. A boxing trainer from St. Louis, Tocco moved to Las Vegas in the 1950s, having worked in the corners of the fight ring of many champions, including Sonny Liston. He described Caifano as one of the toughest characters he'd ever met "Serious as a heart attack." Those were strong words coming from a corner man who worked in a world of tough professional fighters.

About five-foot-five, Caifano was pure psychopath. A gray-eyed ex-boxer, he had a criminal record going back to childhood. When he moved to Chicago he joined Giancana's 42 Gang, collecting debts for the Outfit. Rarely did he return empty handed. His penchant for violence defined his reputation, and he seemed to enjoy brutality. His sadistic nature was as effective as it was unnerving to those around him.

His arrival in Las Vegas as the new mob enforcer didn't go unnoticed. Cowboy Sheriff Ralph Lamb gave Caifano this option: "Keep a low profile, or get out of town." But like the tough Benny Siegel before him, Caifano loved the life of violence, money, and lust. He was also a psychopathic killer, like Siegel, and had no intention of keeping the fact that he had killed many people a secret.

"We were all terrorized by this guy," said Ed Becker, an organized-crime expert and former Riviera publicist. "If he walked into your hotel, you made sure he got whatever he wanted. You never approached him. He always looked at you like he was looking for a gun in your hand. He was such an evil son of a bitch that you didn't dare cross his line. His attitude was, 'I'm a mob guy. Don't fuck with me.'"[18]

Those that did, suffered.

BLAZE AT THE EL RANCHO

Caifano became a prime suspect in the mysterious fire that leveled the original El Rancho Vegas in June 1960, although charges were never filed. County arson investigators determined the fire accidental. Yet Ed Becker, a resident of a bungalow directly behind the El Rancho, recalled that Caifano had made several unsuccessful plays for the resort's chorus girls, earning his tough-guy routine and boorish behavior a boot from the property by the El Rancho owner, Beldon Katleman, mere hours before the fire. The police allegations only heightened Caifano's reputation as a scary psychopath not to be messed with.

Back in the early days of legalized gaming in Nevada, before the Gaming Control Board was established in 1955, licensees were approved despite numerous minor gambling violations, even if they had a history of violence. The Tax Commission kept these behaviors on file, yet with few exceptions the only real background analysis the Commission received came from a satellite office of the FBI.

When visitors from back east came to Las Vegas they often wisecracked at the presence on the casino floor of so many wise guys. Visitors remembered them from the illegal gambling joints back home—Cleveland, Steubenville, Boston, Miami, Chicago, and New York.

Nevertheless, the remote desert oasis of Las Vegas seemed immune to exposure as a town run by men who fronted for the hoodlum element. That was until the infamous Appalachian Mafia conference was uncovered November 14, 1957, at the home of mobster Joseph "Joe the Barber" Barbara in up-state New York. Peter Maas in *The Valachi Papers*, has written, "It was attended by roughly 100 Mafiosi from the United States, Canada, and Italy. Expensive cars with license plates from around the country aroused the curiosity of local and state law enforcement that raided the meeting, causing Mafiosi to flee into the woods and the area surrounding the Barbara estate. More than 60 underworld bosses were detained and indicted."[19]

Discovery of the Mafia meeting helped confirm the existence of organized crime in America, which some, including FBI Director J. Edgar Hoover, had long refused to acknowledge. It also initiated greater police investigation about the presence of organized crime in American society.

Even before New York's Mafia conference was exposed, starting in 1950 with the Kefauver Hearings, Nevada state legislators wanted to avoid federal intervention into Mob activities. Kefauver's focus on organized crime, which led to an overall increase in federal law-enforcement interest in mob activity in the nation, portended a special interest in high-profile Las Vegas. That focus, coupled with the ongoing threat of federal taxation of the state's gaming revenue, produced a significant countermeasure by Nevada legislators: creation of a two-tiered entity of casino regulation in the form of the Gaming Control Board and the Gaming Commission.

The gaming board had the investigative function, gathering information and weighing the data it collected. They then made recommendations to the gaming commission, which had the final say. The new regulatory structure had two positive effects on Nevada. It kept the Feds from getting involved, and it gave Nevada some degree of credibility for controlling its top industry, lacking ever since gaming was legalized in 1931.

New gaming regulations had their first positive result when they brought about the fall of Caifano in Las Vegas. The psychopath had been arrested several times since 1930, yet it was the administrative process of posting him into the *Black Book of notorious people banned from setting foot in Nevada casinos that led to his exclusion. If he wasn't allowed inside the casinos, it would be difficult for him to communicate or intimidate people.

Caifano qualified for the List of Excluded Persons not so much for his alleged brutal slaying of Estelle Carey but for his reputation, based on his being a suspect in a number of other murders. These included the unsolved killing of ex-Chicago police Lieutenant William Drury, the 1952 strangulation of gambler Louie Strauss, and the double-barreled shotgun murder of rackets insider Teddy Roe.

Ed Becker recalled seeing Caifano in the casinos during the 1950s, about the time the killer changed his name to Johnny Marshall. But even an alias couldn't disguise his sadistic nature, or the true reason he was in town: to shake down casino owners such as Beldon Katleman and Benny Binion on behalf of the Chicago Outfit.

*Footnote: Nevada's Black Book, officially known as the List of Excluded Persons, is the state's list of notorious people so unsavory to legal gambling that they are prohibited from setting foot in a casino.

By 1961, Caifano was added to the FBI's Ten Most Wanted List, and he decided to hide out at the Desert Inn, where he had friends. Unfortunately for him, after a few days of room service food, one of the staff reported Caifano's whereabouts, and the authorities put him in custody.

The local news media got wind of Caifano's capture at the DI. When Caifano was escorted from the property, *Las Vegas Sun* photographer Frank Maggio was there on assignment. "Maggio approached Caifano, who took a swing at him, smashing his heavy Speed Graphic camera. Maggio reacted out of instinct, retaliating with a right cross that nailed Caifano flush on the chin, knocking him cold."[20]

Caifano's frightening career was far from over, however. As Sam Giancana's most productive torpedo, Caifano was suspected in another string of murders. These included the 1973 shotgun slaying of corrupt former Chicago chief investigator Richard Cain, and the 1977 car-bombing of oil millionaire Ray Ryan. Earlier, Ryan had testified in court that Caifano tried to extort $60,000 from him. Caifano ended up doing six years in prison for extortion. Unfortunately for Ryan, Caifano held a grudge against him, and two years after Caifano emerged from prison, Ryan's life brutally ended—Mafia style.

Meanwhile, two of Caifano's old pals, Sam Giancana and Johnny Rosselli, had been murdered. Giancana was gunned down in Chicago in June 1975. Rosselli was chopped into pieces and stuffed into an oil drum found floating near Miami in August 1976.

What finally got Caifano put away for a long federal sentence was his connection to the theft of 2,000 shares of unissued

Westinghouse stock worth $2 million. He was sentenced in May 1980, to 20 years at the federal penitentiary in Sandstone, Minnesota. After an early release from prison incarcerated only 11 years, Caifano lived quietly in Fort Lauderdale, Florida. In stark contrast to the lifelines of mob casino overseers Siegel and Greenbaum, doing time in prison seemed to extend Caifano's life expectancy; he died of natural causes in September 2003 at age 92.

"HANDSOME" JOHNNY ROSSELLI

Distinct from the boorish tough guy Caifano with a hair-trigger temper, Johnny Rosselli was the dapper diplomat of the Chicago Outfit. Rosselli represented the boys' interests in both Hollywood and Las Vegas.

Born Filippo Sacco in Esperia, Italy, in July 1905, Rosselli immigrated to Boston in 1911, although at his later trial he testified under oath that he was born in Chicago. He had a checkered career. He fled to Chicago in 1922 after allegedly committing a murder, joined the Chicago Outfit, and changed his name to John Rosselli.

He moved to Los Angeles in 1924 and joined the Jack Dragna crime family. After becoming friends with film producer Bryan Foy, the two of them produced several gangster movies.

By 1940, Rosselli was involved in the Outfit's multi-million-dollar extortion campaign against the motion picture industry. In 1942, he joined the U.S. Army, and a year later was convicted of labor racketeering in the movie industry based on testimony of Willie Bioff. He served six years in prison. Upon his release, Rosselli became the Outfit's go-to guy and maintained his ties to the Dragna crime family.

From 1954 to 1957 Rosselli crisscrossed the country offering "juice" and protection in regions declared open territories by La Cosa Nostra, such as Las Vegas, where no single crime family controlled the city.

"Juice" had two distinct meanings in Mafia lingo. For loan-sharking, juice and vigorish (or the vig), were synonyms for the interest charged on a loan, but in gaming circles, the term referred to connections in the business. Rosselli extended his connections along the East Coast from Boston to Miami, and in the southwest from Arkansas to Vegas to L.A. Outside the country, he migrated to Cuba, where he was well known at Havana casinos, and to Guatamala, where he allegedly involved himself in 1950's politics and developed ties with the CIA.

John Rosselli

ROSSELLI
AND THE TROPICANA HOTEL

In 1957, a consortium of mobsters led by Meyer Lansky, Carlos Marcello, and Frank Costello put together enough money to start construction on the Tropicana Hotel-Casino. Rosselli's role in Las Vegas began to take shape. He was assigned the responsibility of monitoring the project's expenses, for which he received a percentage of the lucrative gift shop concession.

Rosselli's police record and reputation for running with a rough crowd ultimately kept him from becoming a licensed casino owner. He realized, however, that his true calling was establishing high-end connections in legitimate American society. Rosselli went on to become known as the man who made the Tropicana successful. His skill in real estate development and finance was unmatched, as he helped facilitate loans through the Teamsters Central States Pension Fund. In addition, he was on site when the Riviera was built, and he filled its key executive positions with Chicago Outfit personnel.

When the Cuban Revolution ended in January 1959, Fidel Castro nationalized all the Mob's casinos in Cuba and closed them a year later. That put the mobsters out of business there. No wonder that Rosselli, along with Outfit boss Sam Giancana and Tampa boss Santo Trafficante, became involved via recruitment by the CIA in the plot to kill Cuban dictator Fidel Castro. Later, in the mid 1970s, Rosselli became an intriguing subject for the Church committee's attempt to resolve suspicions of conspiracy in the plot to kill President John F. Kennedy, as well as the failed attempt to assassinate Fidel Castro.

In 1963, Frank Sinatra sponsored Rosselli for membership in the exclusive Los Angeles Friars Club. Soon after his acceptance, Rosselli discovered an elaborate cheating scheme in a Friar's Club poker game run by one of his Las Vegas friends, Maury Friedman. Rosselli demanded a cut. Scores of wealthy men, including actor Zeppo Marx and Harry Karl, husband of actress Debby Reynolds, were cheated out of millions of dollars.

After Howard Hughes went on his buying spree of Mob casinos, Rosselli and the men from whom Hughes had made his purchases had a great time pilfering from the casino.

One famous instance of skimming, not connected with The Mob, took place at the Desert Inn when Howard Hughes owned it. One of the three operating craps tables was taken off the books one night, but at the end of the shift one of the conspirators opened the drop box under the table and divided the night's earnings among the floor dealers and other floor personnel before the drop box reached the count room. The thieves carried out their pilfering activities for three months before being discovered.

About this time Las Vegas was beginning to lose its mobbed-up image, especially with the emergence of Howard Hughes. Yet John Rosselli was a mob man and still had his hooks in unwanted places. He maintained a high profile, which some people thought too high. Finally, in December 1966, word got around to Clark County Sheriff Ralph Lamb that Rosselli was extorting money from some of the city's key casino licensees.

One particular evening in December of that same year, Sheriff Lamb learned that Rosselli was in the coffee shop at the Desert Inn with its owner Moe Dalitz. Lamb sent in a rookie deputy with precise instructions: inform Mister Rosselli that the sheriff wanted to see him downtown.

"He told my guy to get lost, which he shouldn't have done," Sheriff Lamb recalled in a later interview. "I went in and helped him brush up on his manners."

What happened next was described by authors Charles Rappleye and Ed Becker: "Lamb strolled into the coffee shop, grabbed Rosselli by his silk necktie, lifted him out of the booth, then pulled him across the table and cuffed him about the head and shoulders all the way back to the patrol car. After handcuffs were snapped on, Lamb slammed Rosselli into the back seat."[21]

At the sheriff's office, Rosselli was thrown in a cage and hosed down with delousing agent like a flea-infested dog. From that mortifying moment on, Rosselli's star status dimmed, and his stature in Las Vegas diminished. Though his falling from grace didn't slow his criminal activity, his profile was slighted.

Just when things seemed bad for Rosselli, they got worse. In 1968, authorities discovered Rosselli never acquired lawful residency or citizenship in the United States, and he was tried and convicted of maintaining an illegal residence. The Immigration and Naturalization Service ordered him deported. However, Rosselli's Italian homeland refused to accept him, so he remained in the United States.

A year after his deportation hearings, authorities were about to get justice for his past criminal activity. The dapper Rosselli, renowned as a genius in the growth of gambling in Las Vegas and notorious as a key figure in the CIA plot to assassinate Fidel Castro, was suddenly convicted of rigging a poker game at the

Friars Club in Los Angeles. In February 1969, he received a five-year prison sentence.

When released, Rosselli was a mere shadow of the well-connected man people once called Handsome Johnny. Nevertheless, he wasn't finished making headlines, which became a huge concern for the Mafia dons back east.

LATER LIFE

When Senator Frank Church's committee held hearings in Washington to discuss publicly, for the first time, several of the CIA's past undercover missions, Rosselli was subpoenaed to testify about the plot to kill Fidel Castro.

Shortly before he was scheduled to appear, an unknown gunman shot and killed the Chicago Outfit's boss Sam Giancana in the basement of his home in Oak Park, Illinois. It happened just days before Giancana was scheduled to testify before the Church committee. Giancana's murder alarmed Rosselli, whose own Mob influence vanished with Giancana's demise and impelled him to permanently leave Las Vegas and Los Angeles for Florida.

During the hearings, the CIA and FBI agents who testified supported their testimony with files of notes. They also prepared working drafts to help them relate events. Rosselli had his own props, which seemed to impress Senator Barry Goldwater. Rosselli testified on June 24 and September 22 1975. The record shows the following exchange:

SENATOR GOLDWATER: Mr. Rosselli, it's remarkable to me how your testimony dovetails with theirs. Tell me, Mr. Rosselli, during the time that all this was going on, were you taking notes?

WITNESS: Senator, in my business, we don't take notes.[22]

Throughout the hearings, Rosselli's testimony was reported as more colorful than informative. He kept his pledge of omertà, the Mafia code of silence, and never exposed his Mob associates. But the powers that be felt differently.

When Rosselli returned to his home in Plantation, Florida, his boredom grew with each passing day. He refused to take seriously the warnings from his friends that his life was in danger.

John Rosselli was last seen alive on July 28, 1976. The following month his decomposing body was found in a 55-gallon oil drum floating in the bay near Miami. When the authorities discovered the drum they found Johnny Rosselli strangled and shot, his legs sawn off. It was believed that he gave public testimony without Mafia approval. Other theorists speculate that Castro paid him back for his participation in the failed plot to assassinate him.

In the absence of Rosselli, the boys back east, once again, began looking at potential candidates to oversee their casino interests in Las Vegas.

THE STARDUST'S
FRANK "LEFTY" ROSENTHAL

Immortalized in the Nicholas Pileggi book *Casino*, Frank Rosenthal was a noted American sports handicapper and casino executive. His career as a mob front man became further inspiration for the acclaimed 1995 Martin Scorcese film *Casino*, a fictionalized adaptation of Pileggi's true crime account. Rosenthal—re-named in the film Sam "Ace" Rothstein was portrayed by Robert De Niro, and his long-time friend and Mafia enforcer Anthony Spilotro—re-named Nicky Santoro—was played by Joe Pesci.

Born on Chicago's West Side in October 1929, Rosenthal often skipped school so he could watch the Cubs play baseball. There, in the bleachers of Wrigley Field, he learned to hone his skills at odds making and successful sports betting.

By 1961 Rosenthal was living in Miami, Florida, a nationally recognized professional sports handicapper and bettor. Often, he was reportedly seen there in the company of notorious Chicago Outfit members Jackie Cerone and Flore Buccieri. About this time Rosenthal was accused of match fixing and subpoenaed to appear before Senator McClellan's subcommittee on Gambling and Organized Crime. As a result of the hearings Rosenthal was barred from all racing establishments in Florida, though he was never charged.

"Despite his frequent arrests for illegal gambling and bookmaking, Rosenthal was convicted only once, pleading no contest in 1963, for allegedly bribing New York University point guard Ray Paprocky to shave points for a college basketball game in North Carolina. To escape police attention Rosenthal moved to Las Vegas in the late 1960s."[23]

Rosenthal's skill as an expert odds maker catapulted his reputation, and given the responsibility of secretly running several mob-controlled casinos, including the Stardust, Marina, Fremont, and Hacienda. Later, he pioneered the first Nevada sports book to operate within a casino, and developed the Stardust into the world's leading venue for sports betting. Those in the know believed Rosenthal was one of a handful of men who set the odds for thousands of bookmakers from coast to coast.

In addition, Rosenthal became known as the first employer in Las Vegas to hire female croupiers; the innovative move proved very profitable. Within a year income nearly doubled at the Stardust, and soon other Strip casinos followed suit in their hiring policy.

Frank "Lefty" Rosenthal

GAMING COMMISSION HEARING

In 1976, Nevada gaming authorities learned that Rosenthal was covertly operating casinos in Las Vegas without a gaming license. The Nevada Gaming Commission held a hearing to judge the feasibility of his obtaining a license. But Rosenthal was denied a license based on his nefarious associations with known mobsters, in particular his boyhood friendship with the notorious Chicago capo Anthony Spilotro.

Unable to obtain a necessary gaming license, Rosenthal designated himself Stardust's "Entertainment Director" and starred in a talk show publicizing the Stardust Casino. Originally televised from a studio, the show was moved to the casino sports book where Rosenthal's first guest was none other than Frank Sinatra in his first ever talk-show appearance.

LATER YEARS

In October 1982, Rosenthal miraculously survived an attempted car bombing when a metal plate under the seat absorbed most of the explosion. Although the person or persons suspected in the attempted assassination were never identified, police suspects included Anthony Spilotro, Mafia boss Frank Balistrieri, and outlaw bikers who were friends of Rosenthal's ex-wife Geri.

Due to his alleged ties to organized crime, in 1988 Frank Rosenthal was entered into Nevada's Black Book, and from then on prohibited from entering Nevada casinos. He returned to Miami Beach, where he worked as a consultant and operated an offshore betting website. Rosenthal died of heart failure in October 2008 in his Miami Beach home at age 79.

ANTHONY SPILOTRO: THE VEGAS ENFORCER

Behind famed odds-maker Frank Rosenthal was his boyhood friend, future overseer of the casino skim, and Vegas point man Anthony Spilotro. By the time of his murder in 1986, Anthony Spilotro, the five-foot-five little tough guy from Chicago, was suspected by the Feds of at least 25 murders, not to mention all the other mayhem he caused during his sordid stay in Las Vegas.

Anthony Spilotro

Spilotro was well-known to the FBI agent investigating organized crime in Las Vegas during the 1970s and 1980s, William F. Roemer Jr. In his biography of Spilotro, *The Enforcer*, the Bureau's most decorated agent told of the FBI's bugging the offices of the casinos, concentrating on those with known Mob ties. Even the FBI was surprised at the amount of cash skimmed and sent off to Chicago. Some estimates placed the amount at $12 million annually, in 1980's dollars.

SPILOTRO'S EARLY YEARS

Born Anthony John Spilotro in May 1938, the man known as the "enforcer" lived most of his life the way he died—brutally violent! Agent Roemer described the pint-sized Chicago hoodlum as ruthless, scheming, and as anti-social as any up-and-coming gangster could be. Just a kid out of Steinmetz High, he exhibited a flair for extreme violence in the way he extorted lunch money from his classmates.

Spilotro dropped out of school in his sophomore year and became known for a string of petty crimes, such as purse snatching and shoplifting. His first arrest occurred in 1955. Before Spilotro hooked up with organized crime, he was arrested 13 times. In 1962 he was befriended by the Outfit's enforcer "Mad" Sam DeStefano, a notorious loan shark and one of the worst torture killers in the annals of crime in a city long recognized for violent inventiveness.

Under the tutelage of Mad Sam DeStefano, Anthony Spilotro started out with the Chicago Outfit as a debt collector and rapidly became occupied in higher levels of criminal activity. DeStefano's preferred torture device was the ice pick. He exhibited his skills with painful impunity to his youthful pupil—Tony Spilotro—a recent high school dropout who seemed to relish the agony of others.

HE "MADE HIS BONES"

In 1962, Spilotro would "make his bones," to commit an ordered murder for the first time, in the notorious M&M killings of Jimmy Miraglia and Bill McCarthy. Spilotro was given orders to wipe out two young thieves who had robbed and shot three people in the mobster-populated neighborhood of Elmwood Park, near Chicago—an area designated off limits to any criminal activity by the Outfit. The two thieves were also reportedly in debt to Spilotro's old boss, Sam DeStefano.

Spilotro found one of the young thieves, Bill McCarthy, clamped his head into an industrial vise, and squeezed it until he got McCarthy's confession to the whereabouts of his accomplice, Jimmy Miraglia. Witnesses later reported that during the torture, McCarthy's eye popped out of its socket before he finally confessed. This head-in-the-vice method was vividly portrayed in Martin Scorcese's film *Casino* by the fictional character Tony Dogs as the victim, and the fictional Nicky Santoro as Spilotro.

On May 15, 1962, McCarthy and Miraglia were found dead in the trunk of a car on the southwest side of Chicago. Badly beaten, they also had their throats slit. Though Spilotro was indicted for his role in what the press popularized as the "M&M Murders," Spilotro was acquitted.

After his acquittal, Spilotro's reputation grew within the Outfit, and his bosses realized he could get information from anyone. A year later he was rewarded when the Chicago Outfit designated him a "Made Man." Spilotro got assigned a territory on Chicago's Northwest side where he controlled the Outfit's bookmaking operations.

MOB POINT MEN IN LAS VEGAS

By 1971 Spilotro was assigned to Las Vegas to oversee the Outfit's unreported profits illegally removed from casino count rooms. The Chicago mob's three "Point Men" who oversaw the infamous Las Vegas skim are described by the FBI as follows: Tony Spilotro was the third in a line of assigned bosses designated to protect mob interests and enforce their policies in Vegas. Johnny Rosselli was the Outfit's first. He served as underboss to

Frank Nitti, Paul Ricca, and Tony Accardo, the Mob mastermind who ruled the Chicago crime family after Sam Giancana's death. Rosselli, who proved more adept as an emissary and negotiator, was quickly replaced by Giancana with Marshall Caifano, aka John Marshall, another pint-sized tough guy who fit right in as the mob's third overseer in Vegas.

The press gave Spilotro the moniker "Tony the Ant" after agent Roemer referred to him as "that little pissant." The media decided Roemer's word was inappropriate for public consumption and shortened it to the "Ant." Tony Spilotro was also nicknamed Tough Tony.

Spilotro set himself up in Jay Sarno's Circus Circus casino, purchasing the lucrative gift shop for $70,000. In this way he would appear legitimate, and he'd be almost next door to Rosenthal and the Stardust operations. From there he took the name of Anthony Stuart, his wife's surname, and under the guise of a legitimate businessman began his nefarious criminal activities.

It wasn't long after Spilotro's arrival in Las Vegas that five murders occurred. Each victim was a loan shark, and curiously, each had been tortured before being killed and buried in the desert.

SPILOTRO AND ROSENTHAL

Noted odds-maker extraordinaire Frank Rosenthal was first linked to Spilotro in 1962, when Spilotro pleaded guilty to attempted bribery of a collegiate basketball player. The two mobsters worked together in Miami in 1964, when Spilotro was sent there to oversee Rosenthal's bookmaking business and make sure no one muscled in on the Outfit's operations. The former boyhood buddies from Chicago became acquainted again in Las Vegas, when Rosenthal began running the operations of the Stardust, Fremont, Hacienda, and Castaways for the Outfit.

OPERATION VEGMON

William F. Roemer Jr. was the lead FBI case agent working "Operation VEGMON" (Vegas Money), which followed the trail of the skim money from Las Vegas back to the Midwest. The courier for the wise guys was the wife of a wholesale meat proprietor who supplied Outfit casinos with choice cuts of steaks and chops. To maintain goodwill and keep his business intact, the meat supplier sanctioned the scheme to have his wife transport the skim from Las Vegas to the Chicago law firm of Bieber & Brodkin, long-time mouthpieces for the Outfit.

The unidentified woman traveled by train and was given the best accommodations at the Ambassador East Hotel, while Bieber & Brodkin divvied the cash among the appropriate people—sweet operation for both the businessman and the Chicago wise guys. Neither the mystery woman nor her husband was prosecuted for their questionable activities.

The tough-guy reputation Spilotro acquired was well-deserved. In addition to the 25 murders in the Chicago area alone that the FBI linked him to, one was a particularly grisly torture and killing of local enforcer and loan shark William "Action" Jackson, whom The Outfit suspected of cooperating with federal authorities. According to Roemer, Jackson "was hung on a meat hook while being slowly tortured to death."

By 1974 Spilotro had sold the gift shop at Circus Circus for $700,000, ten times the price he had paid for it in 1971.

THE HOLE IN THE WALL GANG

In 1976, Spilotro formed a burglary ring with his brother Michael and with Herbert "Fat Herbie" Blitzstein, utilizing eight other associates as burglars. The crew became known as the Hole in the Wall Gang because of its modus operandi for gaining entry—drilling through exterior walls and ceilings. Also in 1976, together with Chicago bookmaker Blitzstein and brother Michael, Spilotro opened The Gold Rush, Ltd, a combination jewelry store and electronics factory located one block from the Strip. It served the gang as a place to fence stolen goods.

By 1979, things went from bad to worse for the Vegas enforcer. Gaming authorities added his name to the infamous Nevada Black Book, barring him from stepping foot in every casino in the state. Spilotro was outraged by the ruling, though it didn't stop him from further criminal activity. Away from Nevada casinos, Anthony Spilotro continued loan sharking, stealing, and fencing stolen goods.

To make matters worse, after his own arrest for an attempted burglary at Bertha's jewelry store in Las Vegas, Spilotro's boyhood friend Frank Cullotta turned federal witness to save himself when he realized Spilotro was out to kill him. Cullotta also admitted that for many years he'd done "muscle work" on Spilotro's behalf, including setting up the infamous 1962 M&M murders of Miraglia and McCarthy.

More heat for Spilotro came when Sal Romano, a crew member who specialized in disabling alarm systems, flipped and became a government informant. Then, during the July 4, 1981, burglary at Bertha's, Romano worked counter-intelligence. FBI Agent Roemer wrote, "Unbeknown to Spilotro, his brother Michael, partner Herbie Blitzstein, and the Hole in the Wall Gang burglars, Romano had turned informant several months earlier; federal agents and police were waiting for the burglars when the heist at Bertha's went down."[24]

DEATH OF ANTHONY SPILOTRO

Sadly for Anthony Spilotro, his once-reliable value as point man had become a security risk to his underworld bosses. He was indicted in Las Vegas for heading a burglary ring. Moreover, he violated mob decorum by conducting an affair with Geri, the wife of Frank Rosenthal. It was also rumored that he was dealing drugs. Meanwhile, though Frank Cullotta had testified against Spilotro, his testimony was found insufficient, and Spilotro was acquitted of murder charges.

Anthony Spilotro, whose affair with Geri sabotaged his friendship with Rosenthal, ultimately met his demise at the hands of mob killers. Much like *Casino*, the film that captured the 1970-80s era of Las Vegas and fascinated millions of moviegoers, Spilotro and his brother Michael were buried in a cornfield in Enos, Indiana. According to the *Chicago Tribune*, Nicholas Calabrese, a former mob hit-man who "testified in the Operation Family Secrets trial, said the brothers were told they were being promoted in the Outfit. Anthony Spilotro was to become a 'capo,' and his brother Michael was to become a 'made member.' They were driven to a mob home in Bensenville, Illinois, and were beaten to death in the basement. Later they were transported to the Indiana cornfield."[25] At the time of his death, Anthony Spilotro was 48.

Looking back, historians today generally believe it was Anthony Spilotro's street crimes that ultimately led to the demise of the Vegas Mafia. Once the authorities began investigating Spilotro's criminal activity, it was a matter of time before other mob-related crimes came to the attention of police and the FBI.

Spilotro was ultimately replaced in Las Vegas by Donald "The Wizard of Odds" Angelini. Anthony Spilotro was survived by his wife Nancy, his son Vincent, and his remaining brothers.

Chapter 3
FASCINATING CASINO OWNERS OF LAS VEGAS

"In the valley of the blind, the one-eyed man is king!"
—Steve Wynn on television's *60 Minutes.*

*W*hen we think of the city's modern-day builders who comes to mind other than Kirk Kerkorian and Steve Wynn, respected, innovative men, corporate self-made visionaries who made a fortune developing massive themed resorts throughout Southern Nevada. The saga of Las Vegas wouldn't be complete without revealing the details of how these intriguing entrepreneurs earned their fortunes building and operating casinos. Theirs is as much a wondrous story as the fabulous casino resorts they created.

Yet, before self-made men like Kirk Kerkorian and Steve Wynn bought into Las Vegas—before the innovative Bill Bennett built behemoth themed resorts that evolved into an empire of casinos—other kinds of captivating men were attracted to Las Vegas.

One man in particular was, at the time of his arrival in Las Vegas, the richest in the world, the eccentric billionaire Howard Hughes. Instead of building casinos as Kerkorian, Wynn, and Bennett did, Hughes bought the casinos as if they were toys—six casinos in all—and went on to amass many other land investments throughout Nevada. Though Hughes wasn't a visionary developer, he ultimately became the state's biggest land owner and employer, owning more casinos than any other private individual.

Another different breed of men came before these respected corporate visionaries, and they too made their mark on Las Vegas. More sinner than saint, years earlier they developed their business acumen during the Prohibition era in America's not-so-hidden underworld of bootlegging, which was often connected to running illegal saloons and gambling parlors.

Two monumental events in the annals of Las Vegas were a magnet for these men and inevitably determined the city's fate for years to come. First was the 1931 legalization of gambling in Nevada—then, two years later, the repeal of Prohibition. Both events persuaded future casino operators—legitimate or otherwise—to come and make their fortunes in Southern Nevada.

Flush with millions in illicit bootleg money, most of these men were sons of Italian immigrants, such as Tony Cornero, who grew up during America's roaring 1920s and desperate 1930s. Many others started out as bootleggers, such as the Desert Inn's Moe Dalitz, supplying illegal booze to a thirsty America. By the 1930s these rumrunners realized it was just a matter of time until

Prohibition would be repealed and they'd be out of business. Thus, almost overnight, a remote whistle stop in the middle of the Mojave Desert became a beacon of opportunity for anyone with a few suitcases full of cash and skill at running a casino. Beginning in the late 1930s, a number of ex-bootleggers looking to own and operate a legitimate casino were lured to Nevada.

One of the more fascinating men of that era was a Texas gambler named Benny Binion. Distinct from the modern-day Ivy-League men such as Steve Wynn and Gary Loveman (the CEO of Harrah's Entertainment and former Harvard professor)—and unlike the immigrant Tony Cornero who had come before him—Benny was an American-born cowboy who earned his gambling education in the "Texas School of Hard Knocks."

BENNY BINION: THE INNOVATOR WHO PUSHED THE LIMITS

The *Review-Journal's* A.D. Hopkins said it well when he described the innovative Benny Binion: "He was a cowboy who pushed the limits. A Texan who knew a thing or two about horse trading, and gambling, and laid his claim on Fremont Street, and changed the face of Western hospitality."[26]

Born the son of a North Texas horse trader in November 1904, Benny spent much of his early years traveling with his father around the Panhandle region. Because of his poor health, his parents kept him out of school, thinking the boy would benefit from being in the open air. Benny learned to gamble playing poker with other traders who gathered with his father at the various campgrounds near western rodeos and other popular

Benny Binion

events where horses were bought and sold, such as county fairs.

By the early 1940s Benny had become the reigning mob boss of Dallas. Soon after he tried to muscle in on the gambling rackets in nearby Fort Worth, the mob boss of that city, Lewis Tindell, was found dead. By the end of World War II, the Chicago Outfit made a successful takeover of Dallas, and following the 1946 elections Benny lost his "connection" with the local government and relocated to Las Vegas.

BENNY MOVES TO LAS VEGAS

Benny Binion purchased the Apache Hotel and the El Dorado Club in 1947, re-opening them as Binion's Horseshoe Casino. The casino promptly became popular, especially among locals, largely due to higher bet limits and Benny's liberal comp policy. In 1951, Benny purchased the building that housed the Las Vegas Club and converted it into the Westerner Gambling House and Saloon.

FBI files reveal that for the most part, Benny Binion stayed within the law after he moved to Las Vegas. Benny's tattered history in Dallas, though, kept the Feds wary, knowing he was someone to be reckoned with.

Jack Binion, Benny's eldest son and president of the Horseshoe Casino, recalled that his father was the first owner to install carpet in a downtown casino, the first to have limousines pick up customers at the airport, and the first to offer free drinks to slot machine players.

"Everybody was comping big players, but Benny comped little players," noted Leo Lewis, comptroller at the Horseshoe. Leo quoted Benny as saying, "If you wanta get rich make little people feel like big people." Comps are complimentary items given out by casinos to stimulate players to gamble.

Benny was also famous for raising the betting limits that all the downtown casinos had, from the usual $50 to $500. The Horseshoe's nearby competition was not pleased with this innovation. They had to raise their limits to stay competitive. Benny's change to that limit produced several death threats.

Throughout the gaming industry, betting limits have always been crucial to protect casinos from the effects of a player's progressive betting system, some form of which many gamblers use. If, for instance, a player wins a $10 bet, his next move is to bet the original $10 again plus the $10 won. True gamblers dream of turning such a parlay into a lengthy streak of luck and winning an enormous amount of money. Casino operators have nightmares about enduring such costly streaks. A $50 house limit blocks a winning streak at the fourth bet, resulting in a $270 win, whereas the same parlay player with a $500 limit can keep doubling up until the seventh bet, winning as much as $1,130 before waiting his next turn.

PLOT TO KIDNAP TED BINION

In 1967, almost 30 years before Binion's youngest son mysteriously died, a couple of local Las Vegans hatched a plot to rival any made-for-television tale of greed and deceit. It left a bullet-ridden cabbie lying dead in the desert.

In *Street Talk*, George Knapp wrote, "In an aging downtown graveyard, beneath a modest headstone and a carpet of grass, are the remains of one Marvin Shumate, remembered only by scattered relatives, and a few stubborn detectives. Shumate worked as a cab driver, and on a fateful night in December 1967, he left work, went to a bar at Paradise and Flamingo, and was never seen alive again."[27]

His body was found in a remote area near Sunrise Mountain with a shotgun blast to the chest and a slug from a 357 in his head, the latter touch an apparent attempt of the killer to leave a message. Police called the shooting a mystery since Shumate wasn't robbed. He had a lengthy police rap sheet of mostly minor infractions, and those who knew him couldn't figure a reason why anyone would do this.

As police learned more, the motive soon became apparent. A homicide detective told the media an informant spilled the whole story, yet no one was ever charged with the crime, and the complete story was never aired to the public—until George Knapp reported the story.

Though newspaper reports at first were vague, police investigators suspected that Shumate and an accomplice, also a cabbie, were plotting to kidnap Ted, son of legendary casino operator Benny Binion. The accomplice got cold feet when he learned that once the ransom was secured, Ted would be killed. The police believe the accomplice reported the plot to Benny Binion and made some kind of deal with him.

Las Vegans remember Benny as an innovative gambler, family man, and goodhearted person, but lawmen knew the real Benny as someone not to be messed with. His extensive FBI file mentions his younger days in Texas as a bootlegger and gambler, where he was known to have killed two men in self-defense. Benny was also alleged to have occasional contacts with guys in the Chicago Outfit. In Sin City, however, he was seen as a bighearted man where family was most dear to him.

Police theorize that Shumate's son was a friend of Ted, and likely helped in the kidnap scheme by providing information. The accomplice turned informant was in on the scheme with Marvin Shumate. Police speculated that whatever deal the second cabbie made with Benny days later Shumate's body was discovered. Homicide detectives are pretty sure what happened, but couldn't make indictments.

The trigger-man in the shooting of Marvin Shumate was never found. Nor was Benny, ever positively linked to the revenge killing of Shumate, despite police suspicions. The kidnapping plot and other events related to it are all part of the legend of a beloved patriarch of downtown Las Vegas.

BENNY'S EARLY DAYS IN TEXAS

In his younger days in North Texas as a bootlegger, Benny carried three pistols—two 45 automatics and a small 38 revolver.

When Benny developed underworld gambling in Dallas, the ocean of money he made attracted ruthless pirates.

In 1931, he suspected fellow bootlegger Frank Bolding of hijacking a truckload of his liquor. He confronted Bolding, who according to Ted Binion "was a real bad man, had a reputation for killing people by stabbing them." In one confrontation, Bolding "stood up real quick and Dad felt like he was going to stab him," so Binion "rolled back pulled his gun, and shot upward from the ground. Hit him through the neck and killed him."

The way he did it is what got Benny his nickname "The Cowboy." It also earned him a murder conviction. During the investigation, authorities discovered Bolding had a knife but hadn't pulled it. Nevertheless, Benny received only a two-year suspended sentence, because said Ted, Bolding's reputation was so bad.

Five years later, Benny killed Ben Frieden, a numbers operator in competition with him. As the story goes, after he shot Frieden, Benny shot himself in the shoulder with a different gun, put that gun in Frieden's hand, then turned himself in, claiming Frieden had shot first. Benny was indicted, but the judge ruled that he acted in self-defense, so the indictments were dropped. You could say that Benny believed it was better to be judged by twelve than to be carried by six. And that's how he killed two men in self-defense.

By 1936, Benny had gained control of gambling operations in Dallas, with protection from a powerful local politician. In addition, Benny's FBI file contains mentions of occasional contacts with wise guys in the Eastern Mob, including Meyer Lansky, as well as connections to the Chicago Outfit.

After establishing himself in Las Vegas, though, Benny became a respected businessman, a philanthropist, and a family man. Nevertheless, throughout this legendary gambler's life, lawmen always said that Benny Binion was not someone you wanted to mess with.

THE BINION/NOBLE FEUD

While running underground casino games in Texas, Benny became involved in a long-running feud with Herb Noble, a small-time gambler—a feud that continued even after Benny moved to Las Vegas. When he demanded a 40 percent cut of a particular game, Noble refused to comply. Allegedly, Benny posted a price for Noble's head that eventually reached $25,000 plus, as a bonus, control of a Dallas craps game. Over the years several people tried to kill Noble, yet even with gunshot wounds he somehow managed to survive.

Noble's wife was killed in a car bombing intended for him. Enraged by his wife's murder, Herb Noble made plans to retaliate by bombing Benny's home in Las Vegas, but he was restrained by lawmen before he could execute his vendetta. In time, a car bomber finally succeeded in eliminating Noble.

In the eyes of syndicate bosses, the nationwide publicity over the Binion/Noble battle was intolerable, drawing unwanted attention to their operations in Dallas and Las Vegas. When Benny's bodyguard killed a man in the men's room of the Westerner Club, the syndicate helped the Feds to incarcerate Benny Binion for skimming casino receipts. In 1951, Benny lost his gaming license, and in 1953 he began serving a five-year term at Leavenworth Penitentiary for federal tax evasion.

Over the years, Binion's Horseshoe became the most profitable casino in Glitter Gulch, a nickname for downtown Vegas. One reason for its success grew from an innovative idea for a tourist attraction: management displayed a large glass-encased horseshoe containing $1 million in $10,000 bills. Tourists loved having their photograph taken in front of the $1 million horseshoe.

Unfortunately, Benny had to sell his share of the Horseshoe to pay $5 million in legal costs resulting from his trial and conviction for tax evasion. The Binion family lost controlling interest in the Horseshoe in 1957, but in 1964 regained full control, although Benny could never again hold a Nevada gaming license. He did, however, maintain an office near the downstairs restaurant and remained on the Horseshoe's payroll as a consultant.

CREATION OF THE WORLD SERIES OF POKER

In January 1949, Benny did something that would forever instill the game of poker in the annals of gambling lore. He arranged for Johnny Moss and "Nick the Greek" Dandalos to play heads-up, or head to head, in a poker tournament, which lasted an incredible five months, with Dandalos losing a reported $2 million. Interestingly, the 42-year-old Moss had to rest by taking naps on a regular basis. During the naps, Nick the Greek, then 57, passed his time playing craps. After months of playing heads-up poker and seeing his opponent, Johnny Moss, win millions, Dandalos uttered one of the most famous poker statements of all time: "Mister Moss, I have to let you go."

Over the years Benny continued establishing heads-up contests between high-stakes players. In 1970 the seed of an idea began to germinate and he invited six of the best-known poker players to compete in a tournament for cash. After a set time the participants voted, by secret ballot, to determine the winner. According to PokerRoom.com, "Johnny Moss, then 63, was voted champion by his younger competition and received a small trophy. The next year, a freeze-out format with a $10,000 buy-in was introduced, and the *World Series of Poker (WSOP)* was born."[28]

Benny's creation of the WSOP encouraged the popularity of poker, and with the help of wide spread television coverage, poker's popularity blossomed and grew. Several memorable moments have occurred during main events. One was Jack Straus's miraculous comeback win at the 1982 final table. He went all-in, and lost. But getting up from the table, he discovered one $500 chip under a napkin, and from that single chip, Straus ultimately won the tournament. The incident eventually became known as "A chip and a chair," which means that's all a player truly needs to win a tournament—one chip and a seat in the event.

Another memorable moment occurred when Chris Moneymaker won the event in 2003, earning over $2 million. All he'd invested was $40 to play in an online qualifying event. This amazing fete, labeled "The Moneymaker Effect," inspired millions of would-be poker players worldwide to try their luck. In 2006, the main event by itself peaked at 8,773 participants, with the eventual champion, Jamie Gold, winning a record prize of $12 million!

DEATH OF A LEGEND

The much loved and colorful gambler's gambler Benny Binion died of a heart attack in December 1989 at the age of 85. A year later he was posthumously inducted into the Poker Hall of Fame. His old friend "Amarillo Slim" Preston, another poker legend, suggested this epitaph: "He was either the gentlest bad guy or the baddest good guy you'd ever seen."

Benny was a key figure in getting the National Finals Rodeo to relocate to Las Vegas. He never forgot his Texas roots, nor did he overlook the cowboys whenever they came to town. He always paid their entry fees for the championship event. When the Las Vegas Horseshoe finally closed, Boyd Gaming continued the bighearted tradition of paying all the entry fees that Benny had generously started.

THE BINION FAMILY

In addition to two sons, Benny and his wife, Teddy Jane, raised three daughters, Barbara, Brenda, and Becky. Teddy Jane managed the Horseshoe's casino cage until her death in 1994. Their daughter Barbara, in a failed suicide attempt, tried to shoot herself, which left her severely disfigured. She eventually succeeded in committing suicide in 1977.

TED BINION

Ted Binion, youngest son of the Horseshoe founder, was born in Dallas, Texas, in 1943. He, his older brother Jack, and all three sisters moved to Las Vegas with their parents in 1947. Ted was a mathematical genius known to mentally calculate odds—or "house percentage"—in gaming transactions. He also had a reputation for aiding people he knew to be in financial difficulty.

Ted Binion

After Benny was convicted of tax evasion and lost his gaming license, Ted and Jack Binion took over day-to-day operations of the Horseshoe. Jack took the role of president, while Ted became casino manager. Ted hosted the Horseshoe's poker tournaments, and during the peak evening hours was often seen partying with high-profile casino guests and pretty women. In 1986 the Nevada Gaming Commission launched an investigation into his involvement with illegal drugs and his association with organized crime figure "Fat Herbie" Blitzstein.

Besides Ted's drug problems and affiliation with mob figures, authorities suspected that he was using his live-in girlfriend, Sandra Murphy, as a bagwoman—the person who removes the uncounted cash, or skim, from the casino count room. Ted had marital problems too. His affair with Murphy, whom he met at

Cheetahs, a topless club in Las Vegas, caused his estranged wife and daughter to pack up and return to Texas.

In 1996 gaming regulators provisionally banned him from participating in the management of, or even entering, the Las Vegas Horseshoe. Meanwhile, Ted struggled with drug addiction. He was said to shave off every hair on his body to avoid testing positive in Commission drug tests. Ted Binion's gaming license was permanently revoked in 1998 and he was banned from associating with the family business. However, Ted had a $7 million silver collection housed in the basement vault of the Horseshoe. And when his ties to the family business were severed, he had to either relocate the silver to a secure location or sell it.

TED BINION'S MYSTERIOUS DEATH

A few months after Ted Binion's gaming license was revoked by the Nevada Gaming Commission, he died September 17, 1998, what at first appeared a self-induced drug overdose. Investigators later determined his death had been staged. After nine months of investigation, they arrested and convicted two people in Ted's alleged murder: Sandra Murphy, Ted's live-in girlfriend at the time of his death, and her new lover Rick Tabish. The apparent motive for murder was $7 million in buried treasure.

Ted had built a concrete-lined vault on the desert floor on a remote property he owned in Pahrump, 60 miles west of Las Vegas. The vault contained most of Ted Binion's treasure, including six tons of silver bullion, paper currency, Horseshoe Casino cheques, and more than 100,000 rare coins—estimated to be worth between $10 million and $14 million—all of which had previously been stored in the Horseshoe Casino's vault.

Soon after Ted Binion's death, Tabish—who'd helped design and build the concrete bunker in the desert—was discovered by police in the middle of the night trying to dig up 12,000 pounds of silver ingots.

Murphy and Tabish were later granted a retrial, which began in October 2004, and were ultimately acquitted of the murder charges. The pair, however, were convicted of lesser charges connected with the Ted Binion case—burglary (1 to 5 years) and grand larceny (1 to 5 years). The retrial determined that the Binion family had paid off several witnesses in the first trial.

In 1998 a legal battle broke out between two of Benny's siblings, Becky and Jack Binion. The resolution was Becky's taking over presidency of the Las Vegas Horseshoe while Jack moved on to operate the family's remaining gaming interests. Cost-cutting measures implemented under Becky's rule became very unpopular with gamblers, especially the closing of the downstairs Horseshoe café which featured a popular 24-hour $1.99 ham and egg special. Becky also sold the $1 million horseshoe exhibit that served as a great backdrop for free pictures of visitors—a well-known tourist attraction. As for the distribution of proceeds from entry fees in the WSOP, she made drastic changes that were very unpopular with casino dealers.

HARRAH'S BUYS THE HORSESHOE, AND RIGHTS TO THE WSOP

Meanwhile, the Horseshoe Casino's bills went unpaid, including Culinary Union benefits owed. Gaming agents seized $1 million from the Horseshoe payroll to satisfy creditors, and eventually the Horseshoe was forced to close. In March 2004 it was purchased by Harrah's Entertainment. They retained the rights to the Horseshoe name and the famed *World Series of Poker* brand. Harrah's almost immediately sold the hotel and casino to MTR Gaming Group, which retained the Binion brand name.

"Cowboy" Benny Binion was thought of by many as a true founding father of a fledgling western town that inevitably matured into the entertainment and gambling capital of the world.

Though never considered a founding father like Benny Binion, another interesting man came to Las Vegas and made a huge imprint on the city, in time becoming the state's largest land owner and employer. His name was Howard Hughes. Unlike Benny, Hughes lacked skill as a casino operator. Even so, he eventually became one of the most interesting characters in the city's history.

HOWARD HUGHES
—THE BILLIONAIRE RECLUSE

Howard Hughes

In contrast to the corporate self-made billionaires who built their fortune developing casino resorts, Howard Hughes was born into wealth. His father had invented a dual-cone rotor drill bit in 1909, the first drill bit that could penetrate solid rock easily. It revolutionized oil drilling by opening up new locations for oil exploration. In *Next to Hughes*, Robert Maheu wrote, "After his father's death, [Howard] inherited Hughes Tool and, thanks to the licensing fees from the drill bit, a sizable fortune."

In 1925, Howard Hughes met Noah Dietrich in Los Angeles, a former race-car driver turned accountant. They immediately hit it off and Hughes hired him. Most historians believe it was Dietrich, who had endured a business relationship with the recluse for 32 years that transformed Hughes from a wealthy man to a billionaire. Dietrich acted as Chief Executive Officer of the Hughes' empire from 1925 to 1957." Authorities came to believe that Dietrich's memoir, *Howard: The Amazing Mr. Hughes*, was a likely if inadvertent source of novelist Clifford Irving's infamous fake autobiography of Hughes.

"There is no doubt about it," affirms Robert Maheu, Hughes' right-hand man for many years. "He was delivering Howard profits of $50 million to $55 million a year. Big bucks in those days."

Meanwhile, Hughes groomed his image as the playboy movie mogul who discovered Jane Russell and Jean Harlow. He also designed, built, and flew his own aircraft, and the daredevil aviator went on to establish new speed records. Hughes became a national hero after his historic 1938 round-the-world flight. While test-piloting the XF-11 photo reconnaissance plane in 1946 he crash landed on a golf course in Beverly Hills. Miraculously he survived the crash but broke nearly every bone in his body. To ease his severe pain physicians liberally medicated morphine, instigating a lifelong dependency to opiates. All the same, the daring aviator remained a regular visitor to Las Vegas during the 1940s and 1950s, occasionally seen in the casinos with a gorgeous young woman at his side. His close associate, Robert Maheu, a former FBI agent, regularly took on assignments, at times spying on girlfriends and increasingly posing as Hughes' emissary. "He decided that he wanted me to become his alter ego so he would never have to make a public appearance."

Robert Maheu wrote in his memoir, "We never met face-to-face. Communications were always by phone or memo. I believe Hughes went into seclusion because he was going deaf and was too proud to wear a hearing aid."[29]

HOWARD HUGHES' AFFINITY FOR LAS VEGAS

How Howard Hughes became Nevada's biggest employer and land owner, and most powerful man during his four-year stint in Las Vegas makes a truly incredible legend. The circumstances that created this legend are even more unusual.

Before the renowned aviator made Las Vegas his home in 1966, he had stayed there several times. On his first visit during World War II he stayed at the Flamingo, El Rancho Vegas, and Desert Inn. Later in 1953, the then 47-year-old rented a five bedroom cottage near the Desert Inn. He referred to it as the "Green House" because its exterior color contrasted with the sandy-brown desert terrain. During this stay he acquired about 40 square miles of land just northwest of Las Vegas from the Bureau of Land Management (BLM), trading 73,000 acres of land he owned in five northern Nevada counties for the BLM parcel. Hughes called his newly acquired parcel Husite. He intended to relocate Hughes Aircraft from Culver City, California, to Husite. Maheu noted that Hughes, "had felt oppressed since California levied an income tax in 1935," but that his "key executives and technicians at Hughes Aircraft had flatly refused to be exiled to the desert, and the Husite property remained vacant." The 40-square-mile parcel, vacant for so many years, is today a prosperous master-planned community known as Summerlin.

Hughes lived in the Green House for nearly a year and continued to pay rent with instructions to keep it exactly as it was, despite his never returning there. He frequently visited the Grace Hayes Lodge—today the site of the Mirage—owned at the time by vaudeville headliner/film star Grace Hayes. Hughes reportedly offered to buy the Grace Hayes Lodge, but he declined to continue negotiations when its proprietor countered Hughes' offer with a price of $250,000, ten times what Hughes wanted to pay.

In the interim, the Kefauver Hearings of 1950-51—officially the Senate Special Committee to Investigate Crime in Interstate Commerce—held America's attention. The first committee of its kind, it was composed of senators from around the country ordered to expose organized crime in America for the evil empire that it was. A second purpose was to gain a better understanding of how to fight it.

The public's sentiment was reflected in a *Life* magazine article of April 6, 1951: "People had suddenly gone indoors into living rooms, taverns, and clubrooms, auditoriums and back-offices. There, in eerie half-light, looking at millions of small frosty screens, people sat as if charmed. Never before had the attention of the nation been riveted so completely on a single matter."[30]

The Kefauver Hearings unfortunately, shed a lot of bad publicity on Las Vegas, exposing to the public the mob's presence and illegal skim operations.

As the years rolled on, the need of Las Vegas for a savior—someone who could cleanse its tarnished mob image—became apparent. He arrived in the Autumn of 1966, but this time he stayed four years and forever shaped the destiny of Nevada for years to come.

PRIVATE TRAIN FROM BOSTON

On a cold November night in 1966, the reclusive billionaire Howard Hughes and his entourage of business aides made a midnight exodus from the fifth floor of a Boston hotel. Needing peace and quiet, desperate to get away from snooping newspaper reporters and other prying eyes, Hughes boarded a private two-car train and headed west to Las Vegas.

Hank Greenspun, *Las Vegas Sun* publisher and friend to the billionaire, had persuaded Hughes to move to Nevada because of its benefits: no state income tax and lots of land available to a man with money.

Hughes and his entourage arrived in Las Vegas the night on Thanksgiving and were immediately whisked to the Desert Inn, where they occupied the top two floors of penthouse suites. Usually the top floors were reserved for high rollers, but the Hughes group of aides were non-gambling Mormon businessmen. Moreover, their reservation was for ten days only at a time when the upcoming holidays would create a large demand for Las Vegas hotel rooms.

Robert Maheu recalled that when he was able to negotiate the rooms at the Desert Inn, the hotel management had not considered the billionaire businessman a high-rolling guest.

Ten days passed, and the Hughes' entourage did not check out. With the holidays approaching, Moe Dalitz, owner of the Desert Inn, was furious. New Year's Eve, one of Las Vegas's busiest holidays, was less than a month away, and the suites the Hughes' ensemble occupied had already been promised to high rollers.

ATTEMPTED EVICTION OF HUGHES

Concerned about Hughes' extended stay, Dalitz phoned Maheu and told him that the entire Hughes group must leave or be physically evicted. When Hughes learned of the situation, he told Maheu, "It's your problem—you work it out."

So Maheu called in an old favor owed to him by Teamster President Jimmy Hoffa. As the story goes, Dalitz got a call from Hoffa requesting an extension for the Hughes group. Dalitz agreed on the condition that no future extensions would be granted. The eviction reprieve lasted through the New Year and several months into 1967. Maheu told Hughes that he had played out his options with Dalitz. "If you want a place to sleep," he said, "you'd damned well better buy the hotel." The billionaire couldn't have agreed more, and so began Howard Hughes's foray into buying up huge amounts of Las Vegas real estate.

Seven months before his Thanksgiving 1966 arrival in Las Vegas, Hughes had been on the defensive over conflict-of-interest concerns involving his ownership of both Trans World Airlines (TWA) and Hughes Aircraft. The U.S. federal court forced Hughes to sell his shares in TWA. The sale of his interest in TWA netted him a gross profit of $547 million. Unless he reinvested this huge sum, which the IRS considered "passive income" and taxed at a higher rate than "active" or "working" income, Hughes would lose much of it to taxes.

To most businessmen, negotiating the purchase of a thriving business such as the Desert Inn was the means to an end. To tycoon Howard Hughes, it was crafty deal making. After months of offers and counter offers, Dalitz and Hughes finally agreed on a price of $13.25 million. Once Hughes owned the DI, he discovered the gross receipts of a casino were considered active income. Overjoyed with the notion of a reduced tax liability,

Hughes phoned Maheu. "How many more of these toys are available?" he inquired. "Let's buy 'em all."

Typically, under jurisdiction of the Nevada Gaming Commission, one becomes a licensed operator of a gambling establishment by appearing in person before the commission, undergoing an extensive background check, being photographed and fingerprinted, and filling out financial disclosure papers— all of which Hughes had no intention of doing. The commission, believing the new billionaire resident would be a great asset to the community, bent the rules to accommodate their new reclusive resort owner. According to K.J. Evans in a *Las Vegas Review-Journal* article, "well-connected Las Vegas attorney Thomas Bell was hired to handle the licensing, and would stay on as Hughes' lobbyist in Carson City. The new governor, Paul Laxalt, persuaded the commission to allow Maheu to appear as Hughes' surrogate."

"Laxalt saw Hughes as a better option than the mob," said Maheu. "He was an excellent businessman, and he was totally legitimate—the kind of sugar daddy Las Vegas needed."

Finally, in 1967, the Nevada Gaming Commission granted to Hughes the license he needed to operate the Desert Inn.

HUGHES HISTORIC SPENDING SPREE

"The Man," as his close associates referred to their unseen boss, began his historic spending spree from his penthouse atop the luxurious Desert Inn. After acquiring the Desert Inn, Hughes began a roll that boggled the mind of most millionaire gamblers.

His next acquisition was the Sands, then a Strip showplace. Its best days when Sinatra and his Rat-Pack pals made the Copa Room their playground, had passed. Even so, when Moe Dalitz was consulted, he told Hughes that the Sands would be a good acquisition. Hughes paid $14.6 million for the casino hotel and 183 acres of prime real estate that, in time, became the Howard Hughes Center.

Hughes then bought the Castaways for $3 million, the Frontier for $23 million, the Silver Slipper for $5.4 million, and the unfinished Landmark, which had stood empty for eight years, for $17 million. But when Hughes tried to buy the Stardust for $30.5 million, the U.S. Securities and Exchange Commission prevented him from closing the deal, concerned over Hughes holding a monopoly on Las Vegas lodging.

"If we had been allowed to buy the Stardust, you wouldn't have had ... all the terrible publicity from that movie *Casino*," wrote Maheu in *Next to Hughes*.

The Chicago Outfit's emissary to Las Vegas and Hollywood, Johnny Rosselli, approached Maheu one time to tell him who would be the new casino manager. Maheu told him to buzz off. Howard Hughes was not in bed with the mob, nor did he have any intention of falling in with organized crime. In fact, he was actually working quietly to ease the mobs out of Sin City.

Hughes had to know something to have bought the Desert Inn, Sands, Frontier, Silver Slipper, Castaways, and the Landmark. Acquiring those particular casinos was not an accident. What he knew was contained in a study commissioned by former Attorney General Robert Kennedy, "a blueprint for exorcising the mob from Las Vegas." The study identified the casinos that had to be cleaned up. Maheu wrote that the study said, "the best way to clean them up was by purchase. So you put all the elements together, and who is better equipped with the money than Hughes?"[31]

Casinos were not his only investments in Las Vegas. During his four-year stay Hughes acquired buy options or purchased outright nearly every plot of vacant land from McCarran Airport to Sahara Avenue, a distance of four miles.

"We didn't make the new Las Vegas," Maheu said in a 2004 interview. "I like to say we got it ready."

HUGHES BUYS KLAS CHANNEL EIGHT

After Hughes moved into the DI he realized to his dismay that he couldn't watch movies on late night television, a pastime he enjoyed since his Hollywood days at RKO Studios. A chronic insomniac, he wanted to watch old movies on television when most Las Vegans were either sleeping or out on the town. Metropolitan Las Vegas had no all-night TV stations. In September 1967, *Las Vegas Sun* publisher Hank Greenspun sold his television station, KLAS Channel eight, to Howard Hughes for $3.6 million. Sin City's newest billionaire resident now had his own 24/7 channel to satisfy his late-night addiction.

Hughes' other non-casino properties included the residential lots of the Desert Inn's Country Club, the North Las Vegas Airport, and all the land surrounding McCarran International Airport. His massive portfolio included Harold's Club in Reno, an airline named *Hughes Airwest*, nearly every vacant lot on the Las Vegas Strip, and some 2,000 mining claims. When he finished buying up Las Vegas in the autumn of 1970, Hughes' Nevada holdings were worth an estimated $300 million, making him the state's largest employer and the holder of more gaming licenses than anyone else in history!

"JUICED IN"

In the old days of the casino business, it was common practice to "skim" the cash in the counting room from the cash boxes. The purpose, of course, was to illegally avoid paying taxes on some of the gross receipts a casino took in. Another common practice whenever experienced operators purchased a thriving business such as a casino was to remove most of the key personnel and replace them with employees they knew to be trustworthy. If they didn't personally know each prospective employee, someone within the organization had to vouch for them. This practice created the term "juice." Being "juiced in" to a casino meant the person being hired had connections and supposedly could be trusted. In the early days of Las Vegas casinos, "juice" was very important, especially in the mob-operated joints. Because the people being hired would most likely have access to large sums of money, operators needed assurance that their employees were not thieves.

HUGHES NEGLECTED TO REMOVE THE BANDITS FROM THE DI

In 1967, when novice casino operator Howard Hughes took over ownership of the Desert Inn, he unknowingly made the crucial mistake of neglecting to remove the bandits already entrenched there. In one instance mentioned in Chapter 2, a craps table stayed on the books as closed, yet actually remained open, while the bosses and the dealers continued daily to remove its cash box, and divvy up the booty. It took three months before the oversight was finally discovered. Even more astounding is the revelation that after Hughes death, from 1971 through September 1976, the Hughes holding company, Summa, lost $132 million. Those responsible were said to be the inexperienced people operating Hughes' casinos.

Hughes did not build a single casino in Nevada, "and had at best a rudimentary knowledge of the casino business," said Robert Maheu, whose *Next to Hughes* cites example after example of the billionaire's missteps. For example, of the six casinos Hughes owned, the most obvious blunder was his purchase of the Landmark, "which both Maheu and Moe Dalitz had strenuously advised against. Though distinctive, it was never a success, and is today a parking lot," wrote K.J. Evans.

On the other hand, Hughes purchased a thin strip of land, adjacent to Caesars Palace that two decades later became seed money for a young developer's rise to fame and fortune. After Hughes left Las Vegas in 1970, his interest in land waned, and in 1971, he traded that narrow strip of land to a young hopeful named Steve Wynn. Eventually, Wynn sold the land to Caesars

Palace and used his profits to buy a controlling interest in downtown's Golden Nugget.

"MORMON MAFIA"

Hughes's massive business holdings were overseen by a small group of aides, most of whom were Mormons. Though Hughes was not a member of their church, they were the only people he found trustworthy enough to handle his business affairs. This group was unofficially dubbed "The Mormon Mafia." In addition to taking care of Hughes' everyday business operations and his health, his aides made every effort to satisfy "The Man's" every whim. Besides his addictions to movies on late-night television, Hughes was fond of Baskin-Robbins' Banana Ripple ice cream. When that particular flavor was discontinued, his aides sought to secure a bulk shipment for him. The smallest special order Baskin-Robbins would supply was 200 gallons. Fine. The aides had 200 gallons shipped from Los Angeles. Soon after it arrived, Hughes said he was tired of Banana Ripple and preferred Chocolate Marshmallow ice cream. Thus, Desert Inn guests and employees enjoyed free Banana Ripple ice cream for the next 12 months.

While living in his penthouse atop the Desert Inn, Hughes became concerned about the explosions occurring at the Nevada Test Site only 65 miles northwest of Las Vegas. He tried to stop the explosions but never succeeded in persuading the authorities to halt them. Hughes feared the atomic blasts would frighten tourists and keep them from coming to Las Vegas. He was concerned too, that the rumbles might damage the many structures he owned.

According to the numerous memos he wrote, Hughes envisioned Las Vegas as a model metropolis, with its own high-speed rail, clean water and clean air, mountains on all sides, and cradled in the midst of the Mojave Desert. As a former engineer he also had concerns about sewage draining into Lake Mead, the primary source of drinking water for most Las Vegans.

HUGHES LEAVES LAS VEGAS

After a four-year stay in the city, Hughes was carried out of the Desert Inn on a stretcher, whisked to Nellis Air Force Base in an unmarked van, and flown by private jet to the Bahamas. With his health failing, a bitter corporate struggle broke out over Hughes' immense business and land holdings in Las Vegas. His trusted aide Robert Maheu, personal physician Dr. Robert Buckley, and other top aides were fired once Hughes had been removed from the DI's penthouse.

The quirky billionaire aviator never returned to his model metropolis, though his strange, almost bizarre legacy continues to nourish the legend of the city's growth and development.

Former FBI agent Robert Maheu, Hughes's virtual mouth, eyes, and ears for 13 years, was fired in December 1970 by Chester Davis, the lawyer who defended Hughes in a successful battle over alleged antitrust violations involving TWA, and Summa Executive Vice President Frank William Gay.

Paul Laxalt, then Governor of Nevada, delivered the news to Maheu at the Sands Hotel on December 7. "He told me he had spent over a half hour talking with Howard, and that Hughes had told him that I was fired," Maheu recalled in *Next to Hughes*.

Once Hughes left Las Vegas in the fall of 1970, his interest in the city diminished. Following his 1976 death, those in control of his estate sold off its casino interests to concentrate on real estate development, namely Husite. Evolving into the planned community development of Summerlin, that was Hughes' real legacy.

DEATH OF THE BILLIONAIRE AVIATOR

Almost five and half years after his abrupt departure from Las Vegas, Howard Hughes at age 70 died on April 5, 1976, in an airplane flying back to Texas where it all began. Two reports, however, told different stories about precisely where his death occurred. One claimed that Hughes died on board an aircraft owned by Robert Graf, en route from Hughes' penthouse in Acapulco, Mexico, to the Methodist Hospital in Houston, Texas. The other claimed he died on board a flight from Freeport, Grand Bahamas, to Houston.

At the time of death, his extensive use of opiates and reclusive activities made Hughes practically unrecognizable. From an imposing 6'2" frame, he weighed barely 90 pounds at the time. His hair, beard, and fingernails were untrimmed. The FBI had to fingerprint the corpse to make a positive identification. When his body was received at the morgue in Houston, an autopsy revealed kidney failure as the cause of death.

Severely malnourished, Howard Hughes was already in very poor health at the time of his death. During the autopsy the coroner reportedly found broken hypodermic needles still embedded in his arms. The coroner also noted Hughes other internal organs appeared healthy, although his kidneys were damaged.

Summa executives and heirs began battling over the billionaire's massive estate. William Lummis, the son of a maternal aunt and a Houston lawyer, became Summa's chairman of the board in 1976, and Gay, who presided over Hughes' "Mormon Mafia" of personal aides, became its CEO that same year. Davis remained board director and chief counsel for Summa.

HUGHES' SUMMA CORPORATION

The name Summa, Latin for "highest," was the name of the holding company adopted in 1972 for the business interests of Howard Hughes. Having been formed immediately after he sold the tool division of Hughes Tool Company, the company remained Summa for 18 years following Hughes' death.

The Summa Corporation contained Hughes' varied holdings, including:

- Hughes Air West
- Hughes Helicopters—a former subsidiary of Hughes Aircraft retained by Summa when the remainder of the aircraft business was donated as an endowment to the Howard Hughes Medical Institute
- Hughes Sports Network
- KLAS-TV—the Las Vegas CBS affiliate
- Hughes Nevada Mining

- Desert Inn
- Sands Hotel and Casino
- Frontier Hotel and Casino
- Landmark Hotel and Casino
- Silver Slipper Casino
- The Castaways Hotel and Casino
- Harold's Club Reno
- Xanadu Princess Resort and Marina

The Xanadu Princess is a 20-acre beachfront casino facility with 215 rooms and 80 boat slips situated in the Bahamas on the southern coast of Grand Bahama Island. Built in 1968, the resort was purchased by Hughes in 1972, and for several years it was celebrated as a Caribbean hideaway for the Hollywood jet set of the era, including Rat - Pack members Frank Sinatra and Dean Martin, and other big-name celebrities such as Cary Grant and Lucille Ball. Hughes subsequently moved into the resort's penthouse floor and made it his residence until days before his death in 1976. After Hughes' death the resort was sold, but the penthouse floor where he lived the final four years of his life remained inexplicably empty for 30 years.

THE MYSTERIOUS "MORMON WILL"

In the years that followed, a number of interesting documents began to surface claiming to be the billionaire's will. One of the more intriguing was a will submitted by Utah gasoline station operator Melvin Dummar, who swore under oath during a seven-month trial, that late one evening in December 1967 he had given Howard Hughes a ride in his car. Dummar stated that he had found a scruffy and dirty man lying along U.S. Highway 95, 150 miles north of Las Vegas. The man said he was Howard Hughes, asked for a ride to Las Vegas, and Dummar obliged, taking him to the Sands Hotel. Dummar also said he never saw the man again. Then, just days after Hughes' death, Dummar claimed that an unknown man showed up at his gas station and left an envelope containing the will on his desk.

Uncertain of what to do, or if the document was genuine, Dummar left the will at the Latter Day Saints office. The Nevada court ruled in June 1978 that the Mormon will was a forgery, and that Dummar was an opportunist who had played a hoax.

After six years of wrangling in the Nevada court in an effort to resolve the billionaire's estate, the judges ruled that none of the wills was legitimate, and that Howard Hughes had died intestate, without a valid will. In 1983, led by William Lummis, the estate was divided among 23 cousins. In 1994, Summa Corporation was renamed the Howard Hughes Corporation to maintain his name on the business and to honor the man.

The extended legal battles endured until 1984, when the Nevada courts ultimately rejected claims by Texas and California that the Hughes' estate owed inheritance taxes.

Administrators were appointed, led by Hughes' cousin William Lummis, and most of Summa's holdings were gradually liquidated. Summa's Nevada mining interests were sold off by the end of 1976, while Hughes Sports Network and KLAS-TV were both sold in 1978. Republic Airlines purchased Hughes Airwest in 1981. McDonnell Douglas bought Hughes Helicopters in 1984. During the 1980s, all the hotel and casino properties were sold. As most of the original businesses were liquidated, Summa changed into a land developer, using the vast holdings of raw, undeveloped tracts of land Hughes had accumulated in Southern Nevada as a starting point.

"My heart still bleeds for what happened to Howard Hughes," Maheu told the *Las Vegas Sun* in a 2004 interview. "I often said after I got off the phone with him that I just finished talking to the poorest man in the world. He was so unhappy."

DID HUGHES IMPROVE THE IMAGE OF LAS VEGAS?

At the time Howard Hughes began his historic spending spree in Nevada, the cohort of men who came to Las Vegas for legitimacy in the 1940s and 1950s were nearing retirement age. Las Vegans believe that mob activity declined during Hughes' four years in Las Vegas, partly because he bought out many of the old-timers when he purchased his six casinos, and partly because the authorities formed the Nevada Gaming Commission in 1955 to become more stringent in licensing, and the Feds turned up the heat when they instigated the Kefauver Hearings in 1950.

The *Las Vegas Review-Journal* included this observation: "Hughes' attorney, Dick Gray, pointed out to the Justice Department attorney that the FBI, Internal Revenue Service, and law enforcement agencies generally are very glad to see Hughes come in and acquire gambling interests from less desirable owners. Just by showing up, Hughes changed Las Vegas forever. If one of the richest men in the world, one of the nation's largest defense contractors and a genuine national hero, was willing to invest in Las Vegas, it must not be such a sordid, evil place after all."[32]

Robert Maheu, who spent 13 years working for Hughes, said, "He cleaned up the image of Las Vegas. I have had the heads of large corporate entities tell me they would never have thought of coming here before Hughes came." All told, during the late 1960s and 1970s, some 14 publicly owned corporations bought into Nevada, purchasing 25 major casinos and generating nearly half the state's total gaming revenue. The emergence of Howard Hughes and a number of publicly owned conglomerates brought Las Vegas the respectability it so desired.

KIRK KERKORIAN—THE QUIET LION

Unlike the eccentric billionaire Howard Hughes, who inherited his money and bought up Nevada casinos as if they were children's toys, a different self-made breed of casino man came to Las Vegas and emerged as one of the city's greatest entrepreneurs.

The story of Kirk Kerkorian, Chief Executive Officer of Caesars Entertainment, which includes the huge $11 billion CityCenter, reads like an All American rags-to-riches narrative that's hard to put down. His multitude of casino resorts began with the International Casino and developed through expansions and acquisitions and today operates on four continents. Kerkorian once noted in a rare interview with the *Review-Journal*, "When you're a self-made man you start very early in life. In my case it was at nine years old when I started bringing income into the family. You get a drive that's a little different, maybe a little stronger, than somebody who inherited."

Growing up in Fresno, California, Kirk was the youngest of four children born of Armenian immigrants, Lily and Ahron Kerkorian. In 1922, when he was four-years-old, the family moved to Los Angeles. At age nine he sold newspapers and hustled odd jobs to earn money. He dropped out of school in the eighth grade, and under his older brother's tutelage became a skilled amateur boxer. He fought under the name "Rifle Right Kerkorian" and won the Pacific amateur welterweight championship. When he went to work for Ted O'Flaherty, his life made a remarkable change.

KERKORIAN MEETS TED O'FLAHERTY

In autumn 1939 at age 22, Kerkorian experienced a defining moment in his early career when he met Ted O'Flaherty. Kerkorian started by helping O'Flaherty install wall furnaces earning 45 cents an hour. "Some days, reported the *Review-Journal*, "Kerkorian would go with him to Alhambra Airport and watch him practice maneuvers in a Piper Cub airplane. Originally disinterested, Kerkorian consented one day to go aloft with O'Flaherty."[33] In the air, Kerkorian discovered he could see the beauty of the mountains on one side and the blue Pacific Ocean on the other. It's when he fell in love with flying. "He was sold on it right then," O'Flaherty later recalled. "He had never been up in a plane before. But I'm telling you, after that first flight he went right at it. The very next day, he was back out at the field to take his first flying lesson."[34]

In 1940, Kerkorian sensed America would inevitably be drawn into the war in Europe, so he decided to become a licensed aviator before he got drafted into the infantry. One day he arrived at a desolate airfield in the middle of the Mojave Desert called "The Happy Bottom Riding Club," adjacent to the USAF's Munroc Field, now Edwards Air Force Base. A combination flight school and dairy farm, it was owned by pioneer aviator Florence "Pancho" Barnes. There, Kerkorian received flying lessons in exchange for milking her cows and tending the cattle.

"I haven't got any money," Kerkorian told Barnes. "I haven't got any education. I want to learn to fly. I don't know how I can do it. Can you help me?"

She obliged, and within six months Kerkorian had a commercial pilot's license and a job as a flight instructor.

But life as a teacher bored him.

"I heard about the Royal Air Force flying out of Montreal, Canada, and I went up there, and I got hired right away," he recalled. "They were paying money I couldn't believe, $1,000 a trip," wrote Dial Torgenson in the 1974 biography *Kerkorian: An American Success Story.*

FLIGHTS FROM MONTREAL TO SCOTLAND

Kerkorian took a job as a transport pilot with the RAF Air Transport Command. He was required to fly Canadian-built de Havilland Mosquito bombers from Labrador to Scotland. Only one in four made it. The problem was twofold: The distance to Scotland was 2,200 miles but the Mosquito's fuel tanks carried fuel for only 1,400 miles, and only two routes were feasible, each more dangerous than the other. "The roundabout route was Montreal-Labrador-Greenland-Iceland-Scotland, but the plane's high-performance wings could be distorted by a paper-thin coating of ice, causing it to fall out of the sky. 'The snowfields and forests around that frozen perimeter were strewn with downed Mosquitoes crushed like matchboxes,'" wrote Torgenson.[35]

He could fly directly across the Atlantic, riding a west-to-east air current described as the "Iceland Wave." Typically, it pushed Mosquitoes toward Europe at jet speeds, yet it wasn't always reliable. During mid-flight, if the Iceland Wave waned, plane and crew were in danger of crashing. During one Atlantic crossing in June 1944, the Iceland Wave lost all intensity. Next the sun set, then the reserve tank indicator pointed to empty, and Kerkorian prepared to ditch. But his navigator, knowing the plane would lose valuable altitude, begged Kerkorian to drop below the clouds to get a visual bearing. Fortunately, he went with the navigator's urging, and as they emerged through the bottom of the clouds, the lights of Prestwick, Scotland, twinkled ahead.

Kerkorian made a perfect landing.

33 FLIGHTS
EARNED KERKORIAN HIS SEED MONEY

During 2.5 years with the RAF, Kerkorian delivered 33 planes, traveled to four continents, and managed to save most of his generous salary, which became the foundation of his future wealth.

In July 1945 after completing his RAF service, Kerkorian made his first visit to Las Vegas. He paid $5,000 for a single-engine Cessna, which he used for flying charters—which grew into a successful business.

During the late 1940s and 1950s, shooting dice engaged his leisure time, and he became well known as a Las Vegas high roller, nicknamed "the Perry Como of the craps table," for the mild-mannered way he won—or more frequently lost—$30,000 to $40,000 a night. Eventually, he quit gambling entirely.

Married three times, Kerkorian's most enduring union—from 1954 to 1984—was to Jean Maree Hardy, his second wife. They met and fell in love while Miss Hardy was choreographing a performance at the Thunderbird in Las Vegas. They had two daughters, Tracy and Linda, whose names Kerkorian combined for naming his massive holding company, Tracinda Corporation.

In 1947, Kerkorian purchased a small charter line, Los Angeles Air Service, for $60,000, which flew gamblers from Los Angeles to Las Vegas. He later changed the name to Trans International Airlines (TIA), and offered the first jet service on a nonscheduled airline. That same year, he took out a loan to buy war surplus bombers. With airplane fuel in short supply, he shrewdly sold the fuel from the plane's tanks, paid off the loan, and subsequently owned the planes free and clear.

Kerkorian operated the charter airline until 1968, when he sold it for $104 million to the Transamerica Corporation, receiving as part of the selling price, $85 million in stock. This made him TIA's largest shareholder.

In 1962, Kerkorian made a land deal *Fortune* magazine called "one of the most successful land speculations in Las Vegas' history." He purchased 80 acres on the Strip across from the Flamingo Hotel for $960,000. The $12,000-an-acre price was low even then, given that a narrow strip of land cut the 80 acres off from the Strip. Landlocked. "We traded the owners four or five acres for all of this thin strip that they could never build on," Kerkorian said. "Then I got a call from Jay Sarno, the principal owner of Caesars Palace, and that's how Caesars got started."[36] By 1968, Kerkorian had already collected $4 million leasing the land to Caesars Palace, which eventually purchased the 80-acre parcel that year for $5 million. Altogether, Kerkorian grossed $9 million in the deal with Caesars Palace. Newly prosperous with the cash from the sale, along with his Transamerica stock, Kerkorian was primed to build his first Las Vegas casino resort.

ORIGINS OF THE INTERNATIONAL HOTEL

In the spring of 1967, Kerkorian purchased 82 acres along Paradise Road for $5 million. He hired architect Martin Stern Jr. and built the International Hotel, which at the time was the largest hotel in the world.

While the International was under construction, Kerkorian's business partner, Fred Benninger, suggested that because the International would be so large, they should purchase an existing casino-hotel and use it to train staff. The Flamingo Hotel and Casino fit their needs, was purchased, and became the training ground for the International. Benninger hired Sahara Hotel executive Alex Shoofey as Flamingo president. Shoofey then raided the best of the Sahara's top managers—33 in all— including veteran entertainment director Bill Miller and casino manager James Newman.

In February 1969, the Securities and Exchange Commission gave the approval for Kerkorian's International Leisure to offer the public about 17 percent of the corporation's stock at an initial price of $5 per share. Meanwhile, the Justice Department had acknowledged that gangster Meyer Lansky, Bugsy Siegel's cohort from the old days of Murder Inc., was a hidden co-owner in the Flamingo. Skimming the gross receipts was suspected, and more or less proven after Kerkorian acquired the infamous resort. The Flamingo reportedly never showed more than $400,000 in profits. However, in 1968, Kerkorian's first year, it earned a reported profit of about $3 million, because its alleged skimming operation had ended. Later in 1971, Kerkorian sold the Flamingo to the Hilton Hotels Corporation.

Regarding the International, "We opened that hotel with Barbra Streisand in the main showroom," said Kerkorian. "The rock musical 'Hair' was in the other showroom and the opening lounge act was Ike and Tina Turner. Elvis followed Barbra in the main showroom. I don't know of any hotel that went that big on entertainment. Streisand and Presley brought in some 4,200 customers (potential gamblers) every day for 30 days straight, breaking in the process all attendance records in the county's history."[37]

Kirk Kerkorian

The location Kerkorian chose for the International was often criticized. Naysayers said that the 30-story, 1,512-room hotel was too big and too far away from the Strip.

"We had the same doomsday people when we were building the MGM Grand, same people, same doomsday," said Kerkorian. "You have to ask a lot of questions and listen to people, but eventually, you have to go by your own instincts."[38]

THE ORIGINAL
MGM GRAND HOTEL & CASINO

At the same time Kerkorian was making his initial imprint on Las Vegas, he became interested in the Hollywood film industry. In 1969 he began buying stock in the troubled MGM studios. By year's end he had acquired enough outstanding stock to control MGM, which he reorganized, merged, sold and resold over the years.

From the MGM studio's acquisition emerged the theme for his next mega resort. On the 43-acre site first occupied by the Bonanza Hotel, in 1973, Kerkorian built the original MGM Grand Hotel & Casino, opening at that time as the world's largest hotel. Again, Martin Stern Jr. was the architect and Fred Benninger his partner.

The resort had a movie theme to reflect Kerkorian's interest in film making, and it offered many amenities and entertainment options, including *jai alai. Visitors could engage in live para-mutual betting on the games as they were played. The resort also featured a large shopping arcade, a movie theater showing vintage MGM films, and eight restaurants—some named after famous movie stars, such as Tracy's, a tribute to the great actor Spencer Tracy. Of the MGM's two enormous theaters, the Ziegfield Stage showcased productions by famed choreographer Donn Arden, such as the long running *Hallelujah Hollywood* and *Jubilee*. The Celebrity Room showcased acts such as Barry Manilow, Dean Martin, Sammy Davis Jr., and Jerry Lewis.

The arrival of the MGM Grand as the Strip's first mega resort set a new standard for luxury and size in old Las Vegas, unmatched until the 1989 opening of Steve Wynn's Mirage.

Footnote: *Jai alai, considered as the fastest game in the world, is Basque in origin and popular in South Florida, where it is used as a basis for pari-mutuel gambling. The game is played on an open-walled playing area called the "fronton," with either two players (singles), or four players (doubles), using a "cesta" attached to the right hand to toss a ball called a "pelota" against the front wall.

MGM GRAND FIRE

On November 21, 1980, the MGM Grand suffered a disastrous fire. It started behind the walls of a first-floor restaurant and smoldered for hours before erupting into the casino and rising into the hotel. The fire killed 87 people, the worst disaster in Las Vegas history to date. Almost three months after that fire, the Las Vegas Hilton—which used to be the International—caught fire, killing eight.

The MGM Grand was refurbished in only eight months. It added another hotel tower and reopened in 1982.

The MGM fire made such an impact that it instigated fire safety improvements worldwide.

Kerkorian sold the original MGM Grand, located at the southeast corner of Flamingo road and the Strip, to Bally's in 1986 along with MGM Reno, for a total of $594 million. The Las Vegas property was renamed Bally's Las Vegas, owned and operated today by Caesars Entertainment.

THE SECOND MGM GRAND

Kerkorian's next MGM Grand Hotel & Casino opened in December 1993. It was built on the old Marina Hotel and Tropicana Country Club site at the northeast corner of Tropicana Avenue and the Strip.

Kerkorian again hired Martin Stern Jr. as the architect. Of course, his long-time partner Fred Benninger aided in the huge resort's development. In the beginning, the intention was to develop the first true destination hotel in Las Vegas by including the MGM Grand Adventure Theme Park behind the casino. The notion at the time was to make the Las Vegas Strip more family friendly by developing attractions for children and young adults too young to be inside the casino.

The resort was originally built with an extensive Wizard of Oz theme, featuring the green "Emerald City" color on the exterior and Wizard of Oz memorabilia decorating the inside. A yellow brick road completed the effect along with a statue likeness of Dorothy, the Scarecrow, the Tin Man, and the Cowardly Lion standing in front of the city.

Besides the theme park, the resort featured a 380,000 square-foot convention facility, a 15,000-seat MGM Grand Garden Arena, the Grand Spa, 16 restaurants, numerous shops and night clubs, 5,005 rooms, and the largest casino in Clark County. Although the resort proved successful, the theme park performed poorly and did not reopen for the 2001 season. The following December, MGM announced that the former theme park would be developed as a luxury condominium and hotel complex called "The Signature."

Three years later the MGM underwent extensive renovations. The Oz Casino was the first to go. In 1998 the main entrance on the Strip changed to a more traditional entrance. No longer would visitors enter through the mouth of a giant cartoon-like version of MGM's mascot, Leo the Lion. The reason: many Asian gamblers avoided the casino or used its back entrance because of the "feng shui" belief that entering the mouth of a lion brought bad luck. Instead, a large bronze statue of Leo was added above the Strip entrance to maintain the MGM lion theme. Leo's new statue stands on a 25-foot pedestal, is itself 45 feet tall, weighs 50 tons, and is the largest bronze statue in the U.S.

Torgenson quotes Kerkorian saying he is "not a firm believer in the rule of needing 30 years of experience if you've got good, common sense." Kerkorian gave full credit to Fred Benninger for building the International, the old MGM, and the new MGM. "I can't take much credit," he said, "except for seeing the big picture; the amount of rooms, what kind of showrooms, I'm into that part of it. But when you get into the nitty-gritty, I don't have the education to really get in there and dissect it."[39]

Nowadays, one of the biggest attractions is the live Lion Habitat nestled in the heart of the MGM Grand. Separated from the huge cats by only one-and-a-half inches of glass, visitors can watch several lions on display at all times.

MGM MERGER

In May 2000, Kerkorian's MGM merged with Mirage Resorts, becoming the world's second largest gaming company, behind Harrah's Entertainment. In 2005, MGM Mirage acquired the Mandalay Bay properties, including many of Bill Bennett's projects under the Circus Circus name, such as the Luxor and the Excalibur. Among Kerkorian's many casino resorts are the MGM Grand Detroit, and the MGM Grand Macau which opened in December 2007.

In 2008, Kerkorian's net worth according to *Forbes* magazine was $16 billion, making him the world's 41st richest person. But by 2010, Kirk Kerkorian was among those hardest hit by the economic downturn, and as a result his net worth tumbled to a mere $3.1 billion.

Not bad for someone who dropped out of school in the eighth grade, sold newspapers and earned a pilot's license by taking flying lessons in exchange for his shoveling cow dung.

STEVE WYNN: A VISION OF LUXURY

Similar to marvel entrepreneur Kerkorian, another innovative, self-made man accumulated wealth by developing huge, luxurious casino resorts in Southern Nevada—Steve Wynn. His first trip to Las Vegas with his family occurred when he was 10 years old.

Steve Wynn

Wynn once told an interviewer in 1983 that when he was young he'd go to bed at night and his father would sneak out to shoot dice at the Flamingo and the Sands. Wynn recalled that it was 1952, and to get to Las Vegas one rode horses through the desert and tied them to a hitching post at a casino's back door. "It was like stepping back into the frontier," Wynn said in a *Review-Journal* interview. "Casino owners were king; they owned the town. They were glamorous; they had beautiful women, and lots of money."

In time, Wynn's vivid observations about casino owners in 1952 would be made about Wynn himself.

WYNN'S EARLY CAREER

Growing up in the cold climate of Utica, NY, Steve Wynn got his first gaming experience in a string of family-owned bingo parlors helping his father call bingo numbers on weekends. Wynn's father, Michael, tried to open a bingo parlor in Las Vegas, but was unable to obtain a license. He returned to Utica, and helped his mother, Zelma, to raise Steve and Kenneth, Steve's younger brother by 10 years.

Later, Steve took classes at Wharton Business School and on weekends continued helping his father run the bingo parlors. His father died in 1963, just before Wynn received a Bachelor of Arts degree in English Literature from the University of Pennsylvania. At the time of his death, Michael Wynn reportedly left $350,000 in gambling debts.

In 1963, Steve Wynn met Elaine Paschal, a hotel promoter from Miami, the daughter of one of his father's gambling buddies. Ironically, Elaine's father and Wynn's father earlier had joked about both their kids meeting and going on a date. Elaine was a blonde beauty, Miss Miami Beach, and at the time of their meeting attended UCLA. After they fell in love, Elaine transferred to George Washington University to be closer to Wynn. They married a few months after Michael Wynn died.

Steve Wynn took over the family's bingo operation and managed to accumulate enough money to pay off his father's debts and buy a small stake in the Frontier Hotel & Casino in Las Vegas. In 1967, he and Elaine moved to Las Vegas. Eventually he became the Frontier's keno and slot manager. It was Wynn's investment in the Frontier that became perhaps the most controversial deal he ever made.

The Frontier came with hidden owners, all of whom were mobsters engaged in the usual skimming activities. Had Wynn's associates been the typical old timers out of the Prohibition-era roadhouses around Nevada, the gaming authorities might have paid little attention. However, within a year of Wynn's assuming his role of keno and slot manager, the gaming authorities pressured him to sell to a buyer they'd found, someone who could come in and clean up the place. He managed to avoid charges of wrongdoing when he sold his interest to billionaire Howard Hughes. Wynn later claimed he made no money on the Frontier deal.

No longer invested in the Frontier, Wynn got involved briefly in promoting lounge shows, and by 1968 obtained a valuable wine and liquor distributorship. He also made the most valuable contact any businessman could make in Las Vegas: banker E. Parry Thomas.

ENTER PARRY THOMAS, THE HELPFUL BANKER

Edward Parry Thomas, CEO of the Bank of Las Vegas (later becoming Valley Bank), was known at the time as the only banker in the country who would lend money to build casinos.

Mainstream financial institutions thought casinos too devious to secure a loan.

A shrewd banker, Thomas acquired a reputation for knowing more about southern Nevada real estate than anyone else. Robert Maheu, Howard Hughes' top aide, couldn't recall any major parcel of Las Vegas real estate Hughes acquired without consulting Thomas—including Hughes' six casinos. One summer while the Thomas family vacationed in southern California, the banker moved into the Desert Inn so he could transact the deals Hughes needed done quickly. Thomas purchased properties in his own name for Hughes. In this secretive way the sellers didn't know that Hughes the then-richest man in the world was bidding for the property.

Thomas and the ambitious Steve Wynn immediately hit it off. Ultimately, Thomas not only loaned Wynn money to begin his casino empire, he also mentored the career of the innovative Ivy Leaguer.

Perry Thomas

Wynn's wealth originated from a huge land deal he pulled off in 1971, which generated the seed money to ultimately make him a billionaire. It started when he learned that Caesars Palace located on the busy corner of Las Vegas Boulevard and Flamingo road, was not the actual owner of a strip of land that ran along Flamingo. Howard Hughes owned it, and Hughes refused to sell it to Caesars. As the *Review-Journal* reports, "But nobody knew more about the Hughes real estate holdings than did Wynn's new mentor, Parry Thomas, who had helped assemble them."[40]

Wynn found another site that Hughes needed, negotiated an option to buy it, then set up a trade with Hughes. Wynn was said to have snatched the Flamingo Road parcel "from under Caesars' nose." If that move wasn't clever enough, the next really was. "Wynn announced plans to build the world's narrowest casino thereon, forcing Caesars to buy the narrow strip for $2.25 million." If Caesars had not paid Wynn for that narrow bit of land, the casino risked having a competitor located at their own front door.

Wynn and an undisclosed partner invested $1.2 million in the transaction, borrowing most of the funds from Thomas. When the deal was done, Wynn paid off Thomas, split the proceeds with his partner, and earned himself a profit of more than half-a-million dollars.

This profit earned in the "Hughes-Caesars Land Swap and Sale" gave Wynn enough money to join with Thomas in what the *Review-Journal* called "the most famous bloodless coup in Las Vegas casino management."

Once again, Thomas played an integral role in a second coup. Thomas informed Wynn that the Golden Nugget in downtown Las Vegas had one of the most desirable locations on Fremont Street. However, it was managed by a group of old-timers content with the status quo and not interested in making any changes. Thomas also informed Wynn that Golden Nugget stock was undervalued, and that the current operators didn't own much of it.

With this knowledge, Wynn and a new group of investors began buying up stock in the Golden Nugget until they had enough to get elected to the board of directors. In due course they gained controlling interest. Next, they began documenting mismanagement, including employee thefts on the casino floor. That led to Wynn's calling for the Golden Nugget president, Buck Blaine, to resign. If he didn't resign, Wynn threatened to sue him.

"We can do it easy or we can do it hard," Wynn recalled saying in his confrontation with Blaine. "Bucky, sitting in that office of his, just caved in," wrote A.D. Hopkins in a *Review-Journal* article Blaine bailed out with a $30,000-a-year tin parachute labeled a "consulting fee." By August 1973, Wynn ran the company, and in one year he increased pre-tax profits from $1.1 million to $4.2 million.

To a Glitter Gulch that over the years had lost its glitter and much of its business to the emerging Las Vegas Strip, in 1977, Wynn added 579 rooms to the hotel, many of them the best Las Vegas then had to offer. Soon the Golden Nugget was making $12 million a year.

As a result, not only did Wynn become the youngest casino owner in Las Vegas, but also the Nugget later received accolades earning its first four-diamond rating from Mobil Travel Guide. By 1987, Wynn offered a total of 2,300 luxurious hotel rooms, which attracted new upscale clientele to downtown Las Vegas and made his empire enormously successful. In time, the Golden Nugget Las Vegas proved the foundation for Wynn's ultimate rise to prominence in the gaming industry.

THE GOLDEN NUGGET PARLAY

Once he transformed the Golden Nugget into the jewel of downtown, Steve Wynn looked to America's East Coast for more opportunities. In an old resort town along the South Jersey shore, gambling had just become legal. Though the old town had lost its tourist appeal, Atlantic City was still an interesting place. During its heyday, it had been a popular vacation spot, with its picturesque boardwalk, sandy beaches, and strategic location between two major cities, New York and Philadelphia. Wynn found an aging hotel, tore it down, and by 1980 had built another Golden Nugget with 506 rooms.

His next move really brought big-money players to both his Golden Nuggets. He paid $10 million for three years of "Frank Sinatra's silver voice and priceless image," which he featured in his showrooms and in the commercials for his casinos. The *Review-Journal* reported that Wynn "bought jets, helicopters and limousines to bring high-rollers there... raided competing casinos for proven casino employees, and lavished money to keep them. By 1984 his net worth was estimated at $100 million."[41]

THE MIRAGE AND TREASURE ISLAND

In 1984 Steve Wynn sold the Nugget's Atlantic City property for $440 million, reportedly for a $230-million net profit, and used $60 million of it to further upgrade the Golden Nugget in downtown Las Vegas, adding the second hotel tower and showroom. In 1986, he used another portion of those proceeds to purchase a large tract on the Las Vegas Strip where it intersects with Spring Mountain Road across from the Desert Inn. This choice location had remained largely undeveloped but was not for sale, primarily because it was owned by the reclusive Howard Hughes. But after Hughes' death in 1976, those who ran his immense holdings began divesting parts of it.

At the same time as Wynn acquired the undeveloped tract he purchased two adjacent casinos from the Hughes estate, the Castaways and Silver Slipper. He developed the entire site into the Mirage, later adjacent to it he developed Treasure Island. At the opening of the Mirage in 1989, it became one of the most glamorous resort hotels in the world. It featured an erupting volcano, an indoor rain forest, and high-quality room appointments with an emphasis on service. The reported price tag to build the Mirage was $630 million, of which $565 million was raised by the sale of junk bonds issued by *Michael Milken.

Critics claimed that the lavish Mirage was an enormous gamble, given that junk bonds required payment of a high rate of interest. The hotel would have to make a million dollars a day to service the debt. In 1989, the *Review-Journal* noted that, "While it had 3,000 rooms to do it, nobody really knew if there was enough business to fill that many new rooms, particularly rooms that had to rent for more than the city average to pay the nut."

Footnote: *Michael Milken, nicknamed the "Junk Bond King," was sentenced in 1989 to ten years in prison and permanently barred from the securities industry by the Securities and Exchange Commission. However, for cooperating testimony, the presiding judge reduced his sentence in exchange for cooperating testimony against Milken's former colleagues. With good behavior considered, the Junk Bond King was released after serving less than two years.

Once again, despite the huge expense incurred, Wynn's endeavors in developing the Mirage proved enormously successful. His next resort project, adjacent to the Mirage, was Treasure Island Hotel and Casino. Built at a cost of $450 million, it opened in 1993 with 2,664 rooms and 220 suites. Nightly, pirate battles were staged in "Buccaneer Bay," an area in front of the casino entrance on the Strip. Inside, performing in the showroom was the first permanent *Cirque du Soleil* show in Las Vegas.

THE BELLAGIO

Inspired by the Lake Como resort of Bellagio in Northern Italy, Wynn expanded further on his vision of luxury, converting the razed Dunes' site into the elegant $1.6 billion Bellagio Las Vegas. This magnificent resort opened in 1998 with 3,993 rooms and approximately 10,000 employees. Its many features include a picturesque 8-acre lake with dancing fountains synchronized to music, an indoor conservatory, a museum-quality art gallery, and branches of high-end boutiques and restaurants from San Francisco, Paris, and New York City.

The Bellagio's poker room was considered special by famed poker players. They referred to it as "The Office," owing to its high table limits. It included the high stakes Big Game that could usually be found in "Bobby's Room," named after poker great Bobby "the Owl" Baldwin, who became the Bellagio's first president under Steve Wynn.

The Bellagio was credited with starting a new spree of luxurious mega resorts along the Las Vegas Strip. Among the more recent developments are Mandalay Bay, The Venetian, Paris Las Vegas, CityCenter, and the Cosmopolitan.

MERGER OF THE MGM AND MIRAGE

In June 2000, the Golden Nugget Las Vegas, along with all of Steve Wynn's other properties, was purchased by Kirk Kerkorian. The consolidated corporation became known as MGM Mirage. To date, it is the second largest casino corporation in the world, after Harrahs Entertainment. The reported price paid to acquire selected Wynn properties: $6.6 billion.

WYNN LAS VEGAS AND ENCORE

Five weeks before closing the deal with Kerkorian, Steve Wynn purchased the historic Desert Inn and its adjoining golf course for $270 million. Then, with the net proceeds from his sale to Kerkorian, and with his ability to secure even greater financing, Steve Wynn took Wynn Resorts Limited public in 2002 with an initial stock offering.

Next, he built his most expensive resort to date, the Wynn Las Vegas, at a cost of $2.7 billion. The flagship property of Wynn Resorts is situated on 215 acres, across the Strip from the Fashion Show Mall. It has 45 floors, with 2,716 rooms that range in size from 640 square feet to villas of 7,000 square feet. This magnificent property opened in April 2005. Notably, one of its casino hosts is Joe Esposito, who was Elvis Presley's road manager, and best friend.

In the summer of 2008, hiring of employees commenced for Encore Las Vegas, Steve Wynn's most recent development in Sin City, modeled after the Wynn Las Vegas structure. Although separate hotels, both share the original Desert Inn site. Encore opened in December 2008 with 3,500 employees.

Abroad, Wynn successfully bid for one of three gaming concessions opened in Macau, a Special Administrative Region off the coast of mainland China.

As for Steve Wynn's personal life, his marriage to Elaine produced two daughters, Kevyn and Gillian. Kevyn had the misfortune of being kidnapped in 1993, although she was later found unharmed. Meanwhile, Wynn paid $1.45 million in ransom for her safe return. The kidnappers were apprehended when one attempted to pay cash for a Ferrari in Newport Beach, California.

Wynn once said he purchased the Desert Inn, the site of his Wynn and Encore Las Vegas properties, as a birthday gift for Elaine. Steve and Elaine were divorced in 1986, remarried in 1991, and filed for divorce again in 2009, yet Elaine Wynn remains a director of the company's board.

Author's Note: In the Spring of 2008, during one of my cross-country "Poker Tours," yours truly and Liz Rouse, my soul mate, stayed at the Wynn Las Vegas and played every day in its 18-table poker room. During that four-day stay, we were so impressed with this wonderful resort that I just had to describe here our memorable experience.

To begin, the view from our 12th floor suite was breath taking. Through floor-to-ceiling and wall-to-wall picture window, with two sets of remote-controlled motorized drapes, we could look down on the original, picturesque Desert Inn golf course, which featured a waterfall. In the background we could see the Las Vegas monorail with Sunrise Mountain behind it. His and hers Wynn-monogrammed bathrobes with matching slippers waited for us in the closet (which I later discovered from our maid were complimentary, and which the staff encouraged guests to take home).

Most luxurious of all was the huge bathroom, with a large glassed-in shower, a Jacuzzi-type bathtub adjacent to it, and a wall-mounted television tuned to the poker room channel that listed the games and the player's names. A private enclosed commode included, of course, a wall phone. The king-size bed was very comfortable, and service overall was impeccable. For the most part we snacked in the poker room and dined at the pool-side café, where the food was delicious.

Congratulations, Mister Wynn, we love your resort!

Chapter 4
INSIDE THE CASINO

*H*ave you ever wondered why Las Vegas table game dealers clap their hands before leaving their post? It's all part of casino procedure to protect the house. This practice of "clapping out" reveals to the nearest supervisor that the dealers are leaving the table with nothing hidden in their hands, such as casino cheques or cash. Clapping out to reveal empty palms is performed not only for the supervisor but also for the surveillance or security cameras housed in the ceiling, known as the "eye in the sky." If the eye detects anything out of the ordinary, the person monitoring the eye usually calls down to the responsible pit boss or floor supervisor.

Before high-tech surveillance cameras were installed in casinos, surveillance people moved about on a series of narrow catwalks above the mirrors in the ceilings. From his acclaimed *Las Vegas: Behind the Tables*, Barney Vinson wrote the following excerpt about an interview with a Dunes' security man Roger Mennie: "In the days of yore it was very unsophisticated. When I first came to work here in 1977, we didn't have this new surveillance system. We had the old catwalk. And you had to go all the way outside the building, go around by the restaurant, climb up two rickety ladders, just to get inside. You're bending down, stepping over rafters, cobwebs getting in your face all the time. And it was dark. You couldn't have any bright lights because they would show through the one-way mirror."[42]

One time, onlookers in one Las Vegas casino were treated to a rare sight. In the days of antiquated surveillance, casino patrons heard the sound of glass shattering. Startled, they looked up and saw a man's leg dangling precariously through what was left of a shattered one-way ceiling mirror.

Mennie recalled another incident. "We had a guy fall through the one-way mirror at the Hilton. He was walking to the eye (in the sky), slipped, and fell into one of the convention areas."

Why all the surveillance? Casinos want people to know how they are protecting their customer's assets and the casino's. One casino-hotel reported that it had the most sophisticated surveillance system on the Strip. In the casino alone, they reported having 51 different cameras wired to 16 TV monitors and recording devices on the second floor. Thirty-one of those cameras, housed in their Plexiglas bubbles, were suspended along the ceiling of the casino. "Operated by controls at the monitoring stations, these cameras—with their pan and tilt functions—systematically train on all gaming tables in the casino. They can move 365 degrees horizontally, and 175 degrees vertically... with focus, iris, and zoom controls. The other 20 cameras used in the casino are all stationary. They are trained on the progressive slot machines; the counting rooms; and the cage where cashiers buy and sell cheques, cash checks, and take care of markers."

WHAT SURVEILLANCE LOOKS FOR

The people who monitor these surveillance cameras are taught what to look for in a 12-week training program. Demonstrations of crooked acts were given by representatives from the Nevada Gaming Control Enforcement Commission and by ex-cheaters, or "crossroaders," as they are called in gaming terminology.

The cheaters and scam artists who prey on casinos and their patrons are given interesting nicknames.

The Rail Bird: These cheaters work around dice tables, usually at the busiest action games. Their target is an unsuspecting player with a lot of high-valued casino cheques resting precariously on the rail of the dice table. Their modus operandi is to move in next to their target, and when he or she is not looking the "rail bird" snatches a cheque or two from the unsuspecting player. Near the beginning of the film *Casino*, Sharon Stone can be seen removing cheques from the rail belonging to another player on a dice table at the Tangiers, and putting them in her purse.

Claim Bet Artist: These thieves also work around busy dice tables, where a naïve player often loses track of his bets on the complex layout. The thieves are good at what they do, and most of the time they get away with a false claim the first time. They might, for instance, claim a $5 hard-way proposition bet on a busy craps layout, especially immediately after the base dealer or the box man goes on break and is replaced by someone unfamiliar with the existing bets on the layout. If the claim bet artist argues long enough and holds up the game, most bosses pay them off just to prevent holding up the game.

Dice Slider: This manipulator first sets the dice, then instead of rolling them and hitting the opposite end of the table as he is supposed to, he slides the dice along the surface in order to get a specific result. For example, the "dice slider" might set the dice on 6-6 to a pair of sixes face up, then bets that 6-6 (12) will be the result of the roll.

Past Poster: The first thing table games dealers learn in dealing school is to always keep their eyes on the layout. That's because a cheater, such as a "past poster," believing no one is watching, sneaks in a bet or adds to his already winning bet after the winner is established.

Slugger: This is a counterfeiter who uses slugs in slot machines instead of genuine coins or acceptable tokens. Roger Mennie explained in *Las Vegas: Behind the Tables,* "In the mid 1980s, authorities estimated that Clark County annually lost $20 million to slot machine cheats." Today, most casinos no longer use slot machines that accept coins or tokens. Instead, the newer machines accept only paper money, or credits, and reject counterfeit bills.

One counterfeiter was so good authorities called him the Counterfeit King. Louis "The Coin" Colavecchio, a master tool-and-die maker, created millions of dollars worth of counterfeit coins for slot machines from Nevada to Connecticut and New Jersey.

By 1998, the law caught up with him. He was convicted on forgery and counterfeiting charges and sentenced to 27 months in prison plus three years on probation. While imprisoned he consulted for Las Vegas casinos on how to detect fake tokens. After his release, the casinos banned him. According to a History Channel documentary, he also consulted for the federal government, earning $18,000 for explaining to the U.S. mint how his method of manufacturing dies outlasted theirs. In 2006, police in Rhode Island arrested Colavecchio for the same crime—counterfeiting casino tokens. He told police his legitimate business had gone under, and when he could no longer make ends meet he'd been forced to return to counterfeiting.

Bender and Crimper: A "bender" puts a very slight bend on the corners of playing cards he wants to remember. The "crimper" simply crimps different areas of special cards.

Dauber: The "dauber" marks certain cards with a bit of special paint from his finger so he can recognize those marked cards later. A sophisticated dauber uses ultraviolet paint that can be seen only with special kinds of glasses or contact lenses.

Hand Mucker: This type of cheater conceals playing cards in his clothing or hands, and switches them with the ones he's dealt. He or she is a firm believer in the ancient proverb "the hand is quicker than the eye." These cheaters—the benders, crimpers, daubers, and hand muckers—are four prime examples of why cards are dealt mostly face-up nowadays on Las Vegas blackjack tables, and why the player is, by rule, not allowed to touch the cards. And in casino poker rooms, it's the reason a card is usually burned prior to dealing each round.

Stringer: A "stringer" concentrates on older-type slot machines that accept only coins. This scam artist typically attached fishing wire to a coin through a small hole. He uses a "yo-yo" motion until the wired coin triggers the coin-acceptance switch of the slot machine. To avoid surveillance, the stringer usually surrounds himself with several partners, called "blockers," whose job is to block the view of surveillance agents.

Light Wand: This device consists of a wire, a tiny light bulb, and a small battery. The cheater probes into the slot machine to confuse the counting mechanism and causes a false payout. This scam works only on coin-payout machines.

Slider or Monkey Paw: This technique requires a steel spring or guitar wire to be snaked through the payout chute of a slot machine in order to trip a micro-switch. Technological advances ended its use in the early 1990s.

One of the greatest slot cheats was Tommy Carmichael, who was caught rigging old slot machines in Las Vegas, served time in jail, and is listed in Nevada's notorious Black Book. He also was featured on the History Channel series *Breaking Vegas.*

Counterfeit Tickets: These days, the preferred method of cheating slot machines is to have computer experts create fake "TITO" tickets (Ticket In, Ticket Out), thereby earning false credits in slot machines.

Besides catching these shady characters in the act, casino surveillance is also responsible for spotting people listed in Nevada's notorious Black Book. Anyone listed in it is forbidden from entering all of the state's casinos.

Card Counters at Blackjack: Surveillance looks for card counters, too—skilled players whom casinos believe have an unfair edge by knowing the cards remaining in a single deck or a multiple-deck "shoe" of playing cards. Bob Brooker, a security man for the old Marina Hotel, once discovered one of the most elaborate cheating scams ever reported. During a Culinary Union strike at the Marina, picketers kept pulling the electrical plug on the marquee lights. Brooker and his assistants ran outside to turn the lights on again and noticed a panel truck in the parking lot with the engine running. Brooker knocked on the door and discovered an elaborate electronic system inside designed for cheating. Its monitors, television cameras, and computers were part of a massive blackjack cheating scheme, the scope of which stunned gaming control agents. Inside the Marina another team member was apprehended. He was found with a miniature camera hooked to his belt buckle, small computers in both boots, and in his ear a tiny headset through which "master control" in the truck gave him instructions.

In the early "Wild West" days of Las Vegas, the Mob took care of cheaters in its own way, which seldom, if ever, involved legal means. Rather than calling the police or politely escorting the cheater out the door, as happens today, cheaters were escorted to a back room. There, as portrayed in the film *Casino*, their hands might be broken. In one notorious incident, a casino had 20 cheaters beaten up. They later sued the casino for $2 million, and the case was settled out of court for an undisclosed amount.

All told, Las Vegas casino-resorts have their own internal security, which resembles the command center of a modern-day army. As Robert De Niro said in Martin Scorsese's film *Casino*, "The dealers watch the players. The floor men watch the dealers.

The pit bosses watch the floor men. The shift boss watches the pit bosses. The eye in the sky watches everybody."

COUNTER MEASURES

How do the casinos counter a team of card counters? Card-counting teams typically enter a casino and begin playing at several blackjack tables. When the remaining deck of cards or multiple-deck shoe is favorable for the player—meaning that the remaining cards are rich in aces, tens, or face cards—the counter signals the big player. The big player enters the game knowing he has a favorable situation and begins placing big bets.

Some of the measures casinos use to reduce the card counters' advantage include an automatic shuffler, which constantly shuffles all discards. If that type of shuffler is unavailable, some bosses use an early shuffle once they detect a card counter, or they instruct the dealer to insert the cut card at least half way. Other casinos may have a sign on the blackjack table that says something like, "Mid-shuffle entry limited to betting table minimum."

THE NEVADA GAMING CONTROL BOARD

In addition to a casino's internal security, agents from the Gaming Control Board have certain responsibilities. One is to issue Sheriff's Cards to casino employees, who are required to have the cards in their possession at all times while working. Each card has an identification number and a color photo of the licensee. The cards must be renewed periodically, much like a driver's license. To be eligible for a Sheriff's Card, which in reality is a work permit, the casino employee must be fingerprinted and pass a thorough police investigation.

Another of the board's functions is to count the number of slot machines and gaming tables inside each casino, so the casino's quarterly reports can be monitored. Every casino pays an annual license fee for each slot machine and table game on its premises.

Gaming control agents often make unannounced visits to the casino floor. A retired Dunes' floor man explains: "They'll take the dice off a table without warning. The dice are put in a sealed envelope and taken to their lab, where they are tested for accuracy to determine that they haven't been altered in any way."

Besides making spot checks on their own, gaming control agents also investigate complaints filed by unhappy customers and sometimes investigate each other. According to Barney Vinson, the pull of easy money in Las Vegas has managed to corrupt a few agents over the years. In 1985, authorities charged one for allegedly using slugs while playing a slot machine. The following year an agent working surveillance at Caesars Palace robbed a group of high rollers inside their hotel room. He made the mistake of locking the five men in their bathroom, which unknown to him was equipped with a telephone. A call to the hotel's security office resulted in an arrest before the corrupt agent could escape.

Barney Vinson, who worked as a table games floor man at the Dunes, wrote, "It all goes back to that human frailty called greed. The people who run these gambling casinos aren't dummies. They know all about human nature, that 'something for nothing' philosophy that gets people to the tables in the first place. They know there is a touch of larceny in every person." That's why they have the eye in the sky, gaming control investigators, and a Black Book.

Security man Bob Brooker described the situation this way: "Your employee today who is a good solid employee may start running around... or having some financial problems... and your good employee is no longer good."

HOW DO THEY DO IT?

If you're wondering whether all this casino security, from hand clapping to camera monitoring to gaming control is really worth the effort, consider some of the following true incidents of uncovered casino scams.

SCAM AT HARRAHS NEW ORLEANS

The most difficult casino scams to uncover are conspiracies in which a dealer commits a crime in cahoots with a player or another employee. The following conspiracy scam happened in 1995, while I was employed as a table games supervisor at Harrah's New Orleans Casino.

Three months after the casino opened, late in the morning on graveyard shift, a young Asian man was dealing mini baccarat to seven Asian players. Baccarat is a popular game among Asians. After the authorities investigate, they discovered that all were relatives, including the dealer.

Another oddity was that every one of the seven players wagered $5,000, the table's maximum limit on the Player, not the Banker. One of the baccarat players must have managed to replace a stacked shoe of eight decks of Harrah's monogrammed playing cards on the mini-baccarat table without the eye in the sky or floor personnel seeing it. Security later suspected a woman of taking the old shoe of cards off the table and replacing it with a stacked shoe from her purse. The shoe was stacked in favor of the Player, and as long as all participants wagered on the Player, and not on the Banker, they won.

The next day, Harrah's figured the scam cost them nearly $500,000 before supervisory personnel stopped the "fixed" mini baccarat game. The dealer escaped somehow and was not captured until six months later. When the police went to the dealer's home, they discovered nearly $1 million in Harrah's $500 denomination cheques—all counterfeit. Later, the police confiscated several new cars the dealer's family members had purchased for cash. Besides the casino's financial loss, because of the counterfeit cheques Harrah's was forced to remove all the old $500 denomination cheques from all their games at the New Orleans casino and replace them with new ones.

SCAM ON ROULETTE
AT RESORTS ATLANTIC CITY CASINO

Another incident that involved collusion occurred soon after Resorts opened in Atlantic City. Unfortunately, for the casino the scam lasted for almost two years before being discovered in 1979. At the time, the Resorts Casino in Atlantic City was jam-packed with customers because it was the first facility to open after the legalization of gaming in New Jersey. Evidently, this rip-off occurred between a Resorts' roulette dealer and a player, and was so clever it took years to expose.

The swindle went like this. The player approached the roulette table and put down a $100 bill. His secret accomplice, the dealer, assigned the player a certain color—which is customary. Instead of correctly marking this player's stack as 20 cheques of $5 (totaling $100), the dealer marked it 20 cheques of $25, giving it the inflated value of $500—representing a $400 loss for the casino. As planned, the player played for a while, then cashed out his cheques, each cheque worth $20 more than what he paid for it.

The same two conspirators apparently ran this scam twice a day for over two years, until they grew even greedier and got caught. In the end, no one really knows how much was stolen from Resorts, but it had to be a considerable amount!

SLIGHT-OF-HAND AT CIRCUS CIRCUS

When I worked at Circus Circus during the early 1980s, we had a box man who was so good at stealing that not even the eye in the sky could catch him in the act. I worked for more than two years with this guy and never suspected a thing. He was finally spotted in the act by another dealer, believe it or not. Turns out the thief was folding all $100 bills into long slender strips before "apparently" shoving them into the cash box with the paddle. About every fourth $100 bill he somehow pushed it up the left sleeve of his jacket. Evidently, folding the bills made them easier for the device up his sleeve to grab, allowing him to continue with the natural motion of shoving the paddle toward the cash box with his right hand.

After surveillance noticed what he was doing, his action was captured on film. The police came to the table one night, put the thieving box man in handcuffs, and escorted him to jail. It was estimated that during the previous two years he'd stolen from Circus Circus over $3,000 a week for a total of more than $300,000.

CONSPIRACY AT CAESARS PALACE

Two separate incidents of employee theft at casinos involved a roulette dealer, a floor man, and a box man. In the first scam, the Caesars Palace dealer hid a $500 cheque among the marker buttons near the roulette wheel. The floor man, as part of his supervisory role, stopped by and casually picked up the marker as he watched the play of the game. When he left the table, the marker and hidden cheque were still in his hand.

At another casino, a dishonest box man attempted to smuggle $100 cheques out of the casino by hiding them, one at a time, under his wristwatch, then going outside to hide them under a bush. A passing security guard spotted the stack and arrested the thief when he showed up to collect his ill-gotten gains.

Over the years, casino dealers have been caught with cheques in their pockets, under their belts, in their mouths, in their socks, in their shoes, up their sleeves, in their underwear—even in secret compartments sewn into their monogrammed apron. Up to the late 1970s, casino cheques were as good as cash at Nevada grocery stores, laundries, and service stations. Then one of the largest counterfeiting schemes in the annals of Las Vegas was uncovered, and that convenience came to a swift end. Nowadays, most casinos are very suspicious of another casino's cheques.

PASSING $1 CHEQUES
FOR $25 COUNTERFEITS

This next multi-million-dollar counterfeit scheme was clever but simple. The culprits came up with the scam after they noticed the $1 cheques from a Reno casino were almost identical to the $25 cheques from a major Las Vegas casino. The counterfeiters purchased thousands of $1 cheques from the Reno casino, made up new $25 inserts, pasted them over the old $1 inserts, and proceeded to pass them off as $25 cheques. Their ruse was exposed when one of the counterfeit inserts became unglued and peeled back along the edges, revealing its "one dollar" value underneath.

A floor man at Caesars Palace explained why dealers today are more honest. Salaries are higher and dealers lead more stable, married-with-kids lives. Responsibilities drive up the cost of dishonest behavior. Like bank tellers, dealers have too much at stake to steal from their employers. Moreover, it will be on their record, and no one in the gaming business will hire them.

In the early days of legalized gaming, before the Gaming Control Board and thorough police investigations, those who ran the casinos were primarily concerned with the dealer not being a thief. Dealers were often hired on their reputation and could be "juiced-in" because an employee or someone important vouched for them.

SURVEILLANCE TAPES ACT AS A RECORD

Sometimes the surveillance tapes come in handy and can help resolve a dispute with a customer. Say a blackjack player disputes a particular hand, which for whatever reason cannot be replayed from the discards. The floor man can call surveillance and have the hand reviewed, and from the results, determine if the player should be paid.

For now, the cameras keep rolling in the Las Vegas casinos, and surveillance people keep walking the aisles looking for dealers who violate procedures—along with slot cheats, purse snatchers, rail birds, and past posters.

COMPS AND CREDIT

When high-roller Kerry Packer (See Chapter 6 for complete story) was invited to the MGM Grand in 1993 and again in 1995, he was treated as a special VIP with full red-carpet treatment. What can the common folk and other less-rich high rollers expect in comps from a Las Vegas casino? It depends on their bank account and on the amount of play they give the casino.

Back in the days when junkets were big business, the formula was easy. The casino typically comped the junket player up to 20 percent of the money put in play. If the player put $1,000 in play, the casino comped up to 20 percent of it, or $200. Today it's less. The days of casino junkets slowly faded into the archives of Las Vegas history. It became apparent that the costs simply didn't warrant the action. Junkets required a lot of preparation and expense, such as chartering airplanes to get junket players to town, chartering buses to get them to the hotel, wining them, dining them, and giving them the choicest rooms. Casinos usually threw parties for the junketeers when they arrived, then a bigger party when they left. It turned out to be a losing proposition for everyone but the players on the junkets.

CASINO HOSTS

Casino host Gene Kilroy observed, "The dice and the cards are the same all over. It's how you treat people that makes the difference."[43]

Hosts make people feel like big shots. Mitzi Gobel, a host at the Frontier, once said, "Everybody wants to be somebody when they come here, and I help them feel like somebody." High rollers like to associate with big-time professional sports figures. That's why big boxing matches in Las Vegas fill up the town. Gene Kilroy, host at the Tropicana, was a former business manager for Muhammad Ali.

The casino host's responsibility is to give the VIP guest all the hospitality the casino has to offer—arranging complimentary accommodations, food, and tickets to the showroom. The treatment can include airfare and limousine service to and from the airport, depending on how much action the high roller VIP intends to give the casino.

"A host romances the customers." That's a quote from Irving "Ash" Resnick, host at the Dunes in 1986. Resnick was on a first-name basis with one of his high-roller clients from Japan, Ginji Yasuda, who wanted a Las Vegas casino all his own. The association ended up with Resnick on a first-name basis with a new boss. Resnick introduced Yasuda to Aladdin Hotel owner

Ed Torres, and as a result, Yasuda bought the Aladdin for $54 million, and Resnick worked for him there.

While Resnick worked at the Dunes he brought the casino an estimated $12 million in business, which gives you an idea of how important hosts really are. "Knowing people, bringing them in, knowing how much credit to give and knowing how to collect the money. That's what it's all about," Resnick noted in an interview he gave four years before his death. Ash Resnick spent more than 40 years in Las Vegas working at a number of casinos. His obituary in the *New York Times* credited him with organizing the first Las Vegas junkets for high-stakes gamblers. The *Times* also repeated longstanding allegations of his ties to organized crime and described two attempts on his life. The first occurred in 1974 when eight sticks of dynamite were placed under his car. Two years later shots were fired at him as he left Caesars Palace.

Then there are "celebrity" hosts, often referred to as "greeters." Johnny Weissmuller of Tarzan fame was the first celebrity host. He worked at the original MGM Grand in the mid-1970s. Joe Louis was a greeter at Caesars Palace Las Vegas until his passing in 1981. Caesars also had Pancho Gonzales as its celebrity tennis pro. If players wanted a game of tennis with him, they simply called the host and he'd set up the match. These days, the Wynn Las Vegas has Joe Esposito as a host. He was Elvis Presley's aide and best friend.

It's much the same in Atlantic City. At Bally's Park Place baseball's Hall-of-Famer Willy Mays rubbed shoulders with the masses. The Claridge had New York Yankee great Mickey Mantle as a host.

No matter how much money visiting high rollers had or how many businesses they ran, it was a hoot for them to return home and do a little bragging to their friends. "I played blackjack the other night with Joe Louis at Caesars Palace in Las Vegas. You remember him, don't you? The heavyweight world champion they called the 'Brown Bomber.'" Or, "My wife and I played doubles with Pancho Gonzalez. Man, he just wore me out. Yeah, he's the tennis pro over at Caesars. Remember when he won the U.S. championship two years in a row at Forest Hills?"

Although the celebrity host's job is essentially to greet the high rollers, the casino host's job entails much more responsibility. Besides arranging transportation to and from the casino, the casino host sees players through their stay at the hotel. Since big players are getting comped, someone has to monitor their play to make sure they keep up their end of the understood bargain. Casinos frown on player's taking advantage of all the comps given but spending most of his or her time on the golf course instead of gambling at the tables.

When the typical high-roller VIP becomes an invited guest at a Las Vegas casino-resort, the criterion for determining the amount of comps given depends on the VIP's rating.

PLAYER RATING CARD

Most players are rated, especially if they have a credit line with the casino or want any kind of comp. The table games floor people do the player ratings on a rating card, which records "time in" and "time out," critical factors since the casino knows it has an advantage over any gambler's long-term play. The rating card also determines net win or loss on a given session, along with the size of the average bet made by the player. The casino host usually monitors data generated off the player rating cards via the computer.

It's all about exposure. The few big players who know how to "hit and run" are not the casinos first choice. A prime example was mister hit-and-run himself, Kerry Packer. If you recall from Chapter 6, after Packer's two visits to the MGM Grand, its president was sent to Australia to respectfully inform Packer that his action was no longer accepted at the MGM.

All said, the final tabulation of sessions at the casino, win or lose, is not that big a factor in determining the extent of anyone's comps. If you gave the casino a good shot at your money and you won, no problem—most casinos won't take your comps away. They want you back soon for another shot at that money. In time, they figure they'll get it.

TRACKING

Have you ever wondered how the casinos know how much the big players win or lose? Some think it's mind boggling when so many different elements are at stake, such as markers, cheques, and cash buy-ins.

Markers are simply counter checks issued by the casino to a player with a line of credit. A line of credit with a casino is typically based on how much money the player maintains in his or her checking account. Thus, players who have at least $10,000 are usually good for that amount of credit when they get to Las Vegas.

The table games floor people track players by monitoring not only the size of their bets but also marker play along with their cash play. The casinos have it all figured out, including when the player leaves a table or leaves a pit to play at another. There's solid communication between the pits, even between the blackjack and crap pits. That's why floor people are often on the phone saying things like, "Frank, that fellow in the red shirt who just sat down at blackjack three."

"Yes."

"He's got 24 black cheques, and he's already in $8,000 cash. We don't have his name, so if he goes over $10,000 cash buy-in, we need a CTR on him." A "CTR" is a Currency Transaction Report the casino files with the federal government. If, for example, the aforementioned unnamed player who was already in $8,000 cash exceeded the $10,000 CTR limit, a floor person would be required to get his name and address to file a CTR. If an unknown player refused to give that information, by law he or she is allowed no additional cash buy-ins.

When the player calls it a night, floor people pass along the rating card to the shift boss, who determines the player's rating. A "6" means a sleeping bag in the RV park, but a "1" usually gives the player in question full comp privileges, including the spa, golf course, shows – on the house. In certain cases that high rating even provides air fare for two!

Each table game has an inventory card on which indicates the total amount of cheques on the game. Should a player cash out with, say, 24 black cheques, that amount is taken off the table inventory, and the 24 black cheques are noted on the player's rating card. Should the player take the 24 black cheques and buy in at another game, the floor person communicates that information to the next floor person.

CREDIT

Credit in a casino cannot be compared to your department store credit account. Actually, what the casino is doing is giving you check writing privileges. The practice of writing checks, known as markers, is not strictly reserved for high rollers. Almost anyone with decent credit and a checking account can receive a line of credit and write markers. The player simply applies for credit at the casino cage, and if approved, the amount is typically equal to the amount of your average checking account balance.

Casinos allow players to write markers, not for the customer's convenience nor to provide status symbols for players but as a way to keep track of customer play and to anticipate future comp offers. Most players write markers "because they're expecting a comp," pointed out Barney Vinson in *Las Vegas: Behind the Tables*. "They give the casino a reckless shot at a few thousand, for a chance to win a few hundred in comps. Does it make any sense?"

Writing markers is of no interest to card counters, who may be professionals but are not to be confused with the high visibility high rollers. Professional card counters maintain a low profile. The last thing they want is to provide the casino with their name, address, and the size of their checking account. Nor are they interested in comps. They're after only one thing—a casino's cash. Vinson observed that a card counter can be found "at the single-deck blackjack tables... making modest-sized bets. And nobody knows who he is."

MORE "INSIDER STUFF"

For those of you who are not high-roller whales, marker players, or, for that matter, professionals, you're considered a casual visitor to Las Vegas. All the same, getting a room without an advance reservation, even a room you expect to pay for, can be a real challenge, especially on weekends. Don't believe for a moment there's such a thing as a completely booked Las Vegas hotel, regardless of what the clerk at the front desk tells you. Hotels follow the airlines in their procedure of overbooking accommodations to protect themselves against "no-shows." Then, in the event everyone does show up, the clerk at the front desk is prepared to say it was some sort of computer error. But that's all a bunch of bull!

Have you ever heard of "the casino block?" It's a number of hotel rooms the casino reserves for special players. These are special high rollers or marker players who may turn up unannounced. So just in case, the hotel keeps rooms available for them. The casino also maintains blocks of showroom seating set aside for its top VIP players.

All the average, unknown visitor has to do to get a room when the front desk clerk says "we're full," or to see a show when the showroom is supposedly sold out, is to visit the cashier's cage and establish a line of credit for at least a few thousand dollars. Be sure to do this during the day on a week day, not on Saturday or Sunday, so the casino can call your bank. After the casino cage establishes your credit line, mention to someone in charge, such as a host or floor person, "I would love to gamble in your casino, but my friend and I do not have a room here."

This should get you a room. And if it does, tell the same person in charge that you and your friend would like to see the show, too.

Which brings up another subject: waiting in showroom lines. Casino regulars who know what's what never stand in those winding lines waiting to file into the showrooms. The way to beat the line is to ask for a "line pass." Just tell a floor person you have reservations but would rather play table games than wait in such a long line.

At last, with your line pass in hand you and your guest can stroll directly into the showroom just like all the special high rollers and "invited guests" do. When you arrive at the desk of the maitre d', tell him you want to sit in the front row and you'll take care of the captain. That's the fellow who actually seats you. When the captain offers you a seat to your liking, tip him, but not before being satisfied with your seat, because it's like pulling teeth trying to retrieve a tip from those guys.

Here's another story for future reference. Back in the early 1980s I took my aunt and uncle to see Dean Martin in the

Celebrity Room at the MGM Grand. When we arrived at our fifth row seats, I offered the captain a $5 tip for better front row seats. He looked at me kind of funny and shook his head. Then I pulled out a $20 bill, he snatched it, and gave us three prime seats in the front row!

Chapter 5
MEMORABLE LAS VEGAS CELEBRITIES

"As long as they're remembered by someone
they're never completely gone."
—Anonymous source.

*O*ver the years an endless list of talented performers graced the showroom stages of Las Vegas. One of the first shows was a lively production performed at the El Rancho Vegas in 1941. It starred film and stage actor, emcee/comedian Frank Fay and the El Rancho Starlets, a chorus line of scantily clad dancers from California. Three years later, the Will Mastin Trio starring Sammy Davis Jr.—who became one of Las Vegas's most popular solo entertainers—also played the El Rancho Vegas.

Thousands of great celebrity performances took place before the remote enclave in the midst of the Mojave Desert was recognized as the world's entertainment capital. From the extensive list of celebrities who performed in Las Vegas, the most renowned were Frank Sinatra, Elvis Presley, Siegfried and

Roy, Wayne Newton, Dean Martin, and Sammy Davis Jr.—all of whose biographies are included in this Chapter of the Chronicles.

FRANK SINATRA: OL' BLUE EYES WAS A LAS VEGAS LEGEND

Frank Sinatra

From his first gig in September 1951 at Wilbur Clark's Desert Inn, until his last performance at the MGM Grand in May 1994, Ol' Blue Eyes was a Las Vegas legend for nearly 43 years. Along with his "Rat Pack" cronies, Sinatra introduced an era of "cool" to Las Vegas at a time when resort owners were walking around in cowboy hats. Lorraine Hunt, former Lt. Governor and entertainer, once said, "All these guys came in with their mohair tuxes and the black satin shoes. That look was so cool. I remember being a teen-ager I was so attracted to those shiny shoes. Prior to Sinatra, we were more of a Western-feeling town," said Hunt.

Sinatra was a legend even before his passing. He brought style and sophistication to the Strip. "That Sinatra aura brought international royalty, and made us a global destination. It was a simpler day in a smaller town, and Sinatra's magic was more easily described: gambling, womanizing, drinking till dawn—

and all of it with style,"[44] added Lorraine Hunt in an interview with the *Review-Journal.*

Sinatra's legacy would be lacking without the great imprésario Jack Entratter, the driving force behind one of the defining casinos of the early Las Vegas Strip—the Sands. In 1946, Entratter became general manager of New York's Copacabana club. A year later he owned stock in the club and within three years held controlling interest. In 1952, the 38-year-old Entratter cashed out to become general manager of a new carpet joint just opening on the Strip that was called the Sands. Entratter was a showman and producer par excellence. He established the Sands—A Place in the Sun—as one of the hottest entertainment spots in the country.

Playing the Sands' Copa Room could not have come at a better time for Sinatra. His first gig in Las Vegas had been less than favorable. He was in the midst of a nationwide scandal after leaving his wife, his childhood sweetheart, Nancy, for Ava Gardner. The young sensation from Hoboken, New Jersey, was a virtual has-been by the age of 34. Sinatra had risen to the top since singing for the Tommy Dorsey and Harry James bands in 1939. His smooth style and distinctive voice, which blended with his boyish charm, made him a super star among the bobby-soxers who packed New York's Paramount theatre during World War II.

By war's end, Sinatra's popularity seemed to stabilize. Yet by the end of the forties, his career had totally tanked. His records with Columbia weren't selling, his movies weren't popular, and the bobby-soxers no longer crowded his live performances.

1949: A ROCK-BOTTOM YEAR

Frank Sinatra as Maggio

For Frank Sinatra, the year 1949 had to be the absolute pits: an all-time low in his legendary career. He was fired from his radio show and six months after that his New York concerts failed miserably. Columbia Records wanted out of its contract with him. Then, in 1950 MGM released him from his film contract. Worse, his own agent, MCA fired him. Sinatra's debut in Las Vegas took place at the Desert Inn on September 4, 1951, just a few days after a reported suicide attempt in Lake Tahoe by Sinatra. Both the crooner and local authorities quickly discounted the incident, calling it a sleeping pill miscalculation: Others insinuated Ava-baiting. The crooner's long-time valet, George Jacobs, the man who found Sinatra in a stupor, said otherwise. Years after the incident in *My Way*, Kitty Kelley quotes Jacobs as confirming that Sinatra did try to commit suicide over Ava Gardner that night. "'Thank God, I was there to save him,' Jacobs said. 'Miss G. was the one great love of his life, and if he couldn't have her, he didn't want to live no more.'"[45]

To make matters worse, in a short period of 23 months Sinatra divorced, remarried, and was almost divorced again.

But good things started to happen. His debut at the Sands on October 4, 1953, was very successful. Six months later, he earned a Best Supporting Actor Oscar for his role as Maggio in the acclaimed film *From Here to Eternity*, which elevated his career even more. Fortunately for the hard-working crooner he saved himself. When he read the script *From Here To Eternity* he knew the part of Maggio, the tough little Italian who refused to be broken, was written for no one but him.

It was Ava Gardner, who at the time was devoted to Sinatra, who helped him get the Maggio role. As the story goes, she went directly to Joan Cohn, the wife of Harry Cohn, head of Columbia Pictures. Ava pleaded with Joan to talk her husband into giving Frank a screen test. Frank was perfect for the part of Maggio, Ava said, which Harry would realize once he saw the screen test. Despite the inappropriate nature of the request, Ava impressed Joan with her devotion to her husband. Joan agreed to talk with Harry and to keep Ava's involvement secret.

The role of Maggio came at a low point in Frank's career and he desperately wanted the part. However, Harry Cohn felt Sinatra was nothing more than a washed-up, has-been crooner. Eventually Cohn agreed to the screen test, whether as a result of Joan's pleas or Sinatra's refusal to take no for an answer. Sinatra tested ahead of five other actors, among them Eli Wallach, and won the part. Once Columbia pictures producer Buddy

Ava Gardner

Adler saw Frank Sinatra's performance he had no interest in testing anyone else.

After his screen test, Frank Sinatra was in: Adler never even looked at the other five candidates, and the rest is history.

Within a few months Sinatra was back on his feet making *Guys and Dolls, The Tender Trap,* and *The Man With the Golden Arm.* During his colorful career Sinatra made 20 feature films. His renewed momentum in cinema carried over to his recording career, too. After leaving Columbia, Capitol Records signed him to a new recording contract, and his singing became better than ever, with three consecutive million-record sellers. Singer Paul Anka said, "Under the arrangement of Nelson Riddle, Sinatra entered into a second, more mature phase in his career." Then, NBC offered him a multi-million-dollar contract for a future unspecified number of television appearances.

His Oscar-winning portrayal of the little tough guy, Maggio, brought him the kind of work that had eluded him for years. In a later interview, Sinatra said, "The greatest change in my life began the night they gave me the Oscar. It's a funny about that statue—I don't think any actor can experience something like that and not change."

SINATRA AT THE SANDS

In time, the Sands became Sinatra's playground, largely due to his allegiance to Jack Entratter, who had stood by him through all his troubles, but also due to his financial investment in the Sands. Only months prior to winning the Oscar, Sinatra became financially revitalized when, after 14 months of deliberation, he was approved for a Nevada gaming license and bought two percent of the Sands Hotel. His interest in the Sands grew to nine percent—a testament to his popularity, his ability to fill the casino with high rollers, and his relations with the underworld, because the new Strip resort was at that time controlled by more Mafioso than any other casino in Nevada.

Besides Bugsy Siegel's Flamingo, only four other casino-resorts were operating on the Las Vegas Strip, and Sinatra could see the future. He knew the city would eventually become a boomtown for gamblers. It couldn't miss—Las Vegas was the only place in the country that had legalized gambling.

Sands marquee

In time, his foresight proved correct and eventually made Sinatra a multi-millionaire.

Justice Department files indicate that Sinatra purchased his initial two percent share in the Sands for $70,000. His additional seven percent ownership of the resort was a gift from Vincente "Jimmy Blue Eyes" Alo.

The number one underworld man at the Sands was Joseph "Doc" Stacher, a gangster out of New Jersey, second only to Meyer Lansky in the East Coast Mob. Doc looked on Sinatra as his son. Stacher's police rap sheet included assault and battery, larceny, robbery, hijacking, and investigation for murder. The Sands' official host was Charles "Babe" Baron, once suspected of murder. A few of the unseen mobsters connected to the Sands included Anthony "Joe Batters" Accardo, future boss of the Genovese family in New York, Joe Fusco of the old Capone mob, Meyer Lansky, and Abraham Teitelbaum, a former consigliere for the Capone mob.

In 1979 "Doc" Stacher admitted, "The mob had offered Sinatra a share in the Sands so that he would draw the high rollers. To make sure we'd get enough top-level investors, we brought George Raft into the deal. The object was to get him to perform there, because there's no bigger draw in Las Vegas. When Frankie was performing, the hotel really filled up."[46]

Sinatra reigned supreme at the Sands for the next 13 years. He eventually became vice president of the corporation, and when performing in the Copa Room he earned more than $100,000 a week. His drawing power was such that he could do no wrong in the eyes of the "boys." They even built him a three-bedroom suite on the property, including a private swimming pool protected by a stone wall. To satisfy Sinatra's culinary whims, they ordered Italian breads, prosciutto, and provolone that he relished flown in from New York.

When Sinatra performed in the Copa Room, he always opened by saying, "Welcome to my room." Because he filled the house with big-money players, the casino became his kingdom, and he could do what he pleased in it. The Sands gave him $3,000 a night to gamble with, but he regularly went through that amount in ten minutes. The Sands' extended him credit, at times allowing him to play no limit games and frequently ignoring his markers.

To his friends, Sinatra was extremely generous, especially when they came to the Sands. Kitty Kelley wrote, "He 'comped' all of his friends with free food and free drinks for days at a time, and expected each of them to perform at the Sands, exclusively. If they didn't, they were no longer his friends, as Judy Garland found out when she accepted a Las Vegas engagement at another hotel."

Garlands' performing elsewhere was "strictly a business deal," but "Frank took it as a personal rebuff."

Frank Sinatra made movies at the Sands, recorded some of his greatest albums, sponsored boxing matches, gave glamorous parties and virtually made it the place to go in Las Vegas. Hank Greenspun, publisher of the *Las Vegas Sun*, wrote in a front page editorial: "He frequently flew in Hollywood celebrities, and crowds jammed the casino just in hope of seeing a star having a drink or placing a few bets." Greenspun added, "When Frank Sinatra was in town, it was the economic equivalent of three conventions."

Gambling to Sinatra was second nature. He grew up in the midst of it. His mother, Dolly, had her own bookie, who regularly aroused the neighbors playing bocce ball, an Italian form of ten pins and challenging truck drivers to five-dollar throws. Early on, he watched his father play poker in weekly games and was exposed to betting on all sports, particularly horse racing and boxing. Sinatra's Uncle Gus ran numbers in Hoboken, and his Uncle Babe reportedly had an extensive police rap sheet for crimes like usury and loan sharking.

Ol' Blue Eyes had begun going to Las Vegas on a regular basis shortly after he moved to the West Coast, frequently dropping thousands of dollars at the tables. In time, he developed an affinity with the men who ran Las Vegas; he seemed to thrive in the nocturnal environment and gambled with abandon. One night he lost over $50,000 playing baccarat. Sinatra first played the fast, big-money card game in Monte Carlo and became so fascinated by the action that as part owner of the Sands, he insisted the casino start its own baccarat game.

At the Sands, Frank Sinatra was known to go up to a baccarat table with $10,000, bet the entire bundle, ride it up to $40,000, lose it, and walk away from the table with hardly a shrug.

This author knows another story about Sinatra's renowned gambling ventures. It was told to me first-hand by the man who dealt blackjack to Ol' Blue Eyes, and who went to work for Sinatra when he purchased his own casino in Lake Tahoe.

CHRONICLE OF OSCAR DEALING BLACKJACK TO FRANK AND SAMMY

In 2002 when I worked at the Casino Magic in Bay St. Louis, Mississippi, one of my supervisors was Oscar Zech. In his late 70s, he had worked in casinos all over the world, including Aruba, Reno, and Las Vegas. The day I told him that I was compiling these *Las Vegas Chronicles* he told me the following story about his early experience working in Las Vegas.

Back in the late 1960s, Oscar was a blackjack dealer at Caesars Palace. One night early in his gaming career, Frank Sinatra sat down at Oscar's blackjack table, took out a marker for $50,000, and began playing heads up for $5,000 a hand. During the first shuffle of the four-deck shoe, Oscar said to Sinatra, "Excuse me,

Mister Sinatra, but I just have to tell you that I grew up in New York City, and on Friday afternoon when we got out of school we would almost always take the subway out to the Paramount and watch you perform."

Sinatra smiled and said, "That's great kid: I really appreciate that."

From then on, Oscar could do no wrong in Sinatra's eyes. Whenever he played blackjack at Caesars, he always favored Oscar's table.

About a month later Frank Sinatra and Sammy Davis Jr. were hanging around together at Caesars Palace and happened to sit down at Oscar's blackjack table. They each took out a marker for $50,000 and proceeded to play at the table's maximum limit of $5,000 per hand.

Within 15 minutes of buying in, at the end of the 4-deck shoe Oscar, had beaten them both out of all their stakes—a sum of $100,000!

The first to react to such a drubbing was Sammy. He stood up with that marvelous smile of his, walked around the table to the inside pit, went up to Oscar and put his arm around Oscar's neck, and planted a big kiss on his cheek. Then Sammy walked off laughing out loud as carefree as could be.

Sinatra reacted to the $50,000 quick loss somewhat differently. And Oscar became concerned, especially since Sinatra had a reputation for berating casino personnel, or worse, physically attacking them for cutting off his credit while gambling.

So when Sinatra got up from the blackjack table, Oscar became rather nervous, not knowing what to expect. Slowly, Sinatra walked around the table, into the pit, and came up behind Oscar whilst he shuffled the cards. Sinatra put his right arm around

Oscar and said, "When I get my own casino, kid, you can come and work for me anytime!"

Whew... Oscar was relieved.

Several years later when Sinatra became part owner of the Cal-Neva Lodge & Casino in Lake Tahoe, he kept his promise and hired Oscar as a table games shift manager.

FRANK SINATRA BUYS THE CAL-NEVA LODGE & CASINO

Twenty years had passed since Oscar dealt blackjack to Frank and Sammy at Caesars Las Vegas. One day shortly after Oscar went to work at the Cal-Neva, Sinatra was shooting the breeze with his pal Jilly Rizzo, whom Frank had met in Miami when he performed at the Fontainebleau. (Jilly's Saloon at 256 W. 52nd Street was Frank's favorite New York bar in the mid-1960s.) The two long-time pals were standing at a closed blackjack table near the women's restroom.

A well-dressed fellow and his lady friend walked past, she said, "See you in a minute, Sonny," and entered the restroom.

Sonny went over to Sinatra and Jilly, waited for a pause in their conversation, then said, "Excuse me, Mr. Sinatra, but my girlfriend

Cal–Neva marquee

and I have always been big fans of yours. She is in the restroom right now, but when she comes out perhaps you would do me a small favor?

Sinatra didn't say a thing, so Sonny continued. "When she comes out would you say 'It was good to see you again, Sonny.' I would appreciate it, and my girlfriend would get a real big kick out of it."

Sinatra looked at Jilly, smiled and said, "Sure, Sonny, I'll do that."

A few minutes later when the girlfriend exited the restroom, she walked over to Sonny and latched onto his arm. The couple began walking away, after a few steps Sinatra said, "Hey Sonny, it was good to see you again." Sonny stopped turned around, and said with a sneer, "Hey Sinatra, fuck you!"

Sinatra was aghast. He couldn't believe what he'd just heard. Realizing that he'd been set up, his face turned red. He jumped up from his stool and moved towards Sonny with his fist clenched. Jilly quickly got up and grabbed hold of Sinatra, saying, "Hey Frankie, it's just a mean joke. He obviously doesn't like you. Besides, I know this guy. He's a torpedo from New York, and he's a Made Man. You'd be better off just letting it go."

Sinatra hesitated, then nodded to Jilly and walked back to the blackjack table.

Sonny continued out of the casino with his girlfriend, a smug look on his face.

GAMING LICENSE REVOKED

By 1963, Frank Sinatra not only was part owner of the Cal-Neva but also held points in the Sands Casino Las Vegas. In September of that year after he reapplied for his gaming license, the Nevada Gaming authorities recommended that his gambling license be revoked for allowing Chicago crime boss Sam Giancana a seven-day stay at the Cal-Neva Lodge. The mere presence of the mobster at Cal-Neva was a violation of Nevada law, since he topped the list of excluded persons not allowed in Nevada casinos.

After giving the issue a lot of thought, Sinatra chose not to fight the Board's revocation order. He surrendered his gaming license and eventually sold his interests in the Nevada casinos for a reported $3.5 million.

Kitty Kelley wrote in *My Way*, "Sinatra never could understand the stigma of friendship with Giancana," said Phyllis McGuire, who was Giancana's girlfriend during the controversy. "He'd been friends with the boys for years, ever since he needed to get out of his contract with Tommy Dorsey."

THE SINATRA/GIANCANA FRIENDSHIP

Sam Giancana was a short, balding man who smoked Cuban cigars and talked out of the side of his mouth. He had a sixth-grade education, drove a pink Cadillac, and was known to have at least 14 aliases—primarily Sam Flood, Momo Salvatore Giancana, and Moe or Mooney Giancana. Often, especially when he needed reservations, or traveled with celebrities, he introduced himself as Dr. Goldberg, or Mr. Morris. Sinatra called him Sam.

By 1960, Giancana had allegedly ordered the killing of at least two hundred men. Many of the victims were hung on meat hooks and tortured with ice picks and electric cattle prods, while some of them were simply shot.

A pint-sized dapper dresser, Sam Giancana wore sharkskin suits, alligator shoes and a star sapphire pinky ring given to him by Frank Sinatra. When Giancana knew the Feds were watching him, he added a black fedora and dark wraparound sunglasses.

Above all else, Sam Giancana was known as Chicago's top Mafia boss, successor to Al Capone. As such, he was a lead member of La Cosa Nostra, a national organized crime syndicate. Anything that involved loan sharking, prostitution, illegal gambling, narcotics, and extortion in the Chicago area, Sam Giancana got a piece of it.

In Las Vegas, Sam owned points in the Riviera, the Desert Inn, and the Stardust.

Kitty Kelley quoted Peter Lawford as saying, "Because of Giancana, he kowtowed to the Chicago mob. Why do you think Frank ended every one of his nightclub acts by singing 'My Kind of Town Chicago Is'?"

Sam Giancana's long-time girlfriend, Phyllis McGuire, reported in an interview that on several occasions Frank and Dean flew to Chicago and sang free of charge for Sam. She remembers them, including Sammy, performing at Giancana's Villa Venice and at Giannotti's Restaurant and Cocktail Lounge in 1962.

Sinatra was also friends with Joe Fischetti, whose friendship dated back to 1938. They ran into each other in November 1947 at the Chez Paree in Chicago and hugged each other like brothers. Sinatra had style, and Fischetti, a distant cousin of Alfonse Capone, was raised in the kind of family whose sense of honor Sinatra admired. Joe Fischetti was amici nostri, Italian for "a made man," someone who had sworn in blood to uphold omertà, the Mafia's code of silence. He was a soldati, a soldier, in the dark society of La Cosa Nostra, or Mafia, an ancient Arabic term meaning "sanctuary."

CHRONICLE OF THE RAT PACK

Over the years several explanations circulated for how the Rat Pack came into being. The name was first used in the 1950s in reference to a group of friends and celebrities, including the young Frank Sinatra. One version claimed that the original group leader was Humphrey Bogart, with Lauren Bacall as the "Den Mother." After observing her husband and his friends enter the house from a night out in Las Vegas, she said words to the effect of, "You look like a goddamn rat pack." Another version is that "Rat Pack" is a shortened version of "Holmby Hills Rat Pack," Bogie and Bacall's home, which served as a regular hangout.

Stephen Bogart said in the TV documentary *Bogart: The Untold Story*, "the original members of the Holmby Hills Rat Pack were Frank Sinatra (pack master), Judy Garland (first vice-president), Lauren Bacall (den mother), Sid Luft (cage master), Humphrey Bogart (rat in charge of public relations), Swifty Lazar (recording secretary and treasurer), Nathaniel

Benchley (historian), David Niven, Katharine Hepburn, Spencer Tracy, George Cukor, Cary Grant, Rex Harrison, and Jimmy Van Heusen." In his autobiography *The Moon's a Balloon*, Niven confirmed, "the Rat Pack originally included him but not Sammy Davis Jr. or Dean Martin."

Rat Pack mainstay

The 1960s version of the Rat Pack, formed after Humphrey Bogart's death in 1957, included Frank Sinatra, Dean Martin, Sammy Davis Jr., Peter Lawford, and Joey Bishop. For a brief period, certain visiting celebrities—Marilyn Monroe, Angie Dickinson, Juliet Prowse, and Shirley MacLaine—were referred to as the Rat Pack Mascots, a designation that apparently made the ladies of the group feel like "one of the boys." The group was as dedicated to drinking as Bogie was. Bogart's principle was, "that the whole world was three drinks behind and it was time it caught up."

The Pack was purportedly referred to by its members as the Summit, or the Clan, until "clan" became "politically embarrassing, and they hastened to make it known that they had nothing to do with the Ku Klux Klan." The name "Rat Pack" was never called that by any of its members, although it was the term commonly used by journalists and outsiders, and today it remains the enduring name for the group.

In Las Vegas whenever one of the Pack members was scheduled for a showroom appearance, the rest of the Pack usually came and gave an impromptu performance, which caused much excitement among audiences. Fans swarmed into Las Vegas, and were said to sleep in hotel lobbies or in cars when they could not find rooms so they could experience a Rat Pack performance. The neon marquee of the resorts at which one of them was performing would read, for instance, "SAMMY DAVIS JR— MAYBE DEAN—MAYBE FRANK," although the mainstays of the Pack, Sinatra, Martin, and Davis, could most frequently be found together at the Sands.

Paul Anka, who first played the Sahara in 1959 when he was only 18, was quoted by Kitty Kelley in Sinatra's biography as saying, "Pop music was at its infancy stage and just growing. It was just a bunch of us kids. So, consequently (the casinos) went to these older established acts from the nightclub circuit."

This was an era when television was coming of age, and the way it changed people's habits helped Las Vegas. Instead of going out to supper clubs and seeing shows, Americans started a revolution by staying at home to watch television. That habit put a crunch on supper clubs in other cities, giving Las Vegas the upper hand in presenting established acts.

Suddenly, the Pack all came together. "Now you've got the greatest, cool, hippest entertainers around," Anka said of the expanding circle of cool cats – By 1960 it included Dean Martin, who began solo nightclub acts in 1957 after a split with partner Jerry Lewis, and Sammy Davis Jr., the multi-talented sensation of the Will Martin Trio. Joey Bishop, already established as a solo performer, was reportedly accepted into the Pack as a gag writer and a warm-up for much of the "improvised mayhem onstage."

By the late 1950s and early sixties, these and other stars were the draw pulling audiences to Las Vegas casinos. The budding Strip wasn't sporting theme architecture then as it is today. And the stars came to see Sinatra.

Sonny King, a veteran Las Vegas lounge singer, and longtime friend of Sinatra, was quoted by Kitty Kelley as saying: "He was actually the king of Las Vegas, because the minute he stepped in town, money was here. King was also quoted saying, "He drew all the big money people. Every celebrity in Hollywood would come to Las Vegas to see him, one night or another."

In 1960, following on the heels of Frank's acclaimed film *Can Can* was *Ocean's Eleven*, the movie that became the on-screen spectacle for the Pack.

PETER LAWFORD'S FALLING OUT WITH SINATRA

The making of the film *Ocean's Eleven* solidified the mainstay members of the Pack while they filmed it on location in Las

Vegas. But events beginning in March 1960, led to major falling out between Frank Sinatra and Peter Lawford. Lawford was the brother-in-law of President John F. Kennedy—dubbed "brother-in-Lawford" by Sinatra—and the Pack actively campaigned for Kennedy by appearing at the 1960 Democratic National Convention. During the convention Lawford asked Sinatra if he would have Kennedy as a guest at his Palm Springs house. According to Kitty Kelley, "Sinatra went to great lengths, including the construction of a helipad, to accommodate the President. When Attorney General Robert F. Kennedy advised his brother to sever his ties to Sinatra because of the entertainer's association with Mafia figures, such as Sam Giancana, the stay was cancelled. Lawford was blamed for this, and Sinatra 'never had a good word for him' from that point onward."[47] Prior to the 1960 Presidential election, Sinatra's daughter Nancy said in a televised A&E documentary, "Her father asked Sam Giancana, because of his ties to the Teamsters, if he could help JFK win the election. Giancana agreed, if in exchange Sinatra would work for nothing in Giancana's night clubs."

Many years later Sam Giancana boasted about his contribution to Kennedy's victory. As quoted in Kelley's *My Way*, Giancana frequently told a former Kennedy girlfriend Judith Campbell, "Listen, honey, if it wasn't for me, your boyfriend wouldn't even be in the White House."

Many people credit Sinatra's mobilization of mob support for getting Kennedy the victory. Years later, the owner of the 500 Club in Atlantic City, Paul "Skinny" D'Amato, claimed that, "Sinatra won Kennedy the election. All the guys knew it."

THE RAT PACK'S HEYDAY

In June 1965, at the heyday of the Pack, Sinatra, Martin, and Davis, with Johnny Carson as emcee sitting in for Joey Bishop, who was ill at the time, performed their only televised concert together. It was a closed-circuit fundraiser for Dismas House (the first halfway house for ex-convicts) and was broadcast at the Kiel Opera House in St. Louis. Today that broadcast is available on DVD, as part of the *Ultimate Rat Pack Collection: Live & Swingin.*

A televised interview showed Frank saying that the Pack broke up because each went his way. As for the group's reputation for womanizing and heavy drinking, Joey Bishop said in a 1998 interview: "I never saw Frank, Dean, Sammy, or Peter drunk during performances. That was only a gag! And do you believe these guys had to chase broads? They had to chase 'em away!"

MARRIAGE TO MIA

Other than the glorious Pack of cronies who usually gathered at the Sands, the 1960s also saw 50-year-old Sinatra marry 21-year-old Mia Farrow. The brevity of their union, 16 months, was said to be the result of two divergent celebrity careers going in separate directions.

The sixties also saw a major change in ownership of Frankie's favorite stomping grounds, when billionaire tycoon Howard Hughes bought the Sands in 1967. Apparently, under Entratter's liberal accounting policies, the crooner had a substantial line of credit at the casino cage. Not so under management of the new regime. One night in September Sinatra's credit was cut off, and he reacted by flying into a rage. According to Eleanor Roth, quoted in Kelley's biography of Sinatra, the altercation occurred when Sinatra was refused credit in front of some of the Apollo astronauts visiting the hotel, and he completely lost his temper. Roth said, "When Frank won, he took his cheques, and when he lost, he didn't pay his markers."

"He got up on that table, and started yelling and screaming right in the middle of the casino," recalled entertainer Paul Anka, who claims to have witnessed the debacle. Hotel staff called management and vice-president Carl Cohen showed up. He was a big burly guy, but Sinatra threw a punch anyway only to have Cohen return the favor. According to a quote in the *Review-Journal*, "The blow knocked the caps off Sinatra's two front teeth." The rumor mill credited the altercation to Howard Hughes' hatred of Sinatra after Ava Gardner passed up Hughes to marry the singer. Limiting Sinatra's credit in the casino was Howard's way of embarrassing Sinatra and evening the score.

FRANK SINATRA PERFORMS AT CAESARS PALACE

In November 1968, Sinatra signed to perform at Caesars. Two years later casino credit would again, be at issue, and it created more trouble for Sinatra when, as Kitty Kelley describes, "casino executive Sam Waterman pulled a gun on him after another argument over casino credit. Sheriff Ralph Lamb threatened to throw the singer in jail, saying 'I'm tired of the way he has been acting around here anyway.'"[48]

Unbeknownst to Sinatra, an IRS investigation was going on into the relationship between the Mafia and the entertainment industry. Sinatra was among the targets of the IRS surveillance.

On September 6, 1970, an IRS agent working undercover on graveyard shift in the cashier's cage at Caesars watched as one of Sinatra's aides came to the window with a large amount of $100 cheques and walked away with $7,500 in cash. The undercover agent had a special interest in Frank Sinatra because for weeks he watched the crooner take vast sums of money in markers—IOUs to the casino—that were not being deducted from his salary or paid back in winnings.

The undercover IRS agent discovered that Sinatra was using the casino for petty cash. Whatever he won off a marker, he put it in his pocket, and whenever he ran out of cheques to bet with, he simply signed another marker for $10,000. It was easy money for him, but concern grew about his paying back his markers. Sinatra told friends it wasn't necessary for him to pay his markers, because when he performed at Caesars and then played the gaming tables, he figured he attracted enough big money around him that the casino earned huge profits, larger than they would without him.

The story related in *My Way* went like this. At about five a.m. the undercover agent got a call from the blackjack pit saying that Sinatra had just signed another marker. The agent phoned Sandy Waterman, casino manager, who had been part owner of the Cal-Neva with Sinatra in 1963. Waterman dressed, came down to the casino floor, and was informed of what was going on. He stood quietly in a corner and waited for the next time Sinatra's aide approached the cage window. When he did, Waterman nodded his okay to cash in Sinatra cheques. Then he walked over to the blackjack table to deal with Sinatra.

Waterman said to the singer, "I want $10,000 in markers," recalled the agent.

"What's the matter? My money isn't good here?" asked Sinatra.

"Yeah, your money is good as long as you've got money. You don't get cheques until I see your cash."

The undercover agent continued, as quoted by Kelley. "That's when the trouble started and Frank called Waterman a kike and Sandy called him a son of a bitch guinea. They went back and forth like that in front of a big crowd of people, including three security guards, until Sandy whipped out his pistol and popped it between Sinatra's eyeballs... Sinatra laughed and called him a crazy Hebe... He said he'd never work at Caesars again and walked out... Frank had carte blanche at Caesars—complete run of the casino—but it's getting heavy when you have built up so much in markers and maybe 50 percent of it is petty cash in your pocket. This must have been going on for a long period of time, because Waterman got pretty excited about it," the agent recalled.[49]

Sheriff Ralph Lamb was irate about the incident. Waterman ended up being booked for pulling a gun. The next day the district attorney dropped the charge against Sanford Waterman.

Kelley quoted the district attorney as saying, "My reports indicated Waterman still had finger marks on his throat where Sinatra grabbed him. There seems to be reasonable grounds for making the assumption that Sinatra was the aggressor all the way."

People who knew him reason that Frank Sinatra's crude behavior at Caesars Palace goes back to his growing up years in New Jersey. His first job was with a newspaper, the *Jersey*

Observer, where he started out riding news trucks and later was promoted to copy boy. One day he took some of his first wages and bought new clothes. While he strutted about Hoboken showing them off, the cops stopped him, wanting to know where he got them. He reportedly wised off by saying to them, "Ya copper, whats it to you?" With that, he was unmercifully beat up, resulting in a smashed nose, cracked ribs, with his face and body a bloody mess, and his tattered and torn new clothes. From that day on, any kind of authority directed his way made him a little crazy.

KIDNAPPING OF FRANK SINATRA JR.

In December 1963, Frank Sinatra Jr., at the age of 19, was kidnapped from Harrah's Lake Tahoe. Two days later he was released after his father paid the kidnappers $240,000 ransom they demanded. To communicate with the kidnappers via payphone, as they demanded, Frank Sr. carried a roll of dimes with him during the entire two-day ordeal. After, friends claimed that carrying a roll of dimes in his pocket became a lifelong habit.

In 1988 at his father's request, Frank Jr. put his career on hold in order to act as his father's conductor and musical director. Poet and vocalist Rod McKuen wrote in an online article: "As the senior Sinatra outlived one by one all of his conductors, and nearly every arranger, and began to grow frail himself, his son knew he needed someone that he trusted near him. Frank Jr. was also savvy enough to know that performing was everything to his dad, and the longer he kept that connection with his audience, the longer he would stay vital and alive."[50]

SINATRA'S ANNOUNCED RETIREMENT

When sales of his famous signature song "My Way" began to decrease, Sinatra announced his retirement. And so began the longest ever farewell engagement. "The Voice" continued to perform until his 79th year. Sinatra had attempted an earlier retirement in March 1971, citing a desire to spend more time with his family, and perhaps write. He returned in April 1973 to record tracks for the LP *Ol' Blue Eyes Is Back*.

Frank Sinatra performed his final public concerts in Japan's Fukuoka Dome in December 1994. Two months later, he sang at a private party for 1,200 guests on the final night of the Frank Sinatra Desert Classic golf tournament. It was his very last performance. *Esquire Magazine* reported of his show that he was "clear, tough, on the money and in absolute control." His closing song was "The Best is Yet to Come."

Twenty years earlier Sinatra had told *Daily News* columnist Kay Gardella that Billie Holiday, whom he first heard in New York's 52nd Street clubs in the 1930s, was the greatest single musical influence on him.

Frank Sinatra's attitude can be summed up in an anecdote about when Quincy Jones was arranging the album *Sinatra at the Sands* in Los Angeles in 1966. Sinatra had phoned Jones at his hotel room and invited Jones to join him in Las Vegas for a weekend. Jones turned him down, saying he had too much to do. Sinatra said, "Q, you gotta live every day like it's your last because one day you'll be right."

Two other quotes attributed to Sinatra are equally memorable: "You only live once, and the way I live, once is enough."

And his closing line to audiences after completing his last song at a live performance, "Thank you for letting me sing for you."

Frank Sinatra passed away on May 14, 1998, at the Cedars Sinai Medical Center in Los Angeles. He was 82 years old. The following night the lights on the Las Vegas Strip were dimmed in his honor. President Bill Clinton said that he had managed "to appreciate on a personal level what millions of people had appreciated from afar." Singer Elton John added that Sinatra "was simply the best—no one else even comes close."

He was survived by his wife Barbara, whom he married in July 1976, and by his three children from his first marriage to Nancy: Nancy Sandra, born in 1940; Franklin Wayne Emmanuel (Frank Jr.), born in 1944; and Christina (Tina), born in 1948.

FINAL TRIBUTE

"He brought unmatched excitement to the Strip, and defined the word 'swinger' for all times," said actor Gregory Peck at the Las Vegas golf tournament that bears Sinatra's name. Peck added, "With his little gang of merry men he established forever a sense of free-floating fun and frolic that captured the imagination of the world."

In the 1960s, Frank Sinatra played a major role in desegregating Nevada hotels and casinos, leading his fellow Rat-Pack buddies and label mates on *Reprise* in boycotting casinos and hotels that wouldn't allow black singers to play, or that wouldn't allow black patrons entry.

Author Stephen Holden wrote, "Sinatra was... the first modern pop superstar.... Following his idol Bing Crosby, who had pioneered the use of the microphone, Sinatra transformed popular singing by infusing lyrics with a personal intimate point of view that conveyed a steady current of eroticism.... Almost single-handedly, he helped lead a revival of vocalized swing music that took American pop to a new level of musical sophistication... his 1950's recordings... were instrumental in establishing a canon of American pop song literature."

In final praise to The Voice, a moniker given the sensational crooner by a talent agency early in his career, the world had never heard anyone like Frank Sinatra before... and likely, never will again!

In the early 1950s when Frank Sinatra was in the midst of a fabulous singing career, an up-and-coming performer named Elvis Aaron Presley was gaining popularity among America's teens for his singing of a new form of music—rock 'n' roll.

Sinatra never came to terms with rock 'n' roll; to him that kind of music was deplorable. And he was appalled by the arrival of the former truck driver from Tupelo, Mississippi, who wiggled and shimmied as he sang his rockabilly songs, driving teenage girls into a screaming frenzy unseen since The Voice himself had thousands of bobby-soxers swooning at the Paramount.

Sinatra also despised the Elvis "look"—the glittery suits and the blue suede shoes. The crooner sang slow, yearning ballads and damned the rockabilly interloper for transposing these traditional rhythms into sexy rock music. Perhaps what Sinatra resented most was Elvis's popularity in a new style of music that threatened to surpass his own. By 1956, that's what Elvis did, becoming the undisputed king of rock 'n' roll. Though Ol' blue eyes believed that rock music didn't deserve a place on the Top 40 charts, Elvis virtually stayed on top for 30 years.

ELVIS HAD A SPECIAL LOVE AFFAIR WITH LAS VEGAS

Picture the Las Vegas Strip circa late 1960s—most of the big showroom stars of the era had either lost their luster, were too old to perform, or had passed away. Those who survived, other than Frank Sinatra, lacked the drawing power to fill the Strip resorts with tourists. That changed in July 1969 when Kirk Kerkorian opened the 1,500 room International Hotel, at the time the largest in the world, and tried to sign a big-time rock 'n' roller such as Elvis Presley to perform in his showroom.

Of the new casino resort's three showrooms, the largest was the 2,000-seat Showroom Internationale. Kerkorian envisioned the city's first megaresort would be a city in itself, with a myriad of entertainment choices. He hired a talented casino man, Alex Shoofey, as general manager, and together they tried to induce Elvis to open as their headliner.

The International Hotel's grand opening just happened to coincide with Elvis Presley's departure from his movie career, which had endured over seven years and 33 films that typically featured his choreographed songs. About this time Elvis had

Elvis

started hinting to his manager, Colonel Tom Parker, that he wanted to go back on the road.

COLONEL PARKER'S INFLUENCE

Naturally, what Elvis wanted was irrelevant when it came to his manager, the "all-seeing" Colonel Parker—who appeared to care more about the singer's career than the singer did. Parker oversaw the details of Presley's rise to fame and fortune with a ferocious dedication. In turn, the Colonel reaped far more than the usual 20 percent management fee, including a whopping 50 percent near the end of Presley's life.

Eventually, Parker took over control of more than Elvis' business' interests—he controlled the way he lived, too. It was the Colonel who insisted that draftee Elvis should carry out all the regular duties of an army recruit. "Parker knew that if Elvis went through basic training, carried his own gear and rifle, marched, and went on guard duty, all just like a normal soldier, that it would help his public image."[51]

While serving in Friedberg, Germany, Elvis met the 14-year-old Priscilla Beaulieu. In her autobiography, Priscilla confirmed that Parker advised Presley that serving as an ordinary soldier would gain popular respect, even though serving in Special

Services would enable him to perform "and remain in touch with the public."

After years of preventing Elvis from getting married, for fear the singer would lose his teen-idol fans, Parker decided it was time for Elvis to wed Priscilla, whom he had courted over seven years and lived with for several years. When the nuptials took place on May 1, 1967, the Colonel extracted every ounce of publicity from the event—he had his old pal Milton Prell, owner of the Aladdin, host the wedding.

TEEN IDOL TO "VEGAS ELVIS"

For the king of rock 'n' roll, deciding in 1969 to reinvent himself in Las Vegas was difficult. Moreover it was an abrupt decision—a calculated career move. Thirteen years earlier in the spring of 1956, a young teen idol named Elvis Presley debuted at the New Frontier. Parker had booked the budding star to a two-week engagement headlining a show that opened "with the soothing strings of the Freddie Martin Orchestra, followed by the Borscht Belt humor of Shecky Greene," reported the *Review-Journal*.

When Elvis appeared on stage before a Las Vegas audience for the first time, he was a 21-year-old budding rock star with a ducktail haircut, long sideburns, eye shadow, wearing mostly black, and his pink shirt collar turned up. He was backed by Scotty Moore, Bill Black, and D.J. Fontana. With his guitar draped over his shoulder he snarled those famous lips, then started those hips gyrating and began to sing.

According to biographer Peter Guralnick in *Last Train to Memphis*, "While Elvis was already becoming a great hit with the teens around the country, he was not the typical Las Vegas Strip entertainer at the time and was met with a cool reception. After the first performance, at which the audience politely applauded, but showed none of the wild enthusiasm to which they were accustomed to."[52] At that point Scotty, Bill, and D.J. knew they were in for a long two weeks.

Newsweek magazine reported that Elvis's presence in the show was tantamount to a "jug of corn liquor at a champagne party," and noted that the stunned audience sat motionless "as if he were a clinical experiment." By the end of the engagement, Elvis moved from the top to the bottom of the New Frontier's marquee, and vowed never again to play night clubs.

But 13 years later in 1969, Alex Shoofey needed big-name entertainers to headline at the International Showroom, and who was bigger than the king of rock 'n' roll, Elvis Presley? Shoofey offered to let Elvis open the hotel. But Parker thought it too risky and declined on the grounds Elvis had performed only once in front of a live audience in 11 years, his "Comeback Special" for NBC in 1968. He was a little out of practice. Nevertheless he looked every bit Elvis, clad in a skin-tight black leather suit. He sang his repertoire of hit singles and finished with his latest hit song, "If I Can Dream."

STREISAND CHRISTENS THE INTERNATIONAL

Barbra Streisand was chosen to christen the Showroom Internationale and Elvis was there to see her perform. It was wise he did, because the experience gave him insight. She was in marvelous voice, but her overall show was lacking. It didn't have the pizzazz of sparkling sets, jokesters, or an entourage of high-stepping performers to enhance Barbra's act. Elvis realized that for Las Vegas talent, by itself, was not enough.

With bad memories of Presley's last Las Vegas gig, Parker reluctantly signed Elvis to a four-week contract with the International at $100,000 per week. After taking in Barbra's performance, Elvis couldn't help remembering 13 years earlier when he had bombed at the New Frontier. Elvis knew he had to build a new act from scratch and he relished the challenge, though he hated the idea of doing Las Vegas—again.

To help find his self-styled "Las Vegas identity," Elvis began scouting lounges and showrooms, studying entertainers and audiences, looking for ideas to stylize into his own show. He found the prototype in Tom Jones, a then-unknown Welsh singer performing at the Flamingo showroom. Performing while encased in a skin-tight black tuxedo, Jones would step to the edge of the stage and lean far back, arching his upper body in such a way that the audience got a good look at the outline of his genitals. The response from the mostly middle-aged female audience impressed Elvis. They cried, screamed, and threw room keys at Jones's feet. During one raucous late-night show they purportedly jumped from their chairs, ripped off their panties, and threw them at his feet.

Elvis admired Jones's vocal skills, although it was his primitive connection with women in the audience that really got Elvis's attention. Instead of relying on the pivoting hips and jerky undulations of his old act, Elvis would use the fluid movements and other martial arts skills he had mastered in studying karate over the years. In fact, he had earned a second degree black belt. On opening night this new "Vegas Elvis" would be supported by a total of 50 artists: a 35-piece orchestra led by guitarist James Burton, his old five-piece rock band, as well as the voices of two soul groups, the Sweet Inspirations and the Imperials.

ELVIS DEBUTS AT THE INTERNATIONAL

With the most elaborate arrangement of "Blue Suede Shoes" ever heard, on that special night of July 26, 1969, Elvis launched his new Las Vegas career when he stepped onto the stage of the Showroom Internationale. There, in a skin-tight black ensemble, he moved along the stage apron kissing one woman after another, passing out his own sweaty handkerchiefs, then more kissing, pushing the energy level of the performance "to a goose-pimply crescendo." Elvis's debut at the International Hotel and Casino was a huge success, due largely to its producers Steve Binder, Bones Howe, and particularly, musical director Billy Goldenberg, who backed Elvis's vocals with a full-sized orchestra. From then on, the king would never again perform without a throng of back-up singers and at minimum a 30-piece orchestra.

Newsweek commented, "There are several unbelievable things about Elvis, but the most incredible is his staying power in a world where meteoric careers fade like shooting stars."[53]

International marquee

When the show ended, Elvis had won over the media and the thirty-and forty-year-olds in attendance. Moreover, he became an overnight superstar—again. Elvis won over the International's top management, too. The next day Alex Shoofey sat down in the showroom with Colonel Parker, and opened the conversation with an offer of a new agreement—for five years.

It was said that the Colonel at first appeared uninterested but signed. Elvis would be paid $1 million a year and appear four weeks twice a year. Biographer Guralnick observed, "Shoofey walked away amazed, calling it 'the best deal ever made in this town.' That was an understatement. Las Vegas showrooms were expected to lose money, and – theoretically – recover it in the casino, "by the time Elvis concluded his first month-long engagement, the showroom had generated more than $2 million. It was the first time a Las Vegas resort ever had profited from an entertainer."[54]

Why would anyone, especially Colonel Tom Parker, known as one of the greatest finaglers in the talent business, sell his hot "new" act for such a pittance? The answer lies in Parker's addiction to gambling. Besides Elvis's weekly salary, the International provided the Colonel with plenty of perks: luxury accommodations, gourmet fare, transportation in hotel planes and limousines, and the crème de la crème of the whole deal-unlimited credit in the casino. Parker usually lost $60,000 to $75,000 a night.

Colonel Tom Parker actually lived in the hotel on the 4th floor from the 1970s to the mid-1980s. When Elvis performed at the International, he lived in the penthouse suite on the 30th floor, room 3000, until his last performance there in December 1976.

FIRST BIG-NAME ROCK 'N' ROLLER TO HEADLINE VEGAS

Unencumbered by the memory 13 years ago of his dismal Las Vegas performance at the Last Frontier, Elvis Presley became the first big-name rock 'n' roller to regularly headline in a Las Vegas showroom. During his first two years at the International, the new, flashier version of Vegas Elvis appeared to go well. He was enthusiastic about his new career and busy experimenting, always trying to improve the show. A noticeable change in Elvis occurred in February 1970—possibly brought on by his increased body weight or he was inspired by Liberace's flowing capes. One night Elvis stepped onto the stage in his famous white bejeweled jumpsuit. "Besides being adorned with ropes of pearls, beads, and rhinestones, the jumpsuit also featured a large belt buckle of sufficient size to hide his burgeoning belly," wrote the *Review-Journal.*

The King's weight gain may have been the result of boredom, especially when he was not performing. Or it may have been his chosen diet of fast food. He also consumed huge quantities of powerful pharmaceuticals to overcome his problems. His use of prescription drugs likely began in the 1950s, about the same time his career started to take off. Driving from county fairs to roadhouse gigs for months on end, he survived by napping in the back seat of a car. A chronic insomniac, he certainly had a legitimate need for sleeping pills, and he had to also discover how to stay awake with amphetamines. He grew more sophisticated with his medication when he discovered *The Physician's Desk Reference*, which detailed the chemistry, the effects, and the proper use of every U.S.-made prescription drug. He purportedly memorized the *PDR,* and carry it with him the rest of his life.

It was also reported that dozens of pill bottles, most from the Landmark Pharmacy across the street from the International, bore the names of several different aides Elvis kept on the payroll.

THE "MEMPHIS MAFIA"

The circle of friends Presley constantly surrounded himself with—until months before his death—came to be known as the Memphis Mafia. The group of "guys" included Red West, Elvis's friend and bodyguard since the 1950s, Sonny West, and David Hebler. The guys could be identified by a necklace displaying a gold lightning bolt and the initials TCB, which stood for Taking Care of Business. While Elvis was onstage, wrote Peter Guralnick, "the guys would be doing just that, combing the hotel and environs, inviting attractive girls to join Elvis in the penthouse for an after-show party."

In July 1976, Vernon Presley—who had begun managing his son's financial affairs—fired the three guys, reasoning a need to lower expenses. Guralnick points out that several observers close to Elvis cited different reasons. One associate, John O'Grady, said the men were fired "because their rough treatment of fans had prompted too many lawsuits." Another Presley associate, David Stanley, said the guys were dropped because they were too outspoken about Elvis's prescription drug dependency.

ELVIS PRESLEY'S LATER LIFE

Years of using too many prescription drugs and suffering from depression, now the singer had another problem: he was consumed with jealousy over his wife's affair with handsome karate instructor Mike Stone. Even worse, it was Elvis who had insisted Priscilla take lessons from the expert martial arts instructor.

One night in 1973, Elvis ordered his best friend and bodyguard, Red West, up to his headquarters room 3000, the King's Imperial suite on the 30th floor topping the Las Vegas Hilton. The reason: Elvis wanted someone dead. The target was to be Mike Stone, who was having an affair with Priscilla since 1970.

As written by the online site *Hollywood Five-O:* "It was no surprise that Elvis turned to Red West for the death warrant the obsessed singer wanted placed on his rival. Red was Presley's most loyal and trusted friend for over 20 years. As Memphis teenagers, Red prevented the budding superstar from being thrashed by high school bullies who wanted to cut his long hair. Rugged and quick-fisted, Red quickly went from small town football hero to senior member of the Memphis Mafia, the squad of musicians, musclemen and business cronies who served The King's every whim.[55]

Later, when he got straight, Elvis rescinded the contract on Stone, much to Red's relief. Even so, the singer lost Priscilla when the couple finalized their divorce in October 1973.

The estranged Elvis couldn't sleep, so he took more sleeping pills. He became increasingly unwell. Twice during 1973 he overdosed on barbiturates and spent three days in a coma in his hotel after the first incident. Near the end of the year, he was hospitalized, semi-comatose from the effects of Demerol addiction. His primary physician, Dr. George C. Nichopoulos, said that Presley "felt that by getting drugs from a doctor, he wasn't the common everyday junkie getting something off the street."

Since his comeback in 1969, Elvis had staged more live shows with each passing year, so that by 1973—his busiest schedule ever—he was doing 168 concerts. Even with failing health, the next year he undertook another intensive touring schedule.

By this point in his life, Elvis was suffering from multiple ailments, including high blood pressure, glaucoma, and liver damage, each reportedly aggravated and perhaps caused by prescription drug abuse. Many years after his death, Dr. Nichopoulus re-examined Presley's x-rays and concluded that he was probably suffering from degenerative arthritis, which fueled his addiction to painkillers.

Once at a concert in Detroit guitarist John Wilkinson recounted, "I watched him in his dressing room, just draped over a chair unable to move. So often I thought, 'Boss, why don't you just cancel this tour and take a year off...?' I mentioned something once in a guarded moment, but he just patted me on the back and said, 'It will be all right. Don't you worry about it.'"

Regardless, Elvis continued to play to sellout crowds. His final concert, unknown to him at the time, was held in Indianapolis at the Market Square Arena, on June 26, 1977. His, prescription drug abuse finally compromised his health, and he was found dead in his bathroom at Graceland. The official cause of death was listed as cardiac arrhythmia, although the autopsy listed 11 different narcotics in his system, any one of which would have been lethal enough in a large dose.

Back in Las Vegas, the Colonel wasted no time in "Taking Care of Business," initiating all kinds of post-Elvis merchandising schemes to earn money for himself and the Presley estate. During the three years following Elvis Presley's death, his name and image earned more than $20 million, the most lucrative period in his career.

SIEGFRIED & ROY:
A PAIR OF AMAZING ILLUSIONISTS

The historical account of Siegfried's and Roy's rise from humble origins to the pinnacle of Las Vegas entertainment is as awe-inspiring as their dazzling stage show. It's a story of two remarkable men who happened to meet working aboard an ocean liner, and through hard work and dedication made their dreams of magic come true.

The masterful Siegfried Fischbacher and Roy Horn were responsible for one of the most successful shows in Las Vegas history. Siegfried's skill at magic, blended with Roy's talent for handling exotic animals, became an extraordinary act that packed Vegas showrooms for nearly 36 years. Their spectacular shows featured breathtaking illusions involving wild, exotic animals, and included their signature white tigers.

After 45 years of performing together, during a live performance at the Mirage a 600-pound Bengal tiger named Montecore sank its teeth into Roy's neck and dragged him offstage in front of a stunned audience. The horrific incident was later ruled an accident, and the popular Siegfried & Roy show having endured more than 13 years at the Mirage, immediately went dark.

After the tragedy Siegfried Fischbacher appeared on the Larry King interview program and explained, "Roy Horn fell during the act, and Montecore was attempting to drag him to safety, as a mother tigress would pull one of her cubs by the neck." Fischbacher went on to add, "Montecore had no way of knowing that Horn, unlike a tiger cub, did not have fur and thick skin covering his neck and that his neck was vulnerable to injury.

If Montecore had wanted to injure Horn, the tiger would have snapped his neck and shaken him back and forth."

The tiger was put into quarantine for ten days to ensure that he was not rabid, then returned to his habitat at the Mirage. Roy Horn's convalescence was long and arduous.

EARLY LIFE OF SIEGFRIED & ROY

Siegfried Fischbacher was born June 13, 1939, in Bavaria, Germany. At eight years old, he attended his first magic show in Munich and was deeply inspired by watching the German illusionist Kalanag. That same year, after finding five German marks lying in a gutter, he bought his first book on magic at the village book store.

Siegfried's future partner in magic, was born Roy Uwe Ludwig Horn on October 3, 1944, at his aunt's house during an Allied bombing raid in Nordenham, Germany.

When Roy was seven, his pet dog, Hexe, a half-wolf, saved his life. Roy had become trapped in a bog while playing in the countryside, and Hexe managed to attract the attention of nearby farmers who pulled Roy to safety.

Seeking a diversion from the misery of postwar poverty and depression, in 1955 Roy began to visit the zoo in Bremen, Germany, where he gained regular access with the help of a close family friend. There, Roy befriended a two-year-old cheetah named Chico, an experience that formed the basis for his love of exotic cats.

After Siegfried finished school and began working at a carpet factory, he made his first attempt at performing magic before an audience—a club of farmer's. His first show was also his first embarrassing disaster, because Siegfried was unable to make a goat disappear. By 1956, Siegfried found work at a resort in Lago di Garda, Italy, starting as a dishwasher. When later promoted to bartender, he began to entertain customers by performing small, informal magic shows.

In 1957, Roy finished school and found work as a bellboy in first class aboard the TS Bremen, an ocean liner cruising between Bremerhaven, Germany, and New York.

Two years later, Siegfried joined the crew of the TS Bremen as a steward and was assigned a cabin across the hall from Roy. Eventually Siegfried was promoted to ship entertainer and asked Roy to help him prepare props for his show.

Roy agreed, but he had a problem—how to get his zoo-liberated cheetah aboard the ship without the crew knowing. Roy asked Siegfried, "If you can make a rabbit and doves appear and disappear, could you do the same thing with a cheetah?" Roy eventually smuggled Chico aboard and became Siegfried's assistant, and the show was upgraded to feature Roy and the trained cheetah.

EARLY CAREER BEYOND THE SEA

In 1964 Siegfried and Roy and Chico left the TS Bremen and began touring the European continent, having their first professional performance on land at the Astoria Theatre in Bremen. Over the next few years they refined their magic act in non-stage venues and small clubs throughout Europe. They received rave reviews for their act at the famous Hansa Theater in Hamburg, Germany, which led to work in Switzerland. The magical German duo then toured Monte Carlo, Madrid, and Paris, where they officially adopted the brand Siegfried & Roy for their act.

THE MAGICAL DUO DEBUT IN LAS VEGAS

In 1967 the partners arrived in Las Vegas with Chico, plus a second cheetah, Simba, and trained flamingos. Their debut was a successful 12-minute specialty act in the Tropicana's popular *Follies Bergere*.

They temporarily left Las Vegas in 1970 to begin a three-month engagement at Puerto Rico's Americana Hotel, where they acquired a jaguar named Jahmal. But because the animal was unmanageable, they had to find another home for it.

Siegfried & Roy returned to Las Vegas and headlined for three years in the Stardust's *Lido de Paris*, this time with a 15-minute act. They also acquired a female Siberian tiger named Sahra for their act. Accolades abounded for Siegfried and Roy, and in 1972, they received the Las Vegas Entertainment Award for Best Show Act of the year.

In 1973 they returned to Puerto Rico with Sahra for a year-long gig at the Americana Hotel. The act's new participants included a Sumatran tiger, Radscha; a black panther, Sabu; and a leopard, Sasha. That same year, producer Donn Arden informed Siegfried & Roy of negotiations with Kerkorian's MGM Grand, at the time under construction, as part of a stage spectacular entitled *Hallelujah Hollywood!* The soon-to-be superstars of magic returned to Las Vegas, signed with Arden, and became an integral act of the long-running show.

Siegfried & Roy with Harriet

When the MGM Grand opened in 1974, Donn Arden staged his biggest extravaganza yet—a $3 million tribute to classic MGM/Hollywood musicals. The legendary *Hallelujah Hollywood* show was performed in the appropriately named Ziegfeld Room. In tribute to the MGM mascot an African lion named Leo was later added to the act.

From that point on, the illusionists performed their incredible feats on stages at several Las Vegas resorts in addition to the original MGM Grand: a second engagement at the Stardust, this time as headliners, and eventually at the Frontier in their own exclusive show.

In 1976 Siegfried and Roy received Magicians of the Year Award from the Academy of Magic Arts in Los Angeles. The following year they met their future manager, Bernie Yuman, whom they fondly referred to as their "five-star general."

In 1978, February 17th was declared Siegfried & Roy day in Las Vegas. That same year the duo agreed to leave the MGM's *Hallelujah Hollywood* to prop up the Stardust's struggling *Lido de Paris*. For their 30-minute closing act, they received star billing as "The Superstars of Magic." Negotiating for Siegfried and Roy was 27-year-old Yuman, who succeeded in making the duo the highest-paid specialty act to date in the history of Las Vegas. Also, showgirl Lynette Chappell and performer Toney Mitchell were added to the show.

The *Review-Journal* reported, "On the night of the Stardust premiere, Siegfried was bitten on his hand and arm by the African lion, who had not adjusted to the new venue. He received 38 stitches backstage, and performed in the second show. Afterward, actor Cary Grant came back stage to congratulate him."

"BEYOND BELIEF" OPENS AT THE FRONTIER

With the help of circus impresarios Irvin and Kenneth Feld, Siegfried & Roy go further than a specialty act and are showcased in their own full-length magic show, called *Beyond Belief*, at the Frontier. It's the first ongoing magic show in Las Vegas, and eventually it racks up 3,500 performances for more than three million show-goers.

In 1982, the Maharajah of Boroada asked Siegfried and Roy for help in saving the white tiger of India, near extinction. In exchange for their assistance, the illusionists were given a gift of tiger cubs. Roy named the male cub Neva, and the female cub Shasadee. Additionally, he was allowed to take from another litter, a third female cub, completely white, which he named Sitarra. Four years later, Sitarra and Neva become Roy's first breeding pair of white tigers with offspring born in Nevada.

Finishing a successful seven-year engagement at the Frontier in 1988, Siegfried & Roy are signed by Steve Wynn to a $57.5 million deal to perform at the Mirage—after it opens. While the Mirage was under construction, the magical pair did a 38-week gig in a custom venue in the Ginza District of Tokyo, Japan. In October of the same year in Las Vegas, Siegfried and Roy are sworn in as United States citizens, along with their assistant Lynette Chappell.

In 1989, Siegfried & Roy took a temporary leave from Las Vegas for a three-week engagement at Radio City Music Hall. Their performance turned out so successful that they smashed a 57-year box office record. Within a year, the masterful illusionists opened in their own exclusive show in a 1,500-seat custom venue at the Mirage. The "Broadway-meets-rock-concert spectacle" was designed by John Napier of *Cats* and *Les Miserables* fame.

By 1992, more accolades abounded when Siegfried & Roy received another award from the Academy of Magical Arts in Los Angeles —this time from the Magicians of the Decade Award. One year later, a Saturday morning cartoon series premiered on television called *Siegfried & Roy: Masters of the Impossible.*

In 1996, Siegfried and Roy were presented with the first white lions ever born in captivity in the United States. The next year, the illusionists celebrated their 15,000th Las Vegas performance. Also that year, the white lioness Prosperity is born.

SECRET GARDEN AND DOLPHIN HABITAT

In 1997, Siegfried and Roy's Secret Garden and Dolphin Habitat opened at the Mirage. Described as a palm-shaded sanctuary, it featured a collection of the planet's rarest and most exotic creatures, where guests of the Mirage could view snow white tigers, striped white tigers, heterozygous tigers, white lions, heterozygous white lions, and an Asian elephant—which the magicians made appear and disappear onstage over the years.

In 1998, Siegfried and Roy are inducted into the Las Vegas Gaming Hall of Fame, and production began on their Imax 3-D biography, "The Magic Box." Within a year, the film premiered nationally on more than 160 Imax screens.

In 1999, the lioness Prosperity was named mascot to the United States Senate, and Siegfried and Roy earned a star on the Hollywood Walk of Fame.

In 2000, they were honored as Magicians of the Century. Steve Wynn also renewed the celebrity pair to a lifetime contract with the Mirage, making them one of top ten highest paid celebrity acts in the world, coming in just behind motion picture producer and director Steven Spielberg.

ROY SURVIVES TIGER MAULING

Sadly, performance under that lifetime contract ran only three years until October 3, 2003, during a 7:30 performance at the Mirage, Roy was critically injured by the Bengal tiger Montecore.

The masterful illusionists gave their final performance for charity, called "The Final Bow," on February 28, 2009, after a hiatus of over five years. Their manager, Bernie Yuman, said about Roy Horn that night, "he's a walking miracle."

Backstage, after a standing ovation, Roy said to his cast-mates, "Are you all ready for the second show?"

DEAN MARTIN: THE KING OF COOL

For more than 30 years, Dean Martin was among the most popular celebrities in the archives of Las Vegas. Entertainment history was made in the 1960s when Martin, along with fellow "Rat Pack" cronies Frank Sinatra, Sammy Davis Jr., Peter Lawford, and Joey Bishop, all performed their impromptu shows at the famous Sands Hotel.

Throughout the 1970s the Riviera Hotel was home for Dean Martin, as was the new MGM Grand, where he performed on its opening night of December 5, 1973. After Bally's purchased the MGM Grand in 1986, he became a mainstay in its Celebrity Room on the Las Vegas Strip, often televising his famous "Roast" specials there. Dean Martin performed more concerts in Bally's 1400-seat Celebrity Room than any other performer.

Also nicknamed the King of Cool, he not only sang but also did stand-up, and was one of the smoothest comics in the business. Besides being a huge star in Las Vegas and a raucous member of Sinatra's Pack, Martin was also a major star in three other areas of show business: motion pictures, television, and recordings.

EARLY LIFE

Born Dino Paul Crocetti on June 7, 1917, in Steubenville, Ohio, to Italian immigrant parents, he was the younger of two sons. Martin spoke only Italian until he started school at age five. As a teenager he became the target of much ridicule for his broken English. He took up playing drums as a hobby, dropped out of high school in the 10th grade, and got a job as a stock boy in a nearby tobacco shop. Later he got work at a speakeasy behind the tobacco shop, doing everything from delivering bootleg liquor to bartending and dealing blackjack. Martin also worked in a steel mill, and by age 15 had begun boxing as a welterweight.

During his prizefighting years, he billed himself as Kid Crochet and earned a broken nose (which was later straightened), and a scarred lip. And according to Nick Tosches' biography *Dino*, Martin had, "several sets of broken knuckles, a result of not being able to afford the tape used to wrap boxers' hands. Of his twelve bouts he would say 'he won all but eleven.'"[56]

Martin gave up prize-fighting and began singing with local bands calling himself "Dino Martini" after the then-famous Metropolitan Opera tenor Nino Martini. Influenced early in his career by the crooning style of Harry Mills of the Mills Brothers, Dean got his first break singing for the Ernie McKay Orchestra. In the early 1940s he started singing for bandleader Sammy Watkins, who suggested he change his name to Dean Martin.

Martin married Elizabeth Anne McDonald in October 1941 and they had four children. Their marriage lasted only eight years before a divorce in 1949. Gradually, Martin developed his own singing style, but in 1943 he bombed at the Riobamba, a high-class nightclub in New York. However, his failure turned out fortuitous because that night he succeeded Frank Sinatra, the setting for their first meeting and eventual lasting friendship.

Up to that time, according to the *Review-Journal,* "Martin had repeatedly sold 10 percent shares of his earnings for up-front cash. He apparently did this so often he found that he had sold over 100 percent of his income. Such was his charm that most of his lenders forgave his debts, and remained friends."[57]

In 1944 Martin was drafted into the U.S. Army and served a year stationed in Akron, Ohio, until reclassified 4-F and discharged. (His reclassification may have been due to a double hernia, which Jerry Lewis wrote about in his autobiography.) By 1946 Martin was surviving as an East Coast nightclub singer, he never reached the fanatic popularity enjoyed by Sinatra. "He seemed destined to remain on the nightclub circuit," cited the *Review-Journal,* "until he met a comic named Jerry Lewis at the Glass Hat Club in New York, where both men were performing. Martin and Lewis formed a fast friendship, which led to their participation in each other's acts, and the ultimate formation of a music-comedy team."[58]

The pair officially debuted at Atlantic City's 500 Club in July 1946. Surprisingly, they were not well received. After their first performance, the owner, Paul "Skinny" D'Amato, took them aside and warned them that if they did not come up with a better act for the second show, they would be fired. The pair went out behind the club to the alley and huddled, agreeing to "go for broke"—that is, to throw out their pre-scripted jokes and improvise.

Dean Martin

When they came out for the second show, Martin sang while Lewis, dressed as a busboy, dropped plates and made a shambles of both Martin's singing and the club's sense of decorum, with Martin pelting Lewis with bread rolls and chasing him off stage. Other skits as part of the night's performance included old vaudeville jokes and lots of improvised slapstick humor. The second show of the evening turned out to be a big hit, with the audience members doubled over in laughter. This success led to several other well-paying engagements that culminated in a triumphant run at New York's Copacabana. Essentially, the act consisted of Martin singing and Lewis heckled him, which typically ended up with the pair having fun themselves as they chased each other around the stage. In a later interview, both said their secret was ignoring the audience and playing to one another.

In 1949 the comedic duo had started doing a radio series. The same year Paramount signed Martin and Lewis as comedy relief for the movie *My Friend Irma*. By the early 1950s, they were the hottest act in America. But frustration set in for the pair with the formulaic similarity of the Martin and Lewis movies, which producer Hal Wallis stubbornly refused to change, as Lewis recalled in his book *Dean & Me*. Martin's dissatisfaction ultimately turned to escalating disagreements with Lewis. Eventually they would no longer work together, and the act broke up in 1956, ten years to the day from their first actual teaming.

SOLO CAREER

In 1957, Martin's first solo film, *Ten Thousand Bedrooms,* was a box office failure. Though still popular as a singer, the era of the pop crooner was waning as rock and roll music surged in popularity. For a while it looked as if Martin's career would be relegated to performing at night clubs and being remembered as Jerry Lewis's former partner. But all that changed when Martin replaced actor Tony Randall as co-star of a war film, *The Young Lions.* As a result, Martin's role in the movie began a spectacular comeback. More success followed when Martin starred alongside Frank Sinatra for the first time, in the highly acclaimed 1958 drama *Some Came Running.* By the mid 1960s, Martin was a top movie- recording- nightclub star.

Martin had claustrophobia and seldom used elevators. So he, despised climbing stairs in Manhattan's skyscrapers and much preferred California over New York, which, because of being earthquake prone, had few tall buildings.

Also in the late 1950s and early 1960s, Dean Martin and Frank Sinatra became close friends. The two of them, along with Sammy Davis Jr., Peter Lawford, and Joey Bishop, formed the legendary Rat Pack. The Pack called themselves "The Summit," made films together such as *Ocean's Eleven*, and formed an important part of the Hollywood social scene in those years.

The Pack was celebrated in Las Vegas, too, especially for their performances at the Sands Hotel. They always wore tuxedos in their act, which usually consisted of singing individual numbers, duets, and trios, and lots of improvised slapstick and chatter. Much of their humor revolved around Sinatra's infamous womanizing and Martin's legendary drinking, as well as cracks about Davis's race and religion. With Davis famously practicing Judaism, he used Yiddish expressions on stage that elicited much hilarity from both stage-mates and audiences. Significantly, Martin and Sinatra refused to perform anywhere that barred Davis, and they were largely responsible for getting Las Vegas casinos to open their doors to African American entertainers and patrons and helped to erase restrictive covenants against Jews.

Despite Martin's reputation as a heavy drinker, he was said to be remarkably self-disciplined. At parties he was often the first to call it a night, and when not on tour or a film location liked to go home to see his wife and children. He also had very strict rules when it came to performances. Phillis Diller said in a Wikipedia article, "He borrowed the lovable-drunk shtick from Joe E. Lewis, but his convincing portrayals of heavy boozers in *Some Came Running*, and Howard Hawks's *Rio Bravo* led to unsubstantiated claims of alcoholism. More often than not,

Martin's idea of a good time was playing golf or watching TV, particularly westerns."[59]

ALLEGED MOB CONNECTIONS

Some written sources alleged that Martin early in his career, had links to the Mafia. Michael Freedland's biography titled *Dean Martin: King of the Road* suggested that Martin was aided in his singing career by the Chicago Outfit. They owned saloons in the Windy city, and later when Martin became a star he performed in their saloons as payback to these bosses—Sam Giancana and Tony Accardo. Freedland also wrote that "while in Las Vegas, Martin was friendly with many mobsters, though not in business with them. Many Vegas entertainers knew the wise guys and were cordial with them personally, without criminal involvement."

A book by John L. Smith, *The Animal in Hollywood*, portrayed Martin's longtime relationship with mob bosses Johnny Rosselli and Anthony Fiato. Smith wrote that "Fiato, aka 'the Animal' did Dean Martin many favors, such as getting back money from two swindlers who had cheated Elizabeth Martin, Dean's ex-wife, out of thousands of dollars of her alimony."[60]

As Martin's career flourished into the 1960s, he both starred in and co-produced a series of four Matt Helm super-spy comedy adventures. A fifth in the series was scheduled, co-starring Sharon Tate with Martin in a dual role, one as a serial killer, but because of Tate's murder and the decline of the spy genre, the film was shelved.

In 1965, NBC launched the weekly comedy-variety series, *The Dean Martin Show*, which exploited his public image as a lazy, carefree boozer. The drinks he consumed, as with his Rat Rack days, were said to be apple juice, though some believed otherwise.

By the 1970s his record albums continued to sell well, even though he was no longer a Top 40 hit-maker, and his weekly television show still earned solid ratings. Meanwhile, in Las Vegas he continued to headline on marquees, guaranteeing casinos standing-room-only crowds wherever he performed. The King of Cool also found a way to make his passion for golf profitable by offering his own signature brand of golf balls. Shrewd investments during his later years substantially increased Martin's personal worth. Friedland's biography of Martin noted that, "At the time of his death, Martin was reportedly the single largest minority shareholder of RCA stock. Martin even managed to cure himself of his claustrophobia by reportedly locking himself in the elevator of a tall building and riding up and down for hours until he was no longer panic-stricken."[61]

LATER LIFE

In 1972 Martin filed for divorce from his second wife, Jeanne. A week later he dissolved his business relationship with the Riviera amid reports that the casino refused Martin's request to perform only once a night. He quickly signed on with the MGM Grand and agreed to a three-year picture deal with MGM Studios.

One year later, two months before his 56th birthday, Martin wed 26-year-old Catherine Hawn. That marriage ended in divorce in November 1976. About this time, Martin reconciled with Jeanne, though they never remarried. That same year he also made a public reconciliation with his one-time partner Jerry Lewis on Lewis's Labor Day Muscular Dystrophy Association telethon that same year.

SON'S DEATH AND DINO'S LATER CAREER

While flying with the California Air National Guard, Martin's son, Dean Paul, died in March 1987 when his F-4 Phantom II jet fighter crashed. One year later, a much-touted tour with Sinatra and Davis sputtered. Freedland notes that on one occasion, he infuriated Sinatra by asking, "Frank, what the hell are we doing up here?" Martin, always responded best to a club audience and felt lost in the huge stadiums that Sinatra insisted they perform in. Freedland adds that Dean was not the least bit interested in drinking until dawn after their performances."[62]

Martin's final Las Vegas performances were at Bally's in 1989. It was there he reunited with Jerry Lewis on his 72nd birthday for their last performance together. Both of Martin's last two appearances on television involved tributes to his former Rat Pack cronies. He attended Sammy Davis's 64th birthday celebration in May 1990, only a few sad weeks before Davis died from throat cancer. Then in December 1990, Martin congratulated Frank Sinatra at his televised 75th birthday special.

By 1991, Dean Martin had unofficially retired from performing. He never fully recovered from losing his son. To make matters worse, he also suffered for many years from emphysema. As Freedland wrote in his biography of Martin, "Except for nightly visits to his favorite Los Angeles restaurants which lasted until

1995, he kept his private life to himself, emerging briefly for a public celebration of his 77th birthday with friends and family."[63]

Not long before that, in 1993, Martin had been diagnosed with lung cancer, and told surgery was needed on his liver and kidneys to prolong his life. He refused. Martin died on Christmas morning of 1995 at age 78. By his side were ex-wife Jeanne and other family members. That night, lights of the Las Vegas Strip were dimmed in his honor.

TRIBUTES AND HIT SONGS

As a tribute to the popular performer, the city of Las Vegas renamed Industrial Road as Dean Martin Drive in 2005. Likewise, a similarly named street near his residence in Rancho Mirage, California, was christened in 2008.

Dean Martin's most memorable hit songs include "That's Amore," "Memories Are Made of This," "Everybody Loves Somebody," "Mambo Italiano," "Sway," "Volare," and "Ain't That a Kick in the Head?"

SAMMY DAVIS JR: A GREAT ONE-MAN SHOW

Sammy Davis Jr. made his Las Vegas debut as part of the Will Mastin Trio at the El Rancho Vegas in 1945, before headlining as a top showroom act at the Last Frontier. "Sammy is definitely a one-man show," wrote *Las Vegas Sun* critic Ralph Pearl, noting, "Davis could sing, pound out drum solos, reprise a Bill Robinson tap routine, and play a variety of instruments in a rousing 'Birth of the Blues.'" Throughout his phenomenal career, Davis amazed fans, critics, and fellow entertainers with his ability to sing, dance, and play numerous musical instruments.

EARLY LIFE

Samuel George "Sammy" Davis Jr. was born in December 1925 in Harlem, New York, and raised by his paternal grandmother. His parents were vaudeville dancers, but they split up when Sammy was three years old. His father, not wanting to lose custody of his son, took him on tour, where the child learned to dance from both his father and "uncle" Will Matsin. Davis became a skilled dancer and eventually joined the act that became the Will Mastin Trio. Davis once said in an interview that while he was young Mastin and his father shielded him from racism. Snubs, for instance, were explained as jealousy.

However, Davis noted in his autobiography that, when he served in the U.S. Army during World War II he was confronted by strong racial prejudice. "Overnight the world looked different. It wasn't one color any more. I could see the protection I'd gotten all my life from my father and Will. I appreciated their loving hope that I'd never need to know about prejudice and hate, but they were wrong. It was as if I'd walked through a swinging door for eighteen years, a door which they had always secretly held open.'"[64]

Sammy Davis Jr.

Davis served in an integrated Special Services unit with the army, finding that the spotlight lessened the prejudice. "My talent was the weapon, the power, the way for me to fight. It was the one way I might hope to affect a man's thinking," he wrote.

As an African American, Davis endured racism throughout his lifetime. In one later-in-life incident Davis was on a golf course with Jack Benny, when he was asked what his handicap was. "Handicap?" he quipped. "Talk about handicap— I'm a one-eyed Negro Jew." In time, this statement became a signature line, recalled in his autobiography.

SOLO CAREER

After his discharge at war's end, Davis rejoined the family trio, which at the time was performing at clubs around Portland, Oregon. Soon, Davis began to achieve success on his own and was singled out for praise by critics. Several albums of his were produced which led to his 1956 appearance in the Broadway play *Mr. Wonderful.*

When Davis debuted in Las Vegas, like other African-American performers he was allowed to entertain but usually not allowed to stay at the same hotels, gamble in the casinos, nor dine or drink in the resort restaurants and bars. In his autobiography, *Yes, I Can,* Davis wrote, "Black performers entered and exited through kitchens, and sometimes were lucky to get a meal at the places where they performed. They stayed in boarding houses or motels in racially segregated West Las Vegas. No dressing rooms were provided for black performers and they waited outside by the swimming pool between acts."

Davis had to endure more than racism and bigotry in Las Vegas. While headlining at the Last Frontier in 1954, Davis made a late-night car trip to Los Angeles for a recording session. His friend Charles Head drove the car while Davis stretched out on the back seat to get some sleep. The trip ended in a horrible collision near San Bernardino. Davis lost his left eye, got a broken jaw, and had other facial injuries. He recovered at the Palm Spring's home of Frank Sinatra, where he was told by his older host, "Relax—You're going to be bigger than ever, Charley,"—Sinatra's nickname for Davis.

Eventually, Davis was fitted for a glass eye, which he wore the rest of his life. While in the hospital, his friend Eddie Cantor described to him the similarities between the Jewish and black cultures. Inspired by Cantor's beliefs, Davis—who was born to a Catholic mother and Protestant father—began studying the history of the Jews, and years later converted to Judaism.

Sinatra's prophecy seemed to come true, because the car crash marked a turning point in Davis's career. Overnight he changed from a well-known entertainer to a national celebrity. He recovered and returned to perform as a solo act on Las Vegas, Reno, and Lake Tahoe stages, and appeared on Broadway and in films.

In 1959, Davis became a member of Sinatra's celebrated Rat Pack. He was initially denied residence at the Sands Las Vegas, until Sinatra threatened to pull the plug on Rat Pack performances unless Davis got his own suite. In due course, Nevada resort owners gave in to the demands of both Sinatra and Dean Martin, opening the doors for other black entertainers who had been forced to find accommodations in West Las Vegas. When performing in the Lake Tahoe area, he enjoyed staying in a home that casino owner Bill Harrah built to accommodate entertainers during their engagements.

As Davis's career progressed, he refused to work at places that practiced racial segregation. His demands eventually led to the integration of Miami Beach nightclubs.

In 1964 at the height of his fame, Davis was starring on Broadway in *Golden Boy* every night and simultaneously shooting his own New York-based afternoon talk show during the day. On a rare day off from the theater, Davis typically spent time in the studio recording new songs or performing live, as far away as Miami, Chicago and Las Vegas, or doing television variety specials in Los Angeles. Later, in his autobiography, Davis wrote, "I knew that I was cheating my family of my company, but could not help myself; because I was incapable of standing still."

LATER CAREER

Although still a big draw in Las Vegas, by the late 1960s Davis's musical career began to decline. Even so, his "I've Gotta Be Me" reached #11 on the *Easy Listening* singles chart in 1969. In an effort to reconnect with younger listeners, he recorded some embarrassing "hip" musical efforts with the Motown label. Then, just when his career reached its nadir, he had an unexpected hit with "Candy Man," the theme song from the television series *Baretta* (1975-1978).

Though "Candy Man" was his last recorded Top 40 hit, he remained a live act beyond Las Vegas, occasionally landing television and film parts, including cameo visits to *All in the Family* in which he planted a kiss on the cheek of Archie Bunker, played by Carroll O'Connor, and on *Charlie's Angels* with wife Altovise Davis. He also guest starred in other television shows, including *I Dream of Jeannie* and *The Patty Duke Show*.

Davis admitted to watching daytime soaps, which led to his making a cameo appearance on *General Hospital*. Later he portrayed the recurring character Chip Warren on *One Life to Live*, for which he received a Daytime Emmy nomination in 1980.

One of his greatest joys off-stage was photography, especially shooting family and acquaintances. Davis's body of work was detailed in a 2007 book by Burt Boyar, who quoted Davis as saying, "Jerry Lewis gave me my first important cameras, my first 35-millimeter, during the Ciro's period in the early fifties. And he hooked me."

Among his many talents, Davis was also an enthusiastic shooter and gun owner. He participated in fast-draw competitions, and was capable of drawing and firing a Colt single action revolver in under a quarter of a second. Additionally, he was adept at fancy gun spinning and often appeared on television showing off his skill. Davis also appeared in western films and as a guest star on several "Golden Age" television westerns.

Davis led a controversial life, which seemed to come to a head when he married white, Swedish-born actress May Britt in 1960. The marriage produced one daughter and two adopted sons. They divorced in 1968. He received hate mail while starring in the Broadway production of *Golden Boy* from 1964 to 1966, a role for which he received a Tony Award nomination for Best Actor. At the time, interracial marriages were forbidden by law in 31 U.S. states, and only in 1967 were those laws ruled unconstitutional by the U.S. Supreme Court. Davis's interracial relationship cost him billing at President John F. Kennedy's inaugural ball in 1961, because of concerns about Davis's "illegal" marriage and the political fallout for Kennedy.

Davis began dating Altovise Gore, a dancer in *Golden Boy*, and they eventually married in May 1970, ten years after his first marriage. They adopted one child and remained married until Davis's death in 1990.

Due to surgery for hip replacement, Davis missed a Rat Pack reunion at the new Thomas & Mack Center in 1983, but returned in 1985 with renewed energy to headline at the Desert Inn. Another hip surgery forced him to ease his workload, and he teamed with comedian Jerry Lewis to perform at Bally's Hotel-Casino. The pair also performed in a successful 1988 HBO special, *An Evening with Sammy Davis Jr. & Jerry Lewis.*

After reuniting with Rat Pack pals Sinatra and Martin in 1987, Davis toured internationally with them and Liza Minnelli. His last performance was at Harrah's Lake Tahoe in 1989, the night before his first radiation treatment. He died May 16th, 1990, at his home in Beverly Hills, California. He was 64 years old.

When Davis died he was in debt to the IRS, and his estate was the subject of several legal battles. After Frank Sinatra learned of Altovise Davis's financial troubles, he reportedly gave Davis's widow $1 million in cash.

Davis wrote in his *Yes I Can,* "Being a star made it possible for me to get insulted in places where the average Negro could never hope to go and get insulted."

Sammy Davis Jr. became the first of the legendary Rat Pack to die, leading to many tributes in his name in Las Vegas and elsewhere. "In Reno, William Harrah named his main showroom in Davis's honor, and today it is still known as Sammy's Showroom. In Las Vegas, Davis was honored in a manner reserved for only a handful of the most prominent entertainers in Las Vegas showroom history. Marquees and neon lights were dimmed along the Strip in testament to Davis's unmatched skills as a singer, dancer, and all-around entertainer."[65]

Author's note: Because I lived 12 years in Las Vegas, I was given a number of opportunities to see, in person, many of the great entertainers perform there: Dean Martin, Siegfried & Roy (when they performed in *Hallelujah Hollywood* at the MGM Grand), Wayne Newton, and Paul Anka. Of them all, I thought Sammy Davis Jr. had by far the greatest act. He was a virtual one-man show. In the late 1970s, I was fortunate to see him perform in the Circus Maximus Showroom at Caesars Palace. Without a doubt, it was the greatest show I have ever seen. His singing literally put goose bumps on my arms, and his dancing was incredible. He was a great entertainer whom I'll never forget.

WAYNE NEWTON: "MISTER LAS VEGAS"

In retirement as of this writing, Carson Wayne Newton was born on April 3, 1942, in Roanoke, Virginia, to parents who were half-American Indian; German-Cherokee on the mother's side and Irish-Powhatan on the father's. Early in his life Newton developed an interest in music, and by six had learned to play the guitar, steel guitar, and piano.

EARLY CAREER

As he grew older Wayne Newton often appeared with his older brother, Jerry, as "The Rascals of Rhythm" on the Grand Ole Opry road shows, and on ABC-TV's *Ozark Jubilee.*

Wayne Newton

Because the future Las Vegas superstar suffered from asthma, in 1952 his family relocated to the drier climate of Phoenix, Arizona. In 1957, when Newton was a junior in high school, a booking agent saw him and his brother, Jerry, perform on a local TV show. Originally signed for a two-week engagement at the Fremont Hotel in downtown Las Vegas but, their act was so well received that the brothers ended up performing six shows a day for over five years at the Fremont. When the gig began, Wayne Newton was only 15 years old, too young to be allowed in casinos. It was at the Fremont where Wayne Newton met hotelier Ed Torres, who took a liking to the brothers and boosted their careers.

In September 1962, the Newton brothers performed together on *The Jackie Gleason Show*, and went on to perform solo on Gleason's show 12 times over the next 12 years. Newton's best known songs include "Daddy Don't You Walk So Fast," "Years," his vocal version of "Red Roses For a Blue Lady," and his signature song, "Danke Schoen."

Jerry eventually got out of show business, and in the 1970s owned WBGY, an FM radio station in Tullahoma, Tennessee. Wayne Newton went on to super-stardom in Las Vegas. He also became the opening act in television's *Jack Benny Show*. After his job with Benny ended, Newton was offered a gig opening for another comic at the Flamingo Hotel, but he asked for and was given, a headline act.

CO-OWNER OF THE ALADDIN AND ALLEGED MOB AFFILIATION

Since its opening in 1966, the Aladdin always seemed to be in trouble. Its inherent problems over the years derived from a number of things but essentially boiled down to poor location, financing, and more frequently questionable ownership. In the spring of 1979 four Aladdin officials were convicted in Detroit of allowing gangsters there to run the resort. In August 1979 Nevada gaming officials closed the Aladdin, but federal Judge Harry Claiborne ordered it reopened immediately. Eleven months later, state gaming officials closed it again.

Newton had earlier invested in the off-Strip Shenandoah Casino, which never got approved for a gaming license and eventually closed. For his next investment, Newton realized that to buy one of the really big resorts he would need a partner, and his old pal from the Fremont days, Ed Torres, seemed the ideal choice.

In September 1980, Newton and Ed Torres, a former CEO of the Riviera and Newton's longtime friend from the Fremont Hotel, purchased the Aladdin Hotel and Casino for $85 million and reopened it the next month. But a month after they purchased it, Newton got a taste of what Frank Sinatra endured much of his life—accusations of mob association. Over the years, Ol' blue eyes seemed to take it in stride, as he regularly snubbed the press and often posed for photographs with known wise guys, which helped enhance his tough guy image. But according to the *Review-Journal,* "similar allegations had the opposite effect on Newton, tainting his clean image."

In October 1980, "An NBC News report said that Newton allegedly had ties to the mob, putting his life and potential gaming career in grave jeopardy," added the *Review-Journal.* "Newton admitted that years earlier he had known Guido Penosi, a reputed member of the Carlo Gambino crime family of New York. Newton, however, insisted that he did not know Penosi had alleged mob ties."[66]

After the airing of that NBC report, other stories surfaced that Newton, who co-owned the Aladdin, allegedly was the front man for the mob. As reported by the *Review-Journal,* "when Newton returned to Las Vegas from an engagement in Los Angeles, FBI agents met him at McCarran International Airport, and showed him a list they had obtained from and informant. It had five names—Newton's and those of four slain men."

For Wayne Newton, that was the proverbial straw that broke the camel's back. Newton eventually sued NBC for libel, which had alleged in its report that the purchase of the Aladdin was tied to the Mafia. He won a $19 million defamation judgment, overturned on appeal. The court ruled "that although the NBC report was inaccurate, there was no malice therefore Newton, a public figure, could not collect damages." Newton later told the *Las Vegas Sun,* that it was not about money. It was about clearing his name. "And I did," Newton said. "It was ridiculous. I'm an Indian boy from Virginia, what do I know about the Mafia?"

Looking back, Newton had bought in to the Aladdin at a difficult time in the development of Las Vegas. It was a grueling period in which the Feds were cracking down on the mob, and corporate ownership of gaming properties was in its infancy.

The Aladdin partnership with Torres ended in a bitter feud, and in 1983 Torres bought Newton's share of the Aladdin for $8.5 million. The partners had quarreled over, among other things, the acquisition of a nearby service station that would have to be demolished to give the Aladdin better access to and from the Strip. Newton was willing to pay the station owner's price of $16 million, while Torres was willing to pay only $4 million for it. Ultimately, that small parcel was never acquired by Torres or Newton, and the Aladdin—now Planet Hollywood—never reached its potential.

NEWTON AS "MISTER LAS VEGAS"

Wayne Newton, who entertains worldwide including at Branson, Missouri, has also performed more than 30,000 shows at several venues in Las Vegas over a 40-year career, earning him the affectionate nickname "Mister Las Vegas." In the 1970s, the hard-working entertainer performed at the Desert Inn, Frontier, and Sands. In the 1980s, it was Bally's, Caesars Palace, and the Las Vegas Hilton. In the 1990s, Newton headlined at the MGM Grand. From 2000 to 2005, he entertained at the Las Vegas Hilton and at the Stardust, where the showroom was named for him.

His last performance at the Stardust on April 20, 2005, was a memorable one. The day after, the *Review-Journal* noted, "News crews were expecting this performance to end on time, to make their 10 pm and 11 pm shows, but the show finally ended around 11:30 pm, thus eliminating the possibility. Mister Las Vegas went on at 7:30 that night, and sang nearly his entire repertoire of songs, along with other Vegas mainstays as well."

NEWTON DECLARES BANKRUPTCY

Wayne Newton spent 10 years of his life and $8 million suing NBC for libel, and it bankrupted him. In 1992, Newton filed for bankruptcy to reorganize an estimated $20 million in debts, much of which was incurred while battling the powerful network. His bankruptcy declaration also included a $341,000 IRS tax lien. By 1999, through hard work and better management of his financial affairs, Newton emerged out of bankruptcy.

In 2000, Newton was elected to the Gaming Hall of Fame. A year later, he succeeded Bob Hope as chair of the USO Celebrity Circle. In 2006, Newton was inducted into the Nevada Entertainer/Artist Hall of Fame at UNLV's Artemus Ham Hall.

LATER CAREER

Although Newton will always be remembered as one of the top-drawing performers in Las Vegas history, in recent years he also showcased other commercial talents including starting up a reality television show in January 2005 with his cable TV show the *Entertainer*, in which the winner earns a spot in Newton's show, plus a headlining act of her or his own for a year.

At the 2007 NBA All-Star Weekend in Las Vegas, Newton sang Elvis Presley's "Viva Las Vegas." Newton was featured in the fall season of *Dancing With the Stars* partnered with two-time champion Cheryl Burke. During the taping he became the first guest on *The Price Is Right* hosted by Drew Carey, which taped next door at CBS Television City.

In October of 2009, Newton began performing his newest show, "Once Before I Go," at the Tropicana in Las Vegas. Newton also appeared that December on the finale of *The Amazing Race 15*. Later, from a suite at the MGM Grand, he told the finalists "the finish line was at 'my house' the Casa de Shenandoah on Sunset at Pecos."

PERSONAL LIFE

Wayne Newton wed Elaine Okamura in 1968, and they adopted a daughter before divorcing in 1985. These days, Newton raises prized Arabian horses at his "casa" where he resides in Las Vegas with his second wife, Kathleen McCrone, and their daughter born in 2002. In his honor, a street near McCarran International Airport was named Wayne Newton Boulevard.

From his beginnings over 51 years ago at the Fremont Hotel, his career seemed to grow along with the town. As far as his title of "Mister Las Vegas," he wears it well.

WALLY COX OPENS AT THE DUNES

Every chapter has its finale, and who better to end this one than with the lovable Wally Cox. You might remember him from the period 1952-1955, when he played a bungling, mild-mannered science teacher in the hit television show *Mister Peepers.*

In 1956 Las Vegas was teaming with celebrities, such as Rose Marie, Noel Coward, and Nelson Eddy. Neon marquees were alight too, with stars such as Tony Martin, Gisele MacKenzie, and the "king of rock 'n' roll" Elvis Presley headlined at the New Frontier. Meanwhile, a new casino hotel was preparing to open across the street from Caesars Palace on the southwest corner of the Strip and Flamingo road: the Dunes. For whatever reason—especially considering the surfeit of great entertainers available at the time —someone made the unique decision that Wally Cox would headline in the showroom on opening night. Money was negotiated, contracts were signed, and the new casino resort began a huge ad campaign aimed at filling its showroom on opening night.

When the big day came, a crowd of reporters and fans appeared at the Las Vegas airport to welcome the famous, easygoing sitcom star seen only on black and white television screens. No one had any idea who would get off the plane, since big-time Las Vegas entertainers usually came with some kind of an entourage. Sammy Davis Jr., for instance, traveled with 8 or 10 go-fers, not counting band members. Other celebrities came with publicists, social secretaries, a chauffeur, or perhaps—as Barry White did—a couple of great-looking babes, one on each arm. Lo and behold, when the plane landed and its door swung open, who emerged but a slightly balding, common-looking man wearing big horn-rimmed glasses. As he made his way down the steps, the only thing of note he brought with him was a newspaper folded under one arm.

Meanwhile, the Dunes entertainment people had flocked to the gangway. "Where's the entourage? Are the babes on another plane?" One reporter said, "Cox just gave one of his meager smiles, much like on *Mister Peepers*. Then he said, "'You only asked for me, and this is what you got.'"

After the first show, one revue reported that Cox's performance was so bad, "he was not allowed to perform in the second show." He was directed over to the cashier's cage, paid his money, and flown back to California. That's one story.

Another version claimed that Cox returned to nightclub work in 1956, was heckled off the stage in Las Vegas, and after a few days voluntarily bowed out of the gig.

Whatever the case, at the time of this writing, Wally Cox retains the record for the shortest showroom engagement in the history of Las Vegas.

Unfortunately, on February 15, 1973, two months after his 48th birthday, the much-loved Wally Cox died of a heart attack allegedly caused, yet never confirmed, by an overdose of sleeping pills.

Chapter 6
SPECIAL PLAYERS AND MEMORABLE TOKES

*H*istorically, casino management's conventional attitude toward most players, win or lose, was that they wanted you back. If you lost, of course they wanted you back. But even if you won they wanted you to return so they could have the chance to win back their money, plus more of yours. Why? Because over time the casino's "house edge" has a greater chance to take effect. Casinos usually have another significant edge over the player—a larger bankroll. This means they can endure huge losses without going broke, an advantage most players don't have.

The exception goes to some of the very special players described in this chapter whose bankrolls exceeded that of the casino they chose to gamble in. These exceptional players were not only considered special, they also became legendary because of the huge amounts they wagered, the generous gratuities they gave to casino staff, and their historic gambling exploits.

WHALES AND GRINDERS

Casino players come in all different forms, from the grinder—the ordinary person who might gamble as little as $50 or $100 a day at the tables—to the "whales"—the super-rich high-rollers. Whales often flew into Las Vegas in their private planes with between $10 and $20 million in cash or more for no other purpose than to gamble for extremely high stakes.

Likewise, all Las Vegas casinos have a marketing strategy designed to appeal to the type of player to whom they want to cater. At the top are the upscale properties such as the Wynn Las Vegas, the Bellagio, the MGM Grand, and Caesars Palace, which have a reputation for catering to the whims of the high-roller whales. At the lower end of the scale, are, for example, the El Cortez downtown, the Strip's Slots-A-Fun, and Circus Circus, with low table limits. Accordingly, they cater to low-limit grinders.

Back in the early 1980s, when I worked at Circus-Circus Las Vegas, the house had a maximum bet limit of $500, strictly enforced with no exceptions. In fact, if high rollers happened to come in and wanted to play at high stakes, they were frankly told "sorry, we don't want the action!"

On the other hand, some of the upscale Strip casinos wanted the high-roller action, and often went out of their way to get it—sponsoring events in which special players such as the whales I describe here made a dramatic impact on a casino's bottom line.

AUSTRALIA'S KERRY PACKER—THE "PRINCE OF WHALES"

Kerry Packer

Kerry Packer is remembered by historians as a billionaire media mogul and one of the most ruthless Australian business tycoons, yet in the gambling world he was renowned for two fascinating attributes, including his nickname, "Prince of Whales," because no one gambled bigger than Kerry Packer. He was also known by casino staff as "King George," a term of affection because he was the biggest tipper in the world. The term "George" in Las Vegas casino jargon translates into a generous tipper or player who makes bets for the dealers.

KERRY PACKER: A GAMBLER LARGER THAN LIFE

We know the house always wins, right? The reason it always wins is that an advantage—the house edge—is built into every casino game. Beyond that, the casino has a bigger bankroll and can endure any winning streak players might throw at it.

When I talk about whales and high rollers, in reality only a few true whales are swimming out there who could put the fear of God into any casino executive and literally bring the house down. One of these was Australia's richest man, Kerry Packer. His gambling exploits in the casinos of the United Kingdom and Las Vegas are legendary.

One observer reported seeing Packer sign several markers for at least $6 million while sitting in the high limit room of the MGM Grand. Although that amount of money would not put the casino in jeopardy, it was Packer's style of play that worried casino management. His favorite games were baccarat and blackjack. His style of play usually began with a betting range of between $300 and $1,000 per hand until he was winning, then he would raise his bets to as much as $300,000 a hand at baccarat. When Packer played blackjack and started winning, he was known to bet upwards of $250,000 per hand on multiple spots, and if permitted, would play two blackjack tables simultaneously.

In the eyes of the casino, Packer was a dangerous player because he lacked the fatal flaw that took down most gamblers—once he got ahead in winnings he seldom lost them. Most gamblers tend to continue playing once they're ahead and end up losing their winnings back to the house. Packer wasn't shy about betting millions, quitting while still ahead of the game. For that, some called him "Hit and Run Packer."

Although Packer's gambling strategy was simple, it was a little more elaborate than that of most high rollers, and it was dreaded by casino executives because it had the effect of forcing the casinos to compete against each other to offer him high-roller comps and discounts. In Packer's case, this consisted of not only the free room and board and free show tickets provided to the average high roller, but much more. Customarily, a casino had to offer Packer a discount on his losses of at least 20 percent.

Thus if Packer lost $1 million, the casino would return $200,000 to him. This strategy reduced the mathematical edge casinos have for guaranteeing its profit. To make matters worse, Packer played blackjack using an expert basic strategy or he wagered on the Banker at baccarat. Against a skilled gambler, baccarat and blackjack have the lowest house edge. In essence, Packer was forcing the casinos to give away the house edge in order to gain his business.

Casino management had mixed feelings about Kerry Packer playing at their tables. True, he gambled large amounts of money, but he could stake himself like no other player. Casinos rely on their huge bankroll—known as the law of large numbers--to guarantee turning a profit. Unlike most players, Packer could afford to go up against the casino's bankroll and sustain large losses until he again hit a winning streak. In addition, his large bets meant his winning streaks involved sizable sums of money, which could easily wipe out a casino's profits—and management's bonuses—for the year. The combination earned him the title Prince of Whales.

PACKER AT THE MGM IN 1993

Like most whales, Kerry Packer was invited to spend some time at the MGM Grand in Las Vegas. Packer agreed, and made the MGM Grand one of his stops for high stakes baccarat and blackjack while on a gambling spree that included Las Vegas and the United Kingdom. Having a billionaire guest like Kerry Packer was seen as a very good thing for MGM's reputation, but not for its bottom line. Nor did it benefit some of the top casino executives who invited him.

On December 18, 1993, the MGM Grand had its gala opening, at which Barbra Streisand earned a notable $4 million for her two performances there. That same night, someone else gained fame in Las Vegas as a result of his gambling excess and generosity with the dealers. Australia's richest man, Kerry Packer, flew into Las Vegas on his private jet. On his arrival at the MGM Grand he deposited $12 million in cash with the casino cage. Packer then began playing baccarat to the tune of $100,000 per hand. (In those days, the per-hand limit at baccarat was set at $10,000, but special players typically were allowed to play at the higher stakes.)

Within a few hours Packer won $10 million. Then something extraordinary happened. After he won a $100,000 bet, which meant $200,000 was bunched in a big stack of 20 placards (cheques) on the table valued at $10,000 each, Packer pointed to the stack and said, "for the dealers." Remarkably, the same thing happened twice more the same night. The total added up to $600,000 in tokes from just one player! There's even more to the saga of Kerry Packer.

According to the *Review-Journal*, during Packer's grand-opening weeklong stay at the MGM, the dealers earned an average of $750 a day in tip income—an amount far exceeding any daily tip average ever reported.

KERRY PACKER
VERSUS THE MGM GRAND IN 1995

Again, two years after Packer won over $10 million, he was cordially invited back to the MGM Grand Las Vegas. Remember, the casino's expectation is that over time, a gambler eventually loses any winnings and will earn the casino a profit at least equivalent to the house edge. That wasn't the case on Packer's return visit in 1995. He took MGM for over $20 million at baccarat and blackjack in a single session. At blackjack, he reportedly requested the entire public area be cleared so he could play by himself. Packer began playing all seven spots on one table, then after getting management permission to play two tables, went from table to table betting $250,000 on each of seven spots on both tables. He had a great run, winning $28 million in 40 minutes. Nevertheless, he continued to play until the wee hours of the morning, finally cashing out with $20 million. For the MGM Grand Las Vegas, it was the largest win ever recorded by an individual player in a single session.

Although no fault of Packer's, several top-level casino executives lost their jobs for inviting Packer to revisit the MGM Grand. Included in the dismissal was Larry Woolf, then president of the MGM Grand Las Vegas. He was reported to have one last obligation to perform before being terminated: fly to Australia and, with all due respect, inform Kerry Packer that his action would no longer be allowed at the MGM.

After, MGM barred Packer from playing at the MGM Grand, I learned that Steve Wynn had said he would happily accept Kerry Packer's action at the Mirage. From then on, until his passing in

2005 at the age of 68, Kerry Packer played blackjack and baccarat at the Mirage whenever he came to Las Vegas.

KERRY PACKER AS "KING GEORGE"

The night of his record $20 million win at the MGM Grand, Kerry Packer left a remarkable $1 million tip for the dealers. On another occasion, during a conversation with a cocktail waitress, he discovered she was married with children. He asked her why she wasn't home taking care of her family. She replied, "It's because I have a mortgage." Packer then asked her how much she owed. The waitress said she still had a balance of $150,000. Packer gave her a tip that was more than enough to cover her mortgage.

These incidents were not mere random generosity but an indication of Kerry Packer's bighearted nature. He had the means to satisfy his habit of helping people with gargantuan gratuities that impacted their lives and livelihoods. Packer's life overflowed with stories like these.

BREAKING CASINOS

Casino executives tend to make big dollars, but to make those big dollars in a fair manner, their pay is based on a percentage of the year-end earnings of the casino. One casino executive from England told of how in one session Kerry Packer wiped out his bonus. Unlike most gamblers, Packer wasn't there to get plastered and have a good time; he was there to win. One year the casino was above its normal year-end profit by about 61 million, and he was projected to receive a six-figure bonus. Kerry Packer came in on New Year's Eve, won 13 million, and virtually crushed our profit margin. The executive got nothing.

This story is a prime example of the size of Kerry Packer's gambling and how it could shake up casinos.

Voiding Christmas bonuses was one thing, busting casinos was something else. The magnitude of Packer's gambling was so huge that only a few casinos in the world would accept his action. Only the biggest casinos with a strong financial statement could absorb the shock of a Packer win.

Sometimes a smaller casino tried to take on the Prince of Whales hoping to get lucky. An online source of gambling stories reports: "The Aspinalls Club was an exclusive high-class casino in London, but because it was so exclusive, it was in the greater scheme of things, quite a small casino. They welcomed Kerry Packer around May 1990. Unfortunately for the Aspinalls Club managers and owners, Kerry Packer had a good winning streak. He took home £300,000 (about $750,000) in winnings, and a week later the Aspinalls Club shut down because of cash flow problems."[67]

One New Year's Eve in the mid 1990s, Packer beat the Las Vegas Hilton, winning over $9 million by playing hands of $150,000 each. The loss dented the year's profit enough that no one got bonuses. "But that night he tipped the dealers over $1 million and gave the lounge singer a gratuity of $100,000. It was his money and he'd damn well do as he pleased with it. That included yearly charitable contributions that paled his occasional casino losses, like millions to a children's hospital."[68]

"I'LL FLIP YOU FOR IT"

Packer was far more than a whale and a generous tipper. His stylish ways lit up a room. In addition, he was a man without fear. Of all the stories about the Prince of Whales, the next one is his most famous gambling exploit.

The Australian billionaire had a run-in with an obnoxious Texas oil millionaire who'd been running his mouth at the blackjack table one night in the Stratosphere's high-limit room. The man tried to engage Packer in a game of poker, annoying Packer. To make matters worse, the loud-mouthed, arrogant Texan kept berating the dealer. Packer asked the Texas gambler to tone it down a bit, but the man got more abrasive. Packer finally told the conceited oilman to shut up. The man turned to Packer and said, "Partner, do you know who I am? I'm worth sixty million dollars!"

According to witnesses, Packer pulled out a coin, and said, "I'll flip you for it, heads or tails?" Humiliated, the obnoxious Texan left the table a few hands later. In Australia there's a general loathing for people who are smug about their wealth.

PACKER HAD BIG LOSSES, TOO

In *The Rise and Rise of Kerry Packer*, author Paul Barry wrote: "As one of his executives put it, he gambles when he's bored, and he gambles often because he's often bored."

Packer's billion-dollar sale of *Channel Nine* must have severely tested the media mogul's boredom threshold. In 1999 the *Sydney Morning Herald* reported that "in March 1987, Packer lost $19 million playing blackjack at the Ritz in London. At Easter he was back in town for the Golden Slipper at Rosehill, where it was alleged that Australia's richest man wagered $20 million in one day, and finished the day $7 million worse off."

The same article said, "Sydney bookmaker Bruce McHugh hung up his bookie's satchel at the end of that autumn's racing after what observers described as an unprecedented betting duel with the media tycoon estimated to have topped $50 million in three days."

In 1999, Kerry Packer had a three-week losing streak at London casinos that cost him almost $28 million – described at the time as the largest reported gambling loss in British history.

The same *Sydney Morning Herald* article mentioned his historic 1995 win at the MGM Grand, and reported that he often won as much as $7 million each year during his annual holidays in the UK. "Packer's visits were a risky affair for the casinos, as his wins and losses could make quite a difference to the finances of even bigger casinos. Packer was also known for his sometimes volcanic temper and for his perennial contempt for journalists who sought to question his activities."[69]

Another report stated that in the late 1990s, Packer walked into a major London casino, gambled £15 million (the equivalent of about $30 million) on four roulette tables, and lost it all. After, he casually walked out of the casino apparently with no regrets.

In September 2001, stranded at the Mirage in Las Vegas when airlines were grounded because of the 9/11 attacks on the World Trade Center, Packer played baccarat at $200,000 a hand and lost $30 million.

"I ONLY GAMBLED
WHAT I COULD AFFORD TO LOSE"

A fitting way to finish this sketch of the Prince of Whales is with a story told by his son as part of Kerry Packer's eulogy. His son claimed that he once asked his father why he gambled such crazy amounts. Instead of trying to justify his gambling with excuses, Kerry Packer replied, "I only gambled what I could afford to lose."

In spite of his mind-numbing wagers and the extent of his gambling proclivities, Kerry Packer was able to accomplish what few heavy gamblers can do – control his habit. How many gamblers, rich or poor, are capable of disciplining themselves to the point of only wagering what they can afford to lose? The magnitude of Packer's wins and his losses, and the size of his bets could fool the mind into thinking, "If he can win $20 million, I can win $20 million." The reality is you can't, not unless you have the richest man on the continent bankrolling you. For the average person, a $150 gamble may be the equivalent of Packer's $150,000 wagers, and a $1,000 loss may be the equivalent of a $10 million loss by Kerry Packer—a matter of perspective. In any case, the key to Packer's success was his discipline, odd as that may seem. Packer gambled the way others play the stock market—never cash out when you're down. He could afford to follow that rule, but the average Joe can't. A tribute to Packer's success at self-control is that despite his propensity for gambling, his family inherited an enormous fortune when he died.

Rest in peace Kerry Packer. You will always be remembered not only as the formidable Prince of Whales, but also, more affectionately, by casino staff who think of you as Earth's Greatest Tipper!

STU UNGAR: POKER'S GREATEST TOURNAMENT PLAYER

Besides the legendary whales and great tippers who are prominent in Las Vegas lore, other types of special players frequented the gaming tables of Sin City.

One of poker's all-time great professional players came to Las Vegas and, in time, made his home here. His genius IQ and photographic memory helped him become famous as a card player in several venues, including gin rummy, blackjack, and, in particular, tournament poker.

Stu Ungar

EARLY LIFE

Born Stuart Errol Ungar, in September 1953, and raised on Manhattan's Lower East Side, "Stuey" was widely considered the greatest tournament poker and gin rummy player of all time.

Stu Ungar was exposed to gambling at an early age at a bar/social club called *Foxes Corner*, owned by his father, a reported loan shark. The club doubled as a gambling establishment. Despite his father's attempts to keep Stu from gambling after seeing the effects of the addiction on customers, the young man began playing underground gin for money and quickly made a name for himself.

Stu's father died of a heart attack in 1966, and with his mother virtually incapacitated by illness, Stu drifted about the New York underground gambling scene until the age of 18. He became friends with alleged organized crime figure Victor Romano, who served as his mentor. Romano was regarded as one of the best, if not the best, card players of his time. Legend has it he could recite the spelling and definition of all the words in the dictionary (a skill acquired in prison), and he excelled at figuring odds.

Those who knew him said Stu was infamous for his arrogance and for routinely berating aloud the play of opponents he considered beneath him, which included just about everyone. Stu's relationship with Romano gave him protection from various slighted gamblers who bristled at his insensitive attitude and assassin-like playing style. One opponent reportedly tried to bludgeon him with a chair after Stu defeated him at gin rummy played at a bar. A few days after the incident the assailant who attacked Stu was found shot to death.

1980 AND 1981 WSOP MAIN EVENT TITLES

In 1980, at age 27, Stu Ungar entered for the first time a Texas Hold'em tournament called the Super Bowl of Poker. He finished 34th out of 41 players. Gabe Kaplan won the title that year. Later the same year Stu entered the World Series of Poker (WSOP) and won the main event, defeating Doyle Brunson and becoming the youngest champion in history. In 1989 he was surpassed by Phil Hellmuth, who later lost to Peter Eastgate in 2008, and to Joseph Cada in 2009.

Stu Ungar, nicknamed "The Kid" because he looked so young, won the main event in 1981, defeating Perry Green heads-up at the final table. Just before the main event, Stu had been barred from Binion's Horseshoe (the sponsor of the WSOP) by Benny Binion, because he spat in the face of a poker dealer after losing a sizable pot in a high stakes game.

Ungar's reputation and his ability to capture media attention won out. After Binion's son, Ted, reminded his father that Ungar's presence would be good for business, Benny allowed Stu Ungar a seat at the table. The experience should have served as a lesson to Ungar, who was notorious throughout his career for abusing dealers.

OTHER WSOP TITLES

Stu Ungar went on to win a third title in 1981, in the $10,000 buy-in Deuce to Seven Draw event, defeating 1978 champion Bobby Baldwin and earning a $95,000 cash prize. He won his third title in the 1983 WSOP $5,000 Seven Card Stud event, out-playing Dewey Tomko, and earning $110,000.

Though dropping out of high school in the 10th grade, Stu went on to win over $30 million in a lifetime spent at the poker table. He became such a great gin rummy player that later in life no one would risk money playing against him; his skill at blackjack was so sharp he was banned from playing in casinos, eventually unable to play blackjack in Las Vegas or anywhere else. Remarkably, Bob Stupak, owner of Vegas World Casino (later the Stratosphere) bet $100,000 that Stu could not count down a six-deck shoe to determine the final card in the shoe. Stu won the bet. That was in 1977.

In 1982 Stu Ungar married, and he and his wife, Madeline, had a daughter, Stefanie, that same year. In addition, he legally adopted Madeline's son from her first marriage, Richie. The boy adored "the Kid" poker great and took his step father's surname.

In 1986 Stu and Madeline divorced. Alas, Richie committed suicide three years later, shortly after his high school prom.

In 1997, a near-broke Stu Ungar convinced executives at downtown's Lady Luck to let him play single-deck blackjack. Aware of his reputation as a card counter, casino management agreed on condition his betting would be restricted to a high and low limit, thus somewhat limiting Stu's edge in counting cards. Stu continued to play blackjack at the Lady Luck for six months, building his bankroll up to as much as $300,000, before going bust.

BETTING THE HORSES AND DRUG USE

Stu Ungar noted in his biography that he first began using cocaine around 1979 on the advice of fellow poker players. The drug was recommended because of its ability to keep a person awake and energized for extended periods, useful during marathon poker sessions. Recreational use, however, soon led to addiction.

His drug addiction escalated to such extreme usage that in 1990, during the WSOP main event, Stu Ungar was found on the third day of the tournament unconscious on the floor of his hotel room from a cocaine overdose. However, Stu had such a chip lead in the tournament at the time that even when the dealers kept taking his blinds out every round of play, Stu still finished 9th and earned $20,500 in prize money. (In Texas hold'em poker the two players to the left of the button are obligated to post "blinds." The large blind is typically twice the amount of the small blind.)

Ungar never managed to lick his drug addiction, hoping only to stay alive long enough to see his daughter grow up. His friends, including poker great Mike Sexton, predicted he wouldn't live to see his fortieth birthday.

Those who knew Stu Ungar well said he would lose most of his poker table winnings betting on horses or sports. He was always hungry for "action." Several of Stu's friends, including Mike Sexton, tried to encourage him to enter drug rehab. Stu refused, saying he knew people who had been to rehab, and told him drugs were easier to obtain in rehab than on the street.

(Apparently, drug dealers targeted rehab facilities specifically because so many addicts are in one place).

STU UNGAR'S LEGACY

Other than the legendary Johnny Moss, Stu Ungar is the only three-time WSOP main event champion. During his poker career, he won a total of five World Series of Poker titles and more than $3.6 million in tournament winnings, over $2 million of which came from the WSOP. In addition, Stu won the main event at the now-defunct Amarillo Slim's Super Bowl of Poker four times, when it was considered the world's second most prestigious poker title. All told, Stu won a total of 10 major no-limit Texas Hold'em events, which required at least a $5,000 buy-in. Yet he entered only 30 major tournaments in his life. Most poker professionals regarded him as one of the great pure talents to play the game.

In 2001 Stu Ungar was inducted posthumously into the Poker Hall of Fame. Michael Imperioli portrayed him in a 2003 movie titled *High Roller: The Stu Ungar Story*. In 2005, his biography by Nolan Dalla and Peter Alson was published: *One of a Kind: The Rise and Fall of Stuey 'the Kid' Ungar, the World's Greatest Poker Player*. A year later, ESPN broadcast the EMMY-winning documentary, *One of a Kind: The Rise and Fall of Stu Ungar*. The film included interviews with his family and several close friends, and excerpts from tapes Stuey recorded in the final year of his life for an autobiography that was never published.

Mike Sexton, Stu's long-time friend, wrote, "Ungar's biggest problem was his sickness. For twenty years he abused himself with drugs. I can't help but think what might have been. What a waste. His life, even with the exciting times and conquests, was a tragedy. Drugs consumed him. I'm astounded when I think of what he achieved in poker, but I shudder to think of what he might have accomplished." Ungar died in 1998 at the age of 45.

CHIP REESE: POKER'S ALL-TIME BEST CASH-GAME PLAYER

Although Stuey "the kid" Ungar was known as poker's greatest tournament player, David Edward Reese, better known as "Chip" Reese, was widely regarded as the greatest all-around cash player who ever lived.

Chip Reese

Reese grew up in Centerville, Ohio, and early in his life suffered from rheumatic fever. The illness kept him home from elementary school for almost a year. During this time at home his mother taught him several card games. Reese later described himself as "a product of that year." By age six he regularly beat much older boys at poker. In high school he played football and excelled on the debate team, winning an Ohio State championship and participating in the National Finals.

Reese attended Dartmouth College, where he played freshman football, joined Beta Theta Pi Fraternity, participated on the debate team, and majored in economics. He also had enormous success in poker games with students and professors. Eventually he tutored his fraternity brothers at a variety of card games, including bridge and different forms of poker. After he graduated, Reese's fraternity named its chapter card room the "David E. Reese Memorial Card Room" in his honor.

Following his admission to Stanford Law School, Reese played in a poker tournament in Las Vegas, ending up in the money with a $60,000 win. By the time he was scheduled to start at Stanford, he'd earned over $100,000 playing poker in Las Vegas. As it turned out, that his first trip to the city was so rewarding and so much fun, he never left. After his first huge win, he resigned from his day job in Arizona over the phone and hired someone to fly to Arizona to clean out his apartment and return to Vegas with his car. Having moved to Las Vegas in the 1970s, Reese became a professional poker player and concentrated on playing in high-limit and no-limit cash games.

POKER CAREER

Chip Reese soon collaborated on the seven-card stud section for Doyle Brunson's best-selling poker book, *Super System*. In the book, Brunson described Reese as "one of the two finest young poker players in the world," noting that Reese was also the best seven-card stud player he had ever played against.

In 1978, Reese went on to win the $1,000 Seven Card Stud Split event at the World Series of Poker and the $5,000 Seven Card Stud event there in 1982. The reason his tournament results appear modest is that he spent most of his time concentrating on cash games instead of playing in tournaments. Later in 1991, Reese became the youngest living player ever to be inducted into the Poker Hall of Fame.

At the 2006 World Series of Poker, Reese won the inaugural $50,000 H.O.R.S.E. event, earning $1.7 million first-place prize money. During his professional tournament career, not counting cash games, Reese's total poker winnings exceeded $3.5 million.

As a tribute, the David "Chip" Reese Memorial Trophy was inaugurated in 2008 and given to the winner of the $50,000 H.O.R.S.E. event at the World Series of Poker.

Chip Reese died at age 56 at his home in Las Vegas in December 2007. He'd just been released from the hospital after a bout with pneumonia. His house on 9024 Players Club Drive in Las Vegas was listed for sale in June 2008 at a price of $5,699,500. Reese reportedly purchased the house with winnings from sports betting at baseball and from an investment in Jack Binion's Horseshoe Casino in Tunica, Mississippi.

THE "SUITCASE MAN,"
WILLIAM LEE BERGSTROM

Other than Chip Reese and Stu Ungar, who were skilled professional gamblers, a second type of player frequented the gaming tables of Las Vegas—a Texas gambler who wanted to try his luck and risk it all on one throw of the dice.

In the early 1980s, William Lee Bergstrom from Austin, Texas, decided to test the claim that Binion's Horseshoe in Las Vegas would book any bet, no matter how large, as long as you made it your first. Bergstrom arrived at the Horseshoe with a suitcase filled with money and said he wanted to bet the entire amount on the Don't Pass Line at craps. A casino supervisor took the suitcase to the cashier's cage, where the amount was verified at $777,000. The suitcase full of money was physically placed on the Don't Pass Line. The shooter, a lady, came out with a roll of six, then sevened out two rolls later. A casino supervisor counted out $777,000 in casino cheques, Bergstrom picked up the winning cheques along with the suitcase full of cash, cashed in at the casino cashier, and departed.

However, Bergstrom couldn't stay away long. He returned to the Horseshoe and won another single bet of $590,000 on the Don't Pass Line. A short time later he made a $190,000 bet, then again made a $90,000 bet, winning both. He always bet on the Don't Pass Line at craps. He returned in 1984 for the last time, making his most famous bet of $1 million. He lost.

Three months later Bergstrom was found dead in a Strip hotel of an apparent self-inflicted wound. Remarkably, he died $647,000 ahead from gambling at the Horseshoe and will forever be known in the annals of Las Vegas history as "the Suitcase Man."

KEN USTON: BLACKJACK TEAM PLAYER EXTRAORDINAIRE

Unlike Bergstrom, who played mostly craps on luck, another special player skilled at blackjack, Ken Uston, beat the casinos in Las Vegas and Atlantic City out of more than $5 million. He utilized a concept called "team play."

Uston grew up in New York City and at the youthful age of 16 attended Yale University, where he became a member of Phi Beta Kappa. He went on to earn an MBA from Harvard, and in the business world he eventually climbed the corporate ladder to become Senior Vice-President at the Pacific Stock Exchange.

After meeting Al Francesco in a poker game, Uston became fascinated with the game of blackjack and its inherent strategies. Francesco eventually recruited Uston to join his "big player" blackjack counting team, using a tactic that involved card counters, the players worked in small teams.

Uston soon broke off from Francesco and went on to form his own unique count teams with big players. Here's how the "team player" strategy worked: Team players took seats at various blackjack tables throughout the casino, where they counted down the remaining cards and used basic strategy to play their hands. When the remaining count turned positive for the player—a surplus of ten-valued cards remaining—the counter signaled the big player (Ken Uston) to enter the game. The big player would make large bets—sometimes at the table maximum of $5,000 or more—and exit the game when the positive count became negative. It was a remarkable scheme that proved highly effective, which some teams still use today. Inevitably, it got Uston unwanted fame, fortune, and the boot from just about every casino in Vegas and elsewhere.

After being barred from casinos around the world, he became famous as a master of disguise. He adopted various costumes to conceal his true identity, thereby enabling him to play blackjack. Uston gained more notoriety when he filed a high-profile lawsuit against the casinos, successfully defending his position. The New Jersey courts ruled that casinos could not bar someone simply for being skilled at counting cards at a blackjack table. In response, many casinos introduced procedural changes, such as increasing the number of decks in games, or limiting a player's bets in mid-shuffle entry to the game, or changing rules to increase the house edge.

Ken Uston was the subject of a 1981 segment on television's 60 Minutes, and in 2005 was featured in the History Channel's documentary series called *Breaking Vegas: "The Blackjack Man."* Uston died in 1987, in Paris, France, at the age of 52.

ARCHIE KARAS
—AN EXTRAORDINARY "RUN"

Perhaps the most legendary of all gamblers was a Greek immigrant named Archie Karas, renowned for one of the greatest winning runs in Vegas history.

After arriving in America in 1967 at age 17, Karas worked in a Los Angeles restaurant situated next to a pool hall. After work, he honed his pool skills, and in time made more money hustling pool than waiting tables. When the pickings got slim at pool and no one would play him for money, he began playing poker in Los Angeles card rooms. Karas quickly became a winning poker player, and building his bankroll to over $2 million. However, by December of 1992, except for a meager $50, he'd lost it all playing high stakes poker. Instead of trying to slow down and re-evaluate his situation, Karas decided to go to Las Vegas in search of bigger money games. What happened during the next three years became a legend—the greatest winning streak in the history of Las Vegas.

THE RUN BEGINS

When Karas arrived in Las Vegas in 1992 with nothing more than $50 in his wallet, he headed to Binion's Horseshoe. There, Karas recognized a fellow poker player from Los Angeles and talked him into staking him to a loan of $10,000, which Karas quickly turned into $30,000 playing $200/$400 limit Razz. Karas returned $20,000 to his backer, who was more than satisfied.

Razz is a form of lowball stud poker played for ace-to-five low. The object of the game is to make the lowest possible five-card hand from the seven cards.

With a bankroll of a little over $10,000, Karas next looked for action around the pool halls of Las Vegas. He found a wealthy and respected poker and pool player whom Karas called "Mister X." Karas was unwilling to reveal the man's identity for the sake of honoring his opponent's reputation.

"MISTER X"

Karas and Mister X began playing nine-ball at $10,000 a game. When Karas had won $200,000, they raised the stakes to $20,000, then to $30,000, and eventually to $40,000 a game. The gamblers and professional poker players who watched Karas play were awestruck. They had never seen anyone play for such high stakes. Karas went on to win $1.2 million at nine-ball. He then played Mister X at seven-card stud poker and ended up winning an additional $3 million from him.

With a bankroll of $4.2 million, Karas felt powerful. Willing to gamble everything he made, he continued to raise the stakes to a level few dared to play. He started playing high-limit craps at the Horseshoe, and after spending only three months in Las Vegas, Karas had worked his bankroll up to $7 million.

By then, many top poker players had learned of Mister X's loss to Karas. Only the top players dared to challenge Archie Karas at poker. Meanwhile, he patiently sat at a poker table in the Horseshoe's poker room with $5 million of his $7 million bankroll in front of him, waiting for any player to play him heads-up for such stakes.

The first to challenge Karas was Stu Ungar, three-time WSOP champion and widely recognized as the greatest tournament poker and gin rummy player of all time. Stu was backed by Lyle Berman, a business executive and co-founder of several Grand Casinos, himself a skilled poker player, Stuey lost $500,000 playing Karas heads-up at Razz. The two then matched up at seven-card stud, which cost Stuey and his backer another $700,000.

Chip Reese, considered the greatest all-time cash player at poker, was next to play Karas heads-up. Reese later said, "Karas had beaten him for more money than anyone else he ever played." Reese ended up losing a reported $2,022,000 in 25 games playing $8,000/$16,000 limit Texas Hold'em. After the drubbing, Reese said to Karas, "God made your balls a little bigger. You're too good."

Karas continued to take on many top players, from Johnny Moss to Doyle Brunson to Puggy Pearson. Many other top players would not play him because they figured his stakes were too high. Of the 15 players who took on Karas heads-up during his winning streak, only Johnny Chan and Chip Reese won from him, and that came after losing to Karas in the first sessions they played. After six months in Vegas, Karas had a great winning streak going and amassed a bankroll of more than $17 million.

Meanwhile, the poker action for Karas had mostly dried up due to the huge stakes involved and his growing reputation. To stay in action he turned to shooting dice. Karas got Jack Binion, the general manager at the Horseshoe, to raise the limit to

$100,000, but according to house rules the $100,000 had to be the first bet. Karas liked shooting dice because he could win $3 million or more quickly. It would take days or weeks gambling to win the same amount at poker. In a later interview with Tom Sexton, Karas said, "With each play I was making million-dollar decisions, I would have even played higher if they'd let me."

Again he got Jack Binion to raise the maximum bet limits. At the peak of his winning streak, Karas was making $300,000 bets on the dice table. Most remarkable though, "At one point in his run Karas possessed all of the Horseshoe's $5,000 cheques—over $11 million," wrote Tom Sexton in his online Sexton's Corner.

By the end of his incredible run playing a combined high-stakes pool, poker, and dice, Karas had won a fortune of about $42 million.

THE DOWNFALL

By the summer of 1995 the tide turned for Archie Karas. During a period of three weeks he lost $30 million. It began with an $11 million loss shooting dice. He then lost another $2 million to Chip Reese at poker. He switched to playing baccarat at $300,000 a hand, losing another $17 million, which all told came to a mind-boggling loss of $30 million.

With $12 million left and needing a break from gambling, Karas took a vacation in Greece. Upon his return to Las Vegas, he began shooting dice and playing baccarat at $300,000 a bet, and in less than a month lost all but $1 million.

With his last $1 million, Karas went back to the Bicycle Club in Los Angeles and played Johnny Chan heads-up poker in a freeze out event. Sexton also noted in his article, "Chan was backed by Lyle Berman, and they both took turns playing him. Karas preferred playing the both of them instead of just Chan, as he felt Chan was a tougher opponent."

Karas ended up winning and doubled his money, only to lose the remaining $2 million in just a few days shooting dice and playing baccarat at the highest limits at the Horseshoe.

In retrospect, one has to ask: How could anyone win all that money without putting some of it away for himself? This is the $42-million question. Perhaps we can answer it, or at least make sense of it, if we try to understand Archie Karas and what made him tick, starting with his own words:

"You've got to understand something. Money means nothing to me. I don't value it. I've had all the material things I could ever want—everything. The things I want money can't buy: health, freedom, love, happiness. I don't care about money, so I have no fear. I don't care if I lose it."

About his phenomenal run that endured almost three years, in an interview Karas brought up four regrets:

1. Not quitting at some point, even though he always wanted to play no-limit craps, in which he could wager $500,000, and would bet it all, from $1 million to $10 million, on the pass line if Jack Binion would let him.

2. Not pressing Jack Binion for at least single odds when he was making $300,000 flat bets at craps.

3. His big run was between 1992 and 1995, before the boom in poker by 2003. Poker was his bread and butter.

He said if he knew how big poker would get, he would have put away $10 million to play high-stakes poker.

4. His biggest regret was keeping too much money in the lock boxes at the Horseshoe, because the urge to gamble it was too intense. Looking back, it would have been wiser to keep most of his winnings in the bank.

During that awesome streak, Archie Karas virtually couldn't be beat. It was apparent that nobody could beat him at heads-up poker. Karas was quoted as saying, "I think today Johnny and Lyle have about 15 gold bracelets between them. I have none. I've always been the heads-up poker king, and truly am the uncrowned champion. If they gave away bracelets for heads-up poker, I would have 80 of them for sure."

In closing, Karas remarked of his legendary run: "To some, the biggest mystery of all was how I lasted so long, gambling this high over two years. Going up and down I had to have wagered over a billion dollars during this amazing streak!"

THE MEMORABLE
$50,000 TOKE AT THE ALADDIN

Prior to Archie Karas's incredible run, another fellow dice shooter had a very profitable night with a big win at the Aladdin.

However, it wasn't the amount of money he won that was so remarkable; it was the generous gratuity he left for the dealers.

The dealers of Las Vegas, especially those who worked at the MGM Grand and the Hilton, adored Kerry Packer largely because of his generosity as a great tipper. Here's a story about another generous man, one who, in one night, won over a half-million dollars shooting dice at the Aladdin Casino in Las Vegas.

This particular incident happened in 1981, when Ed Torres and Wayne Newton were ownership partners in the troubled Aladdin Casino, undergoing foreclosure proceedings at the time. Also noteworthy, the four dice dealers who worked the craps game that dumped some $500,000 that night were "table for table," which means they didn't have to share their tokes with any other dealers in the casino.

Here is what I recall being told to me by one of the crew who worked this particular craps game that night, when, in a short period of about 30 minutes, a craps table on swing shift at the Aladdin ultimately lost half a million dollars. This story is about a marker player, a casino customer who has an established line of credit with the casino where he or she is playing. Upon leaving the premises, the winning marker player customarily pays what is owed. In case of a loss, the amount owing is usually payable within seven to 30 days.

At midnight a marker player stepped up to a craps game. About the same time a big hand, called a "Duke" by seasoned dice dealers, showed up, where one shooter miraculously held the dice for about 30 minutes, the marker player was shrewd enough to bet the table limit, with maximum permitted odds, including big money on all the numbers. Before the dice stopped passing and finally seven out, the marker player had won about $500,000. Meanwhile, once the Duke was over, another player started shooting the dice. The marker player stopped playing and turned in his cheques so the box man could color them up. Once colored up, the marker player thanked everyone and headed to the cashier, appearing to stiff the dealers by not leaving a gratuity. After about ten minutes, the same marker player returned to the craps table where he had just won big and waited for a lull in the action.

When the dice sevened out, the marker player walked up to the stick man, put fifty hundred $100 bills on the table, or $50,000 in cash, and said, "Thanks fellas, this is for you." He smiled, then casually walked off into the night.

Once all the other players at the table were colored up and the game finally broke down, the box man did a count and reported to the shift manager how much the table lost. Because the loss was significant, procedure dictated that the shift manager inform the casino manager of the loss. At the time, the casino manager, Ed Torres, co-owner of the Aladdin, was home sleeping. When he was awakened and informed of the enormous loss he exploded. The situation grew worse when Torres learned that the marker player left the dealers a $50,000 tip, and for whatever reason, had not paid off his marker. Torres' anger turned to rage. He dressed and quickly drove to the Aladdin. The time was three in the morning.

Torres arrived at the craps table before the dealers' eight-hour shift ended. The dealers had already locked up their generous $50,000 gratuity in their toke box, which when divided four ways, came to $12,500 a man. Not too bad for one eight-hour shift at work. Torres explained to them that the marker player had checked out of his room without repaying his marker. He wanted the crew of dealers to give the $50,000 tip back to the house. If they didn't, he threatened to fire all four of them.

The result—each one kept his one-quarter share—$12,500. The next day, of course, all four were looking for new jobs. Ultimately, the $50,000 gratuity went down in the annals of Las Vegas lore as one of the greatest tokes ever given, even though it came with a lot of heat from the casino manager.

The night of that famous $50,000 toke, I was working at Circus Circus just north of the Aladdin on the other side of Las Vegas Boulevard. I was employed there as a dice dealer on swing shift for over five years, from February 1981 to August 1986, including six months as a break-in dealer next door at Slots A' Fun, also owned by Circus Circus. One night in 1982 my crew and I had a similar big toke event, though the money wasn't as huge and no dealers lost their jobs. The interesting part of the story concerns Gary O'Keefe, the table games shift manager on duty that night. Because of the unusual events that occurred, he almost lost his job. To the best of my memory, this is what happened.

NIGHT OF THE $100 YO-ELEVEN

Circus Circus is what in the gaming business we call a "grind joint." It's a family-orientated operation with small betting limits —$500 maximum on all table games—compared with some of the more upscale casinos, such as the Riviera across the street with a $5,000 bet limit, or *Caesars Palace* with a $25,000 maximum limit. Circus management was not interested in catering to big-money players. In fact, they typically discouraged it. Moreover,

Circus typically "sweated the money," meaning that under co-owner Bill Bennett's incentive policy, shift managers got a piece of the action, which averaged three times their annual salary. Therefore, when the casino began losing, the shift managers actually sweated the loss, as if it were their own personal money being given away.

The night in question, I was positioned on third base at the crap table. The stick man was Craig, an African-American from Alabama with a deep southern accent. Because we were so busy, the craps game had two people sitting box, along with two floor men standing over the game, not to mention the shift manager, Gary O'Keefe, watching over everyone.

Shooting the dice on third base was a well-to-do man who was betting the table limit with full double odds, as well as $2,700 in place bets on all the numbers. Every come-out roll, which occurs after a seven out or an established point was made, the shooter liked to bet a two-way eleven—which is a $100 bet for himself along with a $25 bet for the crew of dealers on the "Eleven." Every time the shooter made the bet on the 11, with his left hand he tossed out one black $100 cheque for himself, and a green $25 cheque for the crew. With his right hand he shot the dice.

I emphasize this two-way eleven of $100 for the player and $25 for the crew of dealers because at the time it was the maximum limit permitted on proposition bets. Proposition bets are wagers on the hard way numbers, such as an 8 for 1 payoff that a 5 -5 will roll before a 6-4, and on one-roll bets, such as 16 for 1 that an 11 will roll. These proposition bets are located on the center of a craps layout between the box man and the stickman.

As the game progressed, the dice were hot, the table was running out of cheques, and more cheques had been ordered. Everyone was making money but the house. The shooter, having just made another point, was on a come-out roll. By mistake, he tossed out two black $100 cheques and called out "two-way eleven," simultaneously shooting the dice. Gary O'Keefe, the shift boss, was first to react by saying "bet." The dice landed at the other end of the table, and Craig the stickman called out, "Yo-Eleven, Pass Line Winner."

I loaded up both hands with cheques and started paying the pass line. When I got around to where Craig stood, he bent down and said privately to me, "Hey, Andy, how did you like that mother-fucking call?"

I grinned back at Craig, and then thought, wow, that call was worth $400 a man!

Meanwhile, Gene the box man looked up at O'Keefe and said, "What do I do, boss?"

O'Keefe said, "Cut out $1,600 in green for the dealers." (The one roll proposition bet on 11 pays 16 for 1 at Circus). Craig already had so many green cheques in his shirt pocket he had to ask permission to put the $1,600 in green cheques in his rear pants pocket.

All told, that night each member of our crew made $1,450 in tokes, which included a $200 layoff to Gene ($50 from each of the crew). When our shift ended, as we walked out to the parking lot I slipped Gene two $100 bills folded into a pack of matches.

The next day, the casino manager, Tony Alamo, reprimanded Gary O'Keefe for booking a bet over the table limit. In the end, though, everything worked out. Gary O'Keefe kept his job and was eventually promoted to casino manager when Tony Alamo moved on.

Chapter 7
THE LAS VEGAS DEALER

*T*he American Heritage Dictionary defines "croupier" as "an attendant at a gaming table who collects and pays bets."

In 2009, the croupiers who dealt craps at the Wynn Las Vegas earned over $100,000 in tokes. That's not including their typically minimum-wage salary or other perks, such as free meals during an eight-hour shift. That $100,000 is the pinnacle of earnings for dealers in Las Vegas. For the rest of the city's table games croupiers, it is downhill from there.

If you wonder what it took for a craps dealer at the Wynn to acquire such a prestigious, high-paying job, or for that matter how anyone could obtain such a great dealing job at some of the other top Strip casinos, the answer is—unless you knew somebody influential—it was not easy!

Being a dealer in Las Vegas is kind of a crazy way to make a living. Early on, when I decided to make Las Vegas my home, I was advised to learn how to deal craps because it was more interesting and more challenging than other table games. And dice dealers were in greater demand. That advice was given to me by the late Tony Pack, the casino manager at the Sahara Hotel-Casino in the late 1970s.

I first came to Las Vegas in the autumn of 1963. I stayed and gambled at the Dunes, and I'll always remember being impressed when I saw a young dealer climbing into a late-model red Ferrari. I could tell by his monogrammed Dunes apron that he was a dealer at the Dunes.

Even back then I loved the city. I thought, why not live here? Later, in 1981, the opportunity came for me to make a career change, and Las Vegas became my home for almost 12 years.

WHAT'S IT REALLY LIKE "INSIDE" THE CASINO?

I'll try to share with you what dealing is like from a point of view "inside the pit," beginning with my breaking into the business downtown to my experience working out on the Strip. Overall, I worked in gaming 19 years, primarily as a craps dealer, although during the later years I was employed as a table games supervisor and pit boss.

When I first got into gaming it was a lot different than it is today. We worked table for table as dice dealers, which meant we kept our own tokes. When I broke into the business in 1981, there were two worlds in Las Vegas to work in—downtown, or on the Strip. You typically broke in, that is, earned your apprenticeship, downtown.

Once you gained some experience, you eventually got a job out on the Strip in one of the more up-scale casinos where the money could be ten times what you could earn downtown. The only way you avoided the downtown apprenticeship and broke in on the Strip immediately was to know someone influential, referred to as "juice." This term evolved from the days of The Mob, just before the mid-1960s when The Mob ran Las Vegas casinos. Before personnel departments made thorough background checks, casino dealers were hired on their reputation. Since dealers handle a lot of money, casinos were primarily concerned with hiring someone who wouldn't steal. Thus, if someone vouched for you, you were said to be trusted, or "juiced in," and the person who vouched for you was your "juice."

There was a time when table games dealers in many Las Vegas casinos went for themselves—in other words, didn't pool their tokes. In time, though, the human frailty of greed showed its ugly face. For instance, in order to be assigned a prime table and earn more tokes, blackjack dealers often bribed the scheduler. Soon, there was too much dissention, with dealers quibbling amongst themselves about other dealers earning more money. As a result, management at some unknown casino decided to have blackjack dealers pool their tokes to make it fair for everyone. In time, most of the casinos citywide followed suit and began pooling tokes among most table games dealers, although craps dealers— especially on the Strip—usually went for themselves.

STRIP VERSUS DOWNTOWN

Casino dealers are paid an hourly wage and earn about the same amount citywide. The difference shows up in the tips they earn, which can vary from $20 a day downtown to $200 or more out on the Strip.

Before the Internal Revenue Service got involved and casinos didn't pool tips as they do today, the most profitable jobs were dealing baccarat, then craps, and last blackjack. Other good tip-earning jobs were cocktail server at some of the more upscale joints on the Strip, to showroom captain, bartender, and valet driver.

When I worked downtown the money wasn't very good, yet there was a lot to do, which made the work fun. All the dealers and the locals alike hung out at the Horseshoe, where drinks were 50 cents, you could play 25-cent craps and $2 blackjack, and the sky was the limit. You could dine at the downstairs café and enjoy the 24-hour, $1.99 ham-and-eggs special with toast and potatoes, a slice of bone-in ham the size of the plate itself. The poker games were the best there, too.

Down Fremont Street at the Four Queens, you could listen to the Platters singing in the Lounge Show and snack on a 50-cent shrimp cocktail at the Golden Gate. The best place to work downtown as a dealer, especially after Steve Wynn bought it in 1972, was the Golden Nugget. There the money and working conditions were the best.

With few exceptions, everywhere around town the dealers wore the customary black and whites—black pants, white tuxedo shirts. What visibly set the dealers apart from each other was the monogrammed apron of their casino. At Circus Circus, we were distinguished by pink, fluffy dealer shirts and the Circus monogram on our apron.

THE APPRENTICESHIP

Typically, Las Vegas dealers learned their trade in a special dealer's school and after graduation went to work downtown. Eventually they worked their way out to the higher-paying jobs on the Strip. When I broke into gaming in 1981, the downtown break-in joints were the El Cortez, the Fremont Hotel, and the Golden Gate. These places were renowned for turning out experienced personnel, especially craps dealers. Seasoned management people were patient with the rookies and had been breaking in dealers for years.

One exception to dealer's school were the downtown casinos who hired shills, gave them on-the-job training, and made them student dealers. Kenny Perry, a craps dealer who broke in at the Fremont Hotel recalled, "A shill is a casino employee who acts like he's gambling, in order to entice others to the table. It's called 'breaking in,' and it's a tough nut to crack." When you were a break-in dealer, the order of the day was to "Dummy up and Deal." This meant, do what you're told without asking any questions.

Graduation from dealer school meant a quick interview with the casino shift boss, who—if he liked you—looked at your application and hired you on the spot. If you had a lot of experience he gave you an audition on a live game. At one time casinos gave an applicant a polygraph test. Nowadays, the personnel department does the hiring along with a background check, credit check, and finally a drug test.

BREAKING IN AT THE GOLDEN GATE

After graduating from the International Dealers School in February 1981, I headed downtown to the Golden Gate Casino. There I met the day shift manager named Mack, who told me to fill out an application. Fifteen minutes after Mack looked over my application, he hired me. He signed a license application, which I took to gaming control, paid a $6 license fee, got fingerprinted, and received my Nevada gaming license.

I returned to the Golden Gate that afternoon. I was immediately handed a meal voucher and told to go, at the top of the hour, to craps table three to relieve the stick man. There I would be part of a five-man crew working only the stick, off and on, with another break-in dealer. Mack told me I would have to stay on the stick until I become proficient. Then I could learn to work both second and third base on a craps game.

At the top of the hour I did what I was told and replaced the stickman on craps table three. He left for his break and my nightmare began. At dealer's school we worked with five dice and a stick about 42 inches long. Not here, not on a live game at the Golden Gate. On craps table three, I had to deal with a stick 72 inches long and seven dice. Man, it was murder.

To give you an idea of how bad it was, Mike the box man had to periodically stand up to align all seven dice so I could push them with the stick to the next shooter. He picked up two dice and shot them. My first call was "six." Mack, the shift boss, yelled over the game, "How did it come?"

"Oh, the six came easy," I said. (It's important to clarify for the shift boss which way an even number of the dice lands, because of hard way proposition bets, such as an "easy" 4-2 versus a "hard" 3-3).

Mike, the box man, looked up at me and said with a smile, "Relax Andy, you'll be all right." Even with Mike's compassion, I still felt intimidated. Despite my having spent eight weeks in dealer's school learning this game, it seemed as if every player knew more about craps than I did. Holy crap, with Mack barking at me, I felt almost as if I was back in army boot camp. Then I got nervous, and the stick started shaking in my hand as I tried to hand off seven dice to the next shooter. I must have knocked over every place and come bet on the second base layout. Meanwhile, my nerves were a wreck and sweat poured from my brow.

Then the incident happened. Just before my first break, I handed off the dice to a man about six feet to my right. He selected two dice, and I put the remaining five back in the dice bowl. But this new shooter was a dice setter. Casino bosses hate dice setters, because they waste valuable time playing with the dice before they shoot them, and lost time equals lost money on a craps game. In the meantime, Mike the box man said to me, "Andy, tell the shooter to pick 'em up and shoot 'em."

As this was my first 20 minutes ever on a live craps game and having no tact whatsoever as a professional stick man, I abruptly told the shooter, "Sir, pick 'em up and shoot 'em!"

The customer glared at me but did exactly what I told him to do. He picked up a pair of dice and threw them—not down to the end of the table as a player would, but squarely into the side of my head. Ouch. It happened so fast I had no chance to duck. Mike quickly stood, grabbed the other end of the stick I held, and tried to settle me down. "Don't do it, Andy," Mike said. "I know you want to go over there and clobber that guy, but you can't! Relax, take a deep breath, and next time use a little more discretion with the shooter."

I shook it off, took a deep breath, and nodded. Mike sat back in the box. The guy who threw the dice at me really didn't hurt me. It was more of an insult than anything else. Mostly, my pride was hurt.

After arguably the most exasperating 20 minutes in my life, my relief finally tapped me out and told me to go on a 20-minute break. I was a nervous wreck, yet relieved. On the way to the break room I began thinking, "Why was this table so big? Why is this stick so long? Why are there seven dice on this God-forsaken layout?" Just as I got to the break room, Mike the box man walked up behind me, put his arm around my shoulder, and said, "Andy, remember that stick you just handed to that relief dealer?" Mike grinned at me. "Well, that friggen stick is still shaking!"

We laughed. My nerves felt better after those first 20 minutes working a live craps game. Mike and I became good friends after that. Later, in 1986, we worked together for two years at the Flamingo.

SWEATING THE MONEY

When Bill Bennett owned Circus Circus, the management, down to the table games shift bosses, got a piece of the action, which could amount to salary bonuses of $90,000 or more per person. However, getting a piece of the action came with a downside—the stress of worrying about the casino's money as if it were their own, especially if a heavy bettor started wining big. The bosses' lack of control over wins and losses only increased their frustration levels, which they managed to pass along to their employees.

If you operate a basic casino table game your p.c. (house percentage) stays within a certain range, typically between 11 and 15 percent. But what happens in most of these joints is that the bosses try to manipulate things. One guy wants the stick man to turn the dice every roll, another guy wants the deck cut half way, the guy relieving him wants the deck cut deeper, another floor man wants a shuffle now, his boss doesn't want a shuffle, one place allows players to surrender half their bet, another place disallows the surrender option. It's confusing and frustrating working for all these superstitious bosses. If they simply left the damn dice and cards alone, the p.c. will be there.

When I worked at Harrah's New Orleans Casino, I saw something in the employee handbook that said, "No sweating the money." I liked that company policy.

At Circus Circus, stress was part of the job. On the craps table, we dealers had to hustle to make any money, but if we got caught hustling bets, we usually got fired. One problem was we were not allowed to turn around to see who was standing behind us.

So, we learned to recognize who stood behind us by the shoes the bosses wore. When bending across the craps table to pay or take a bet, we could look down between our arms to the floor. Of course, at the beginning of a shift, the dealer had to be an expert at knowing the bosses' shoes if you wanted to keep your job.

CASINO JARGON

After an apprenticeship, the dealer learns the casino terminology—those secret words only casino people know. "George" is a person who tips or bets for the dealers. "Super George" is a very generous person who bets for the dealers. A "stiff" is a non-tipper, or someone who does not bet for the dealers. A "flea" is a bum. Vegas fleas come in two basic varieties depending on where they play: the downtown flea and Boulder Highway flea.

A "duke" is a long, extended hand shot on a craps table by a player who holds the dice for 20 to 30 minutes or more before a seven out. "Box cars" is a 12, and "aces" are snake eyes on a dice table. A "Skinny Dugan" is a loser seven at craps. A "snapper" is a blackjack. A "paint" is a face card. And a "barber pole" is a mixed stack of different color casino cheques.

BIG SCORES

Las Vegas dealers dream of that big score—making a lot of money. Fletcher Jones Sr., a big car dealer in Las Vegas, once won a great deal of money on a craps game at Caesars Palace.

For a tip, he reportedly gave each of the four dealers a choice of any new Chevrolet at his dealership. That was a great score.

In my 19 years in the gaming business, the biggest single score I ever made was $1,450 at Circus Circus in 1982, when we were table for table. At the Flamingo I earned a little over a thousand dollars in tips several times. One night a crew of craps dealers at the Aladdin each made $12,500 from one player.

Big scores like these are few and far between. The average is much smaller. In the 1980s, dice dealers at Circus Circus averaged $65 a day in tokes in addition to their salaries. During those years, dice dealers at the Dunes and Caesars Palace earned, on average, over $200 a day in tokes. At the Flamingo in 1986, our average was $150 a day. I remember three days at Circus Circus in February 1982 when we made zilch.

MAKING LAYOFFS

Whenever we scored, it was customary to make a "layoff" to the box man who worked the craps table at the time of the score. This was usually done discreetly by folding $100 bill(s) inside a matchbook, and after the shift was over handing it to the box man on our way out the door.

The reason for the openings for several dice dealers at the Flamingo, when I was hired in 1986, was that the entire graveyard crew had been fired—the dealers, box men, floor men, and pit boss. Apparently, hustling got out of hand at the Flamingo, a player complained to someone, and management discovered floor supervisors were accepting layoffs (payoffs) from the dice dealers in exchange for allowing the dealers to aggressively hustle. In the gaming business, to "hustle" means to ask or suggest to players that they make bets for the dealers.

PROMOTION FROM DEALER TO SUPERVISOR A PROBLEM

Another reason for excessive stress in gaming, especially on the Vegas Strip, is that table game supervisors usually earn less than the dealers they supervise. This often creates dissension among the ranks.

The irony is that to advance your career from a dealer to a supervisory position, such as to floor man or box man, one usually had to take a large cut in pay. In other words, in most Strip joints the dealers earn more than the floor people who supervise them, in some cases twice as much. At the Wynn Las Vegas, for instance, dice dealers earn twice the money the box and floor people who supervise them earn. When Steve Wynn owned the Mirage, he gave his floor people the added perk of free golf at his private golf course, a perk the dealers did not have. To make up for the difference in pay, other casinos have tried to take 10 to 20 percent of the dealer's pooled tokes to give to the floor. The decision to do that is currently on hold, until it can be reviewed by the courts.

As a countermeasure, many casinos introduced the position of dual rate, which means a dealer could hold a "dual" position as a combination dealer and supervisor, which plays out as follows: working one day as a dealer at one rate of pay, and another day as a supervisor at a different rate.

CHANGE IN PERSONNEL

Is there any security in gaming jobs? Lately, health insurance has been an issue. It costs a lot more to insure older folks compared with hiring casino staff in their twenties or thirties. That's why in 1995, many experienced table games people from Las Vegas over the age of 40 were laid off.

This doesn't happen to cocktail waitresses, because they have a union; so do busboys, restaurant waiters, and cooks. Nor does it happen to stagehands, musicians, and change girls, who also have a union.

For many people, including me, a job as a casino dealer represented a means to an end. The money was good, and the work interesting, yet after awhile, with all the stress, along with the fools who sweat the money—the work really gets old. Working as a Las Vegas dealer supported my unpublished writing, provided a basic living, and gave me money to invest in several rental properties that I eventually purchased during my 12 years in Las Vegas. Most people I knew in the business were in it for the money.

Casino dealers except poker dealers—usually work an hour at a time with a 20-minute break. If you like being busy, swing is the best shift to work. Swing shift tokes are usually the best. Day shift is slow, and graveyard even slower, but if tokes are pooled over 24 hours, all shifts make the same money. Back in the 1980s, making $150 to $200 a day extra in tokes was great money.

Unfortunately, the days of dealers going for themselves are long gone. Many tip earners under-reported their income or paid no taxes whatsoever. Pooling tokes through the cashier's cage, which is the customary procedure nowadays, gives the IRS a way of getting their fair share of income taxes.

A JOB SATISFACTION SURVEY OF DEALERS

Author on Fair Princess, 1993

Casino dealer jobs are in high demand, and casinos have long lists of applicants waiting to take on a job most dealers characterize as stressful and boring. In the 1980s, UNLV sports sociology professor James Frey conducted a job satisfaction survey of casino dealers in which 80 percent of respondents indicated a preference for a job outside of gaming, and 68 percent reported they saw themselves holding a non-gaming job five years down the road. Of the croupiers, 70 percent said they disliked their job and found it dull. The issue of job security fared even worse, with 86 percent of dealers indicating they had no job security, could be fired at any time, and were in the job for the short term only.[70]

As for me, my favorite times as a casino dealer occurred away from Las Vegas. When the Dunes closed in 1991, I took a job with Princess Cruises as a croupier, and for two years worked in the casinos aboard several of their luxurious "loveboats."

Chapter 8
TIMELINE OF SPECIAL EVENTS IN THE ANNALS OF LAS VEGAS

*S*urrounded by the vast Mohave Desert, a high-desert oasis beckoned the first humans to the region that in time would become Las Vegas. Encircled by barren mountains, the arid inhospitable region was nurtured by two fresh-water artesian springs—geological remnants of an underground river that had flowed 30,000 years in the past. Some 10,000 years ago, the springs erupted through the desert floor and created a lush oasis.

Gushing fresh-water springs attracted Native American Southern Paiutes, the first humans recognized to inhabit the area. Spanish explorers were known to have also passed through the region in 1776.

Undiscovered for centuries, except by local Indians, not until the early 1800s did explorers establish the bubbling water holes through travel diaries and maps.

1829: ORIGINS IN THE HIGH DESERT

Led by Spanish Scout Rafael Riviera, a tattered band of New Mexican traders stumbled upon the desert springs in 1829. They named it Las Vegas, Spanish for the Meadows.

Fifteen years passed before explorer John Charles Fremont led a group of scientists, scouts, and observers for the U.S. Army Corps of Engineers into the Las Vegas Valley, which was still part of Mexico. They made camp near the headwaters of the Las Vegas Springs in May 1844.

Over the years, the water in the high meadowland attracted other people too, such as cross-country mail carriers and prospectors that came to Nevada's famed gold and silver mines. Other than the Paiute Indians, and 30 Mormon missionaries who established a way station on the road between Utah and San Bernardino, California, most visitors to Las Vegas in 1849 found it distinctly uninviting. The climate was hot, of course, because the desert lay only 280 miles from one of the harshest places on earth—the Grand Canyon.

1855: MORMONS ESTABLISH A FORT

Encouraged by the availability of fresh water, Mormon leader Brigham Young sent a party of 30 missionaries from Salt Lake City to the area. At a site four miles east of the Las Vegas springs, the missionaries, led by William Bringhurst, constructed an adobe fort for protection, and farmed crops there. That same year, the first post office was established, named Bringhurst. The Bringhurst group learned of lead deposits in nearby Mount Palosi from the Paiutes. Nathaniel Jones was ordered by Brigham Young to evaluate the find. As the ore was mined from the ground, Jones had the miners mold the lead, but every time the smelted molds were opened the lead fractured. Unknowingly they were not smelting pure lead but a mixture of lead with a precious metal, and in January 1857 the inexperienced Jones abandoned the mining operation leaving the discovery of silver to future settlers.

1858: Missionaries abandoned the adobe fort they had established at the springs. Forty-five years later the missionary fort became part of the Las Vegas Rancho property acquired by the San Pedro, Los Angeles, and Salt Lake Railroad.

1861: March 2, the Nevada Territory separated from the Utah Territory and adopted its present name, shortened from Sierra Nevada, Spanish for "snowy range".

1864: NEVADA ADMITTED INTO THE UNION AS THE 36TH STATE

After the Mormons departed, the land surrounding the fort, about 2,000 acres, was taken over and farmed from 1865 to 1881 by Octavius D. Gass. A farm couple, Archibald and Helen Stewart, subsequently acquired the property when Gass defaulted on his loan. In 1882, Helen Stewart gave birth to Evaline La Vega Stewart, named after Las Vegas.

Archibald was murdered in 1884 by an unknown assailant, and Helen became responsible for the 2,000-acre Las Vegas

Rancho. She sold 800 acres to the railroad in 1902, and it was this acreage that eventually became downtown Las Vegas.

1869: Gambling is legalized for the first time in Nevada.

1902: Just over 33 years later, Montana Senator William Clark needed land for a railroad to realize his dream of connecting the Great Salt Lake with the Pacific Ocean. In those days, the steam locomotive required an abundance of water. For the price of $55,000, Clark purchased Helen Stewart's 800-acre site, which included the rights to the bubbling springs, and in time the railroad became part of the Union Pacific line.

The springs served as a water supply for Las Vegas until water stopped flowing in 1962. By then the Water District had tapped into Lake Mead. The region's historical significance earned the Las Vegas springs an entry on the National Registry of Historical Places in 1978. After extensive restoration, in 2007 it was named "The Las Vegas Spring's Preserve" and opened to the public, with several attractions including the Nevada State Museum.

1905: AUCTION HELD
BY MONTANA SENATOR WILLIAM CLARK

Senator Clark knew that his railroad required a town. From his acquired 800-acre parcel, Clark subdivided some of the land he didn't need for the railroad, and on May 15, 1905, sold each lot at auction for $500. Lured by newspaper advertising and $16 refundable round-trip train fare, more than 3,000 potential investors came to town—100 times as many people as had lived in Las Vegas three years before.

The sale of lots took place under a mesquite tree where the Plaza stands today, marking the birth date of the City of Las

Vegas. From these sales, Clark grossed $265,000, making a tidy 500 percent profit. With his successful land sale, Senator Clark earned not only the distinction of becoming the first person to make a fortune in Las Vegas but also lasting fame when the county in which the city is located was named after him.

In 1905, the first train arrived in Las Vegas, and the Overland Park Hotel opened. It became the Las Vegas Club in 1931. Mel Exber and Jackie Gaughan became its owners in 1961.

1906: THE INFAMOUS BLOCK 16 WAS BUILT

Located on First Street between Ogden and Stewart Avenues, Block 16 got its name from its designation on the town map that was used to create Las Vegas. Planners originally designed Block 16 to cater to the worker and traveler—a twofold intention of accommodating weary rail travelers needing a place to hang out between train stops, and rail yard workers who needed a place to relax after work. Inevitably Blocks 16 and 17 gained notoriety as the only downtown area where liquor could be served without licensing restrictions. Block 16 eventually distinguished itself from Block 17 by blatantly offering prostitution. In time, Block 16 became infamous as the source of the Las Vegas nickname of Sin City.

Other saloons on Block 16, such as the Turf, The Gem, and The Arizona Club, did not maintain a brothel. The first saloon and gambling hall was the Arizona Club, considered by most Las Vegans as the best bar in town until 1912. That year it changed management, and the new owner added an entire second floor over the bar to serve as a house of prostitution.

As the years rolled on, the brothels became cheap rooming houses—until 1946, when the city declared them hazardous. Block 16 was condemned and ordered demolished, and in time it was paved over for parking lots. Today, this infamous "Block" of Vegas lore can be seen behind Binion's Casino, just east of the California Hotel.

1906: The Hotel Nevada was soon renamed the Golden Gate, and in 1931 renamed again as the Sal Sagev—Las Vegas spelled backwards. In 1955, a casino was built underneath the hotel. Nineteen years later Golden Gate assumed the entire operation and the property became the Golden Gate Hotel & Casino.

1906: The Union Pacific Depot was built, just west of where the Plaza stands today.

1907: FIRST LAS VEGAS TELEPHONE

The first telephone in the city was installed in the office of Charles Pop Squires at the Hotel Nevada, today the Golden Gate Hotel & Casino. That instrument is on display on the first floor of the casino.

1909: The first block on Fremont Street was paved.

1910: GAMBLING OUTLAWED

Legal since 1869, gambling in Nevada was outlawed in October 1910 when the Nevada Legislature bowed to public pressure nationwide and revoked all legalized gambling in the state. Overnight, operating a gaming establishment became a felony and throughout Nevada discontented operators locked down their swinging doors.

By 1910, Block 16 businesses began moving towards prostitution instead of remaining sawdust saloons. Its brothels rented upper floors or back rooms to prostitutes, who gave a cut of their profits to saloon management for use of the rooms. The customers would get a dance, buy drinks, and both would go to the rented room. Many working girls did not actually drink alcohol while on the job, even though the customer bought her a drink; her glasses were actually filled with colored water. The prostitutes also got a cut from the saloon for getting the men to buy them drinks.

In the following years, Nevada law was relaxed a bit. Social games of chance were permitted, but prizes were restricted to items such as drinks and cigars, which had to be valued under $2. Soon, nickel slot machines became legal as well. But none of this appealed to America's crap-shooting, poker-playing gamblers, nor did it please the disgruntled operators who were required to pay annual license fees to local governments to run their clubs. Gradually the operators began going "underground," enraging state officials because nobody was paying licensing fees. Realizing that a change was necessary, the 35th session of the Nevada Legislature passed the so-called wide-open gambling bill in 1931.

1911: May 16, Las Vegas became an incorporated city with Peter Buol as its first mayor.

1919: WELCOME HOME STREET DANCE

To welcome home the doughboys returning from World War I, a Fourth of July celebration was held on Fremont Street. Festivities included a parade and a "street dance" complete with a full orchestra. After, attendees were treated to a baseball game played on a new field built on the railroad property west of downtown.

1920: PROHIBITION ENACTED

Under pressure from the temperance movement and other anti-alcohol groups, the United States Senate had proposed the 18th Amendment, which prohibited the sale, manufacture, transportation, and consumption of alcohol in the United States. The "Volstead Act," the popular name for the National Prohibition Act, became the 18th amendment in December 1917, was ratified by 36 states in January 1919, and went into effect on January 17, 1920.

The new law prohibited the sale of alcohol, but authorities did little to enforce the law. By 1925, New York City alone had at least 100,000 speakeasy clubs that served illegally produced alcohol to thirsty drinkers, who thought nothing of flouting the law.

Historians generally agree that Prohibition ushered in the Roaring Twenties and heightened criminal activity, especially the bootlegging of illegal alcohol.

During the 1920s, Prohibition was a law to be flouted by locals and visitors alike in downtown Las Vegas. Old-timers reported that the Sheriff often sat on a chair at the corner of First Street and Ogden Avenue watching patrons of Block 16 enter the saloons, which, by law, were supposed to be closed. Prohibition endured over 13 years, finally repealed in December 1933 by the ratification of the 21st Amendment to the U.S. Constitution.

1920: The first airplane landed in Las Vegas, a Jenny piloted by Randall Henderson.

1920: FIRST LOCAL CASUALTY OF PROHIBITION

According to Fremont Street historical facts online, "Where the Coin Castle stands today was the site of the Northern Club, opened by Lon Groesbeck of the Salt Lake City Brewing Company. He sold large glasses of American Beauty beer for five cents. In 1920, he was the first local casualty of Prohibition, when the district attorney found 23 pints of Old McBrayer in his room. He fled from the state to avoid a three-month sentence, and died a few months later."[71]

1922: CREATION OF THE BOULDER DAM PROJECT

To determine the equitable apportionment of waters from the Colorado River, a commission was formed with a representative from the federal government and one from each of the Basin states, Arizona, California, Colorado, Nevada, New Mexico, Utah, and Wyoming. The federal representative was Herbert Hoover, then Secretary of Commerce under President Warren Harding. Hoover presided over the governors of the Basin states and the resulting Colorado River Compact was signed in November 1922. Known as the Hoover Compromise, it paved the way for the Boulder Dam Project. Building of the dam would offer many benefits to the region, including the generation of hydroelectric power, flood control, and water for irrigation.

1920s: By mid decade, the Union Pacific Depot, which had been built in 1906, ran five through passenger trains daily to Los Angeles. Later, in 1940, the old Union Pacific station was razed to make way for a modern facility.

In 1923, Las Vegas sponsored its first rodeo.

THE LAS VEGAS CHRONICLES

1925: Fremont Street was paved from Main Street to Fifth Street. Four years later the Bureau of Reclamation visited Las Vegas to evaluate the city's potential as a housing center for the Hoover Dam workers. Also in 1925, the first long-distance phone call to Las Vegas was taken at the Union Pacific dining room, fondly called the "Beanery" by locals. It was located next to where the Plaza stands today and was known as the town's most popular spot for social gatherings.

Late in the 1920s, the building where the western part of the Pioneer Club stands today was operated as the Smokehouse. In 1930, it became the Las Vegas Club, and a year later received one of the first gambling licenses in Clark County.

1926: The first commercial airline flight, Western Air Express, was initiated from Las Vegas and a year later the first golf course was built in the Las Vegas area.

1929: The *Las Vegas Review-Journal* became a daily newspaper.

1929: Las Vegas High School opened.

1930: Pair-O-Dice Club opened, the first nightclub to locate on Highway 91, also known as the "Los Angeles Highway," which later became the Las Vegas Strip. The Pair-O-Dice operated as a speakeasy that offered alcoholic beverages (illegal during Prohibition), as well as gambling, also illegal. In 1931, the club was licensed to operate one blackjack game, one craps table, and one roulette table. By 1933, after the repeal of Prohibition, the club was licensed to serve beer.

By the mid-1930s, the Barrel House Beer Garden on Fremont Street became the city's hottest night spot. It featured a complete orchestra and dancing every night. A unique characteristic was a hole cut into the wall between the Barrel House and the adjacent

State Cafe through which patrons could order food. The State Cafe opened during Prohibition, but regardless of the law, you could get a coffee pot full of whiskey—if you knew the owner.

1931: GAMING IN NEVADA LEGALIZED

Gambling had been outlawed in the state since October 1910, but that changed in 1931 when passage of Nevada Assembly Bill 98 authorized all types of gambling—except lotteries. Within seven days of this historic bill's enactment, Governor Fred Balzar approved a new six-week divorce law. Together, these actions meant visitors could come to Nevada to both gamble legitimately and legally divorce a spouse faster than anywhere else in the country.

1931: CONSTRUCTION BEGINS ON HOOVER DAM

Thirty miles southeast of Las Vegas, six of America's biggest contractors began construction on a project of gargantuan scale, eventually spending almost $50 million, building what would become one of the world's great wonders: Hoover Dam. Originally known as Boulder Dam, it was planned to be built in Boulder Canyon, but the dam site was moved downstream eight miles to Black Canyon. The project name remained Boulder Dam until 1947, when it was renamed for Herbert Hoover, who played an instrumental role in its creation, first as Secretary of Commerce, then as President of the United States.

When it was completed in 1935, two years ahead of schedule, it was the largest hydroelectric generating station and the world's largest concrete structure, towering 726-feet high. It tamed the mighty Colorado River and created the huge reservoir, Lake Mead. The dam's completion provided Las Vegas with sufficient water to satisfy its needs for years to come.

Here are some pertinent facts related to Hoover Dam:

- Described as a concrete-arch-gravity dam, it is situated in the Black Canyon of the Colorado River on the border between the states of Arizona and Nevada.

- 112 deaths were attributed to its construction.

- Its hydroelectric generators produce 2080 megawatts of electricity.

- Water flows from Lake Mead through narrowing penstocks—the "pipe" that delivers the water to the generator's turbine in the powerhouse—reaching a speed of about 85 mph by the time it enters the turbines.

- It is presently the world's 38th-largest hydroelectric generating station.

- The dam created a reservoir named Lake Mead after Elwood Mead, the man who oversaw construction of the dam.

- In 1985, Hoover Dam was designated a National Historic Landmark.

1931: TONY CORNERO'S "GREEN MEADOWS" OPENS

Known as the Admiral Tony Cornero by virtue of the two gambling ships he operated off the California coast before he moved to Las Vegas, became the first casino operator to build a resort away from the downtown area. He and his brothers purchased a 30-acre site along Fremont Street near East

Charleston, and in 1931 built the plush Green Meadows resort. Although the hotel had only 30 rooms, it became a big hit with the upper echelon of local Las Vegans. Newspaper reports of the era mentioned that the resorts' popularity was likely due to the Corneros' serving the best bonded whiskey, unlike the Prohibition's "bathtub gin" that was usually poured at the nearby downtown sawdust joints.

Though the Corneros were reputed to be bootleggers in California, when they invested in Las Vegas their intentions were to become legitimate casino operators. That would change in the early 1940s, when the notorious East Coast Mob and the Chicago Outfit came to Las Vegas. They had nefarious intentions about how to run their casinos.

1931: Alice Wilson Morris opened The Red Rooster Night Club where the Mirage is today, later as the Grace Hayes Lodge, Hi Ho Club, San Souci (1955), and the Castaways (1963).

1932: THE APACHE HOTEL OPENS DOWNTOWN

Originally built with 100 rooms and the town's first elevator, during the years of Hoover Dam's construction the Apache Hotel became a frequent stopover for Hollywood celebrities such as Clark Gable and Carole Lombard. Prior to the opening of the Horseshoe (the Apache is the oldest part of today's Horseshoe), the casino was also known as Tony Cornero's SS Rex and as the Eldorado Club. Later, in 1947, Benny Binion purchased the Apache and the El Dorado and converted them both into the renowned Binion's Horseshoe.

1933: Prohibition, enacted in 1920, was repealed.

1935: FRANKLIN DELANO ROOSEVELT DEDICATES HOOVER DAM

On September 30 President Roosevelt dedicated Boulder Dam, later named Hoover Dam, with a celebrated motorcade down Fremont Street.

1937: BUGSY SIEGEL AND MOE SEDWAY COME TO LAS VEGAS

East Coast Mob boss Meyer Lansky ordered mobster Benjamin "Bugsy" Siegel and Moe Sedway to Las Vegas to set up the national race and wire business in 1937. Ten years later, Siegel opened the famed Flamingo Hotel, after he muscled out its founder, Billy Wilkerson.

1938: Guy McAfee bought the Pair-O-Dice Club and renamed it the "91 Club." During the 1920s and 1930s before McAfee came to Las Vegas, he operated nightclubs in West Los Angeles. Most historians agree that McAfee was the first person to refer to State Highway 91 as "The Strip," figuring that a line of nightclubs would form there, as did the clubs he had owned along the Sunset Strip in Los Angeles. State Highway 91, aka the Los Angeles Highway, was originally known as the Arrowhead Highway.

1938: Also, a law was enacted banning saddled horses from entering casinos.

1939: In January, Ria Langham divorced husband Clark Gable, spurring Las Vegas to earn the title of "Divorce Capital of the World."

1940: The population of Clark County reached 16,414 residents; Las Vegas, 8,422.

1940: Beginning signs of the fabulous "Strip" appeared when resort casinos flourished by booking big-name entertainment. The development of colorful neon lighting began the transformation of then drab-looking Fremont Street into "Glitter Gulch," the nickname given to the downtown area of Las Vegas.

Without stringent control of gaming, a cohort of bootleggers and gangsters with suitcases full of cash came to Las Vegas to open legitimate casinos.

1941: The U.S. Army created a gunnery school that became Nellis Air Force Base.

1941: THE EL RANCHO VEGAS OPENED

The first casino resort to spring up on the hallowed boulevard called the Strip was the El Rancho Vegas. History books tell us that in 1941, on his way to California, hotel baron Tommy Hull had a flat tire. While sitting in the car waiting for his driver to put on the spare tire, Hull counted the number of cars passing what is now the southwest corner at the intersection of Sahara Avenue and Las Vegas Boulevard. He gazed at the open desert with picturesque mountains in the background, and had the vision to build his Las Vegas hotel right there. During its heyday, Hull's El Rancho offered its "Chuck Wagon Buffet," the largest in town accommodating 250 people. It boasted no charge for coffee. And breakfast was on the house from 4:15 to 6:30 a.m.

Later, about 1967, as part of his legendary $300 million spending spree, Howard Hughes paid nearly $8 million for the same parcel of land.

The El Rancho Vegas burned to the ground about six in the morning on June 17, 1960, and to date the 66-acre site remains vacant, with nothing on it but desert cacti and a huge price tag from its owner, Hughes's Summa Corporation.

1941: The El Cortez opened downtown.

1941: Infamous Block 16, the town's notorious red-light district since 1906, was forced to close with the opening of the air base in 1941.

A year later, California gamblers Chuck Addison and Tutor Scherer opened the Pioneer Club.

1941: R.E. Griffith bought the 91 Club, which had been the Pair-O-Dice Club. He later added a hotel and renamed the resort the Last Frontier, becoming the second resort built on the Strip. After that, it was renamed the New Frontier, and finally the Frontier.

1942: CAROLE LOMBARD'S TRAGIC DEATH

During a war bond rally, actress Carole Lombard and her mother boarded a Transcontinental and Western Airline DC-3 airplane in her home state of Indiana to return to California.

Her flight refueled in Las Vegas, then took off. It crashed 23 minutes later into Double Up Peak near the 8,300-foot level of Mount Potosi, 32 miles southwest of Las Vegas. All 19 passengers and three crew members were killed.

1943: The Nevada Biltmore and El Cortez were constructed downtown. Three years later, the Golden Nugget, and more significantly the notorious Flamingo Hotel were erected.

The surge of carpet joints continued when the Thunderbird opened on the Strip in 1947, and the Desert Inn began operations in 1950. Then in 1952, the Sahara opened, with each of the following resorts opening in consecutive years; the Sands, the Riviera, the Dunes, the Hacienda, the Tropicana, the Mint downtown, and the Stardust in 1958. The Castaways opened its doors in 1963, and three years later, Caesars Palace, the Aladdin, and the Four Queens opened theirs. In 1967, the Frontier Hotel emerged, with Circus-Circus, the Landmark, and the International—which became the Las Vegas Hilton—opening in consecutive years.

1944: In October the Huntridge Theater opened, the first non-segregated theater in Las Vegas. In November of the same year Liberace made his Las Vegas debut at the Last Frontier.

1945: Wilbur Clark opened the Monte Carlo Club where the Northern Club used to be, and where the Coin Castle is today. Later, he started construction on the renowned Desert Inn, but he ran out of funds—like so many others of that era—and found that he'd been cleverly taken over, ending up in a precarious secondary position to mob ownership.

1946: BENNY BINION MOVES TO LAS VEGAS

As the reigning mob boss, a Texas gambler named Benny Binion was muscled out of Dallas. Along with his wife and five children, he moved to Las Vegas in 1946 and went into partnership with Kell Houssels, owner of the Las Vegas Club. Their venture created the Westerner Club. When the Las Vegas Club relocated across the street, Binion purchased the Apache Hotel and the El Dorado Club in 1947, opening them as Binion's Horseshoe Casino.

The Eldorado Club was also built in 1946. The site formerly housed Cornero's SS Rex, and before that, the Apache Club. The Golden Nugget also opened that year, distinguished as the first structure designed from the ground up to be a casino. It featured the world's largest gold nugget, the "Hand of Faith," displayed in the hotel's lobby. When Steve Wynn purchased the Golden Nugget Casino in 1972, it became his flagship property and the foundation for his future billions in wealth. Wynn ultimately remodeled the Golden Nugget, adding its first hotel tower in 1977, and developed the resort into the jewel of Glitter Gulch.

Significantly, 1946 was the first year the state levied a gaming tax on casinos.

1947: FILM STAR OPENS THE GRACE HAYES LODGE

Vaudeville headliner/film star Grace Hayes purchased the Red Rooster Club in 1947 and renovated it, naming it the Grace Hayes Lodge. In time, because of its prime location, this property changed hands several times, before evolving into the site where developer Steve Wynn built the Mirage.

1948: Clark County purchased Alamo Air Field and opened its first airport, later renaming it McCarran International Airport.

1950: THE DESERT INN (DI)
OPENS AS THE FIFTH STRIP RESORT

Opening as Wilbur Clark's Desert Inn, the DI became a very popular upscale resort featuring a picturesque 18-hole golf course. In 1967, where owner Moe Dalitz tried to eject Howard Hughes and his group of aides from the two top floors of the DI, the eccentric billionaire purchased the resort. It stayed in operation until 1997 when Steve Wynn bought the property, in time becoming the Wynn Las Vegas and Encore resorts.

Since the DI's 1950 opening, almost every major star of the last 50 years has played its famous Crystal Showroom. The many greats who performed there include Liberace, Bobby Darin, Cher, Frank Sinatra, Noel Coward, Neil Sedaka, and more. Comics and variety acts such as the Smothers Brothers, Dean Martin and Jerry Lewis, and Rich Little all performed at the DI, as did thousands of other top entertainers.

1950: In December the Kefauver hearings, officially named the *Senate's Special Committee to Investigate Crime in Interstate Commerce*, began their investigation into organized crime.

1950: In July, Hank Greenspun published the first edition of the *Las Vegas Sun* under the name the *Las Vegas Morning Sun*.

1951: MUSHROOM-SHAPED CLOUDS

Beginning in January, tourists headed to Las Vegas to witness distant mushroom clouds from their downtown hotels. Sixty-five miles northwest of Las Vegas lay the Nevada Test Site where nuclear devices were exploded above ground. Their distinctive clouds could be seen from 100 miles in any direction. The last "above ground" test detonation occurred at the site in July 1962; afterwards, only underground testing of nuclear weapons occurred continuing until September 1992.

1951: A 48-foot tall neon sign featuring "Vegas Vic" was erected in front of the Pioneer Club—a waving cowboy who greets downtown visitors with a hearty "Howdy, pardnuh. Welcome to Las Vegas!" Soon, the huge sign became the most recognized symbol of Las Vegas.

1952: SANDS HOTEL OPENS

The Sands was the seventh casino resort that opened on the Strip. It stayed in operation from December 1952 to June 1996. During its heyday, the Sands Hotel was the center of entertainment, playground to Frank Sinatra and his raucous cronies. Arguably the Sands' most famous claim to fame took place over a three-week period in 1960 during the filming of *Ocean's Eleven*. A special event was set up in the Copa Room called the "Summit at the Sands" in which the stars of Ocean's Eleven—Frank Sinatra, Dean Martin, Sammy Davis Jr., Joey Bishop, and Peter Lawford—performed together on stage for the first time. From that point on they were forever known, particularly by the media, as the Rat Pack.

Sands marquee

Besides the renowned Rat Pack, some of the greatest names in entertainment graced the Sands' Copa Room stage—the showroom named after New York's famed Copacabana Club: Judy Garland, Bobby Darin, Lena Horne, Shirley MacLaine, Marlene Dietrich, Jimmy Durante, Tallulah Bankhead, and Jerry Lewis.

The Las Vegas scenes of *Con Air* were also filmed at the Sands.

Today, the Venetian and Palazzo resorts stand where the Sands once stood.

1953: In July, Hank Greenspun and other investors launched KLAS Channel Eight, the city's first commercial TV station.

1955: NEVADA LEGISLATURE FORMS
THE GAMING CONTROL BOARD

Licensing of gaming in Nevada had been under the jurisdiction of the Sheriff's Department since 1931. The Gaming Control Board was developed in 1955 to implement and enforce the state laws and regulations governing gaming, thereby protecting the stability of the gaming industry.

1955: THE DUNES OPENS
AS THE STRIP'S 10TH CASINO

Much fanfare greeted the opening of the Dunes in 1955, making it a special Las Vegas event. However, it struggled from its inception because of its location at the southernmost part of the Strip. Frequently the troubled Dunes had to borrow money to stay afloat. Years later, that particular intersection evolved into one of the best locations on the Strip once development of Flamingo road was finished and the other three corners were built upon with casinos: Caesars Palace, the first MGM, and the Barbary Coast.

In 1956 the lovable Wally Cox, early television's Mr. Peepers, appeared in the showroom as a stand-up comedian. In January 1957 the Dunes became the first resort in Nevada to offer a topless show. It was called *Minsky's Follies.*

1955: The Moulin Rouge opened downtown on West Bonanza Road, the first African-American-owned hotel and casino in Las Vegas. Heavyweight boxing champ Joe Louis was co-owner. Unfortunately, the Moulin Rouge lasted only seven months before closing its doors. Joe Louis eventually became a casino host at Caesars Palace. After his passing in 1981, a memorial statue of the hard-hitting "Brown Bomber" was sculpted and placed on display near the Sports Book in Caesars Palace.

1956: ELVIS PRESLEY OPENS AT THE NEW FRONTIER

Elvis Presley's Las Vegas debut at the New Frontier was panned by critics, and within two weeks his name was moved from headliner to the bottom of the Frontier's marquee. After his four-week engagement he vowed to never again perform in night clubs. Nevertheless, 13 years later Elvis returned to Las Vegas projecting a new "Vegas Image" for his opening at the International, and he received rave reviews.

1956: The Fremont Hotel-Casino opened as the tallest building in the state of Nevada. Built by Sam Levinson for a cost of $6 million, the hotel originally had 155 rooms. In 1963 the hotel was expanded to include the 14-story Ogden Tower and one of the city's first vertical parking garages. In 1974, the Argent Corporation bought the Fremont, and it was subsequently purchased in 1983 by the Boyd Group.

1957: THE MINT OPENS
ON THE SITE OF THE APACHE HOTEL

The Mint Casino began operations in 1957, and in 1965 a 26-story hotel was added. In 1988 the entire property became part of Binion's Horseshoe.

1957: In September the University of Nevada at Las Vegas (UNLV) held its first classes.

1958: THE STARDUST OPENS

When it opened July 2, it had both the largest casino and the largest swimming pool in Nevada and was the biggest hotel in the Las Vegas area. The Royal Nevada had previously occupied the site where the Stardust was built.

The opening night lounge lineup featured dusk-to-dawn performances by Billy Daniels, the Happy Jesters, the Jack Martin Quartet, and the Vera Cruz Boys.

In the film adaptation of Nicholas Pileggi's novel *Casino*, Robert De Niro portrayed Sam "Ace" Rothstein, the general manager of the Tangiers, and actor Joe Pesci portrayed the fictional Nick Santoro, whose personality was made to resemble that of gangster Anthony Spilotro. Although the movie *Casino* was actually filmed across the street from the Dunes, several blocks south of the Stardust, bits and pieces of the Hoagy Carmichael song *Stardust* can be heard in the movie's soundtrack, a subtle hint as to the casino's true identity.

1959: WAYNE NEWTON OPENS AT THE FREMONT HOTEL

Affectionately known as "Mister Las Vegas," Wayne Newton, began his career at age 15 with his older brother, Jerry, and a group called "The Jets."

Also in 1959, the state legislature created the Nevada Gaming Commission to aid the existing Gaming Control Board in its duty to implement and enforce state laws and regulations governing gaming.

The Las Vegas Convention Center opened in April of the same year.

The famous "Welcome to Fabulous Las Vegas, Nevada" sign was erected, designed by Betty Willis.

Welcome to Las Vegas

1960: EL RANCHO VEGAS BURNS TO THE GROUND

Howard Hughes eventually bought the 30-acre parcel during his famous $300 million spending spree in the late 1960s. To this day, the location at the southwest corner of Sahara Avenue and the Strip remains vacant.

Also in 1960, the Nevada Gaming Commission developed Nevada's infamous Black Book, officially known as the state's List of Excluded Persons—a roster of people considered so unsavory to legal gambling that they are prohibited from setting foot in a casino.

This is the year Clark County population reached 127,016 residents and Las Vegas, 64,405. The downtown sign was erected on I-15.

1963: THE CASTAWAYS OPENS

Barely open a year, the Castaways ran into financial trouble in 1964. Six years later it was sold to Howard Hughes for $3 million.

Since 1989, the Mirage has occupied the site where the Castaways once stood.

1963: The Westward Ho Hotel and Casino opened on the Strip just north of the Stardust. Marketed as "the friendliest casino in Vegas," it operated for 42 years and was known as the world's largest motor inn.

1964: LADY LUCK OPENS DOWNTOWN

Set on 6.27 acres at East Odgen Avenue and 3rd Street, the hotel casino originally opened with 631 rooms. The property eventually fell on hard times and remains closed since February 2006.

The Beatles arrived in Las Vegas and performed two sold-out shows at the Convention Center.

1966: HOWARD HUGHES USHERS IN THE CORPORATE ERA

A crucial turning point in the chronicles of Las Vegas occurred when, in November of 1966, billionaire Howard Hughes came to town and began buying up casinos.

In 1966, Ben Goffstein opened the Four Queens on Fremont Street, named for his four daughters, Faith, Hope, Benita, and Michele. Originally the hotel contained only 120 rooms, but currently boasts 690 rooms. The casino is home to the Queen's Machine, the world's largest slot machine. The Four Queens was also a partner in renovating the downtown area and creating the Fremont Street Experience, completed in 1995.

1966: THE GLAMOROUS CAESARS PALACE OPENS

Built at a cost of $35 million in 1966, the creation of entrepreneur Jay Sarno, Caesars Palace was possibly the most beautiful casino resort in the world.

Furthermore, in 1966 Milton Prell opened the Aladdin. Before the Aladdin, the site was home to the Tally-Ho and Kings Crown Hotel. The Aladdin received a $3 million renovation, including a new 500-seat showroom named the "Baghdad Theater."

1967: SIEGFRIED & ROY DEBUT AT THE TROPICANA

The magical partnership originated in 1959 when these two men worked aboard a German ocean liner, the TS Bremen.

They debuted in Las Vegas at the Tropicana, and later became headliners at the Stardust performing in the popular show *Lido de Paris,* and *Beyond Belief* at the Frontier. In 1990 they signed a reported $57.5 million contract to headline in their own exclusive show at the Mirage.

1967: In May, Elvis and Priscilla married at the Aladdin.

1967: PLOT TO KIDNAP TED BINION

Late in that same year, Ted Binion, youngest son of the Horseshoe's Benny Binion, became the target of a near-kidnapping.

1967: EVEL KNIEVEL'S JUMP AT CAESARS PALACE

Visiting Las Vegas in November to watch Dick Tiger defend his WBA and WBC light heavyweight titles, Evel Knievel first saw the fountains at Caesars Palace. As an upcoming daredevil performer he decided to jump them on his motorcycle. After weeks of coaxing to get an audience with Caesars' CEO Jay Sarno, he succeeded in setting up the event for December 31, 1967.

Knievel tried to get ABC to air the event live on *Wide World of Sports,* but agreed only to consider airing a film of the jump later if Knievel had it filmed, and if it was as spectacular as Knievel promoted it to be. Knievel used his own money to have director John Derek produce a film of the Caesar's jump. Derek's wife at the time, Linda Evans, was the camera operator out of several on the set at the time who filmed the daredevil's famous crash landing. Knievel suffered a concussion and several broken bones that kept him in a coma for 28 days. After he recovered, he was more famous than ever. ABC-TV ended up buying the rights to the film of the jump, paying far more than if they had televised the jump live.

1967: The Nevada legislature passed a law enabling publicly traded corporations to obtain gaming licenses. The law was further refined in 1969.

1968: CIRCUS CIRCUS OPENS ON THE STRIP

Jay Sarno's Circus Circus opened its doors directly across the Boulevard from the Riviera. Remarkably, it was built without an adjoining hotel, causing the property to struggle financially until 1972 when Bill Bennett and his partner, Pennington, built a 395-room tower.

Anthony Spilotro, the mob's "enforcer" and point man in Vegas, later purchased the gift shop concession at Circus Circus from Jay Sarno at a price of $70,000.

1969: THE INTERNATIONAL OPENS WITH BARBRA STREISAND

Kirk Kerkorian's $60 million off-Strip creation along Paradise Road emerged as an enormous success, and in time propelled Kerkorian to multi-billionaire status. According to the *Review-Journal,* "The first song ever sung in the International showroom was by Barbra Streisand, and the song, believe it or not, was 'I've Got Plenty Of Nothing.' She was singing it in a hotel that—at the time—had 1,519 rooms, six restaurants and an eight-acre roof with a putting green on it."

1969: ELVIS PRESLEY'S COMEBACK AT THE INTERNATIONAL

Following a 13-year absence from performing in Las Vegas, the "king of rock 'n' roll" headlined an entirely new show when he stepped onto the stage at the International as "Vegas Elvis." He performed with more pizzazz, backed by a 35-piece orchestra and 15 gospel-soul singers. He went on to perform successfully at the International to sellout crowds until his tragic death in 1977. Today, a life-sized statue of him stands adjacent to the showroom, along with a display containing one of his guitars and several of the outfits he wore.

1969: ORIGINS OF THE MINT 400 DESERT ROAD RACE

Norm Johnson, public relations director for the Mint Hotel in Las Vegas, established the first "Del Webb Mint 400 Desert Rally." The idea had taken root for Johnson in 1968, and the rally endured for two decades in Southern Nevada as one of the top off-road races in the world. The Mint 400 was scratched in 1968 for reasons unknown.

1970: ORIGINS OF THE WORLD SERIES OF POKER (WSOP)

Sponsored by Harrah's Entertainment since 2005, the WSOP is a world-renowned series of poker tournaments held annually in Las Vegas. The first WSOP was held at the Horseshoe in downtown Las Vegas, wherein Benny Binion invited six of the best-known poker players to play over a set period, with the winner determined by secret ballot.

Early on, the WSOP expanded slowly. It took 12 years before the WSOP attracted 52 participants. In the early 1980s satellite tournaments were introduced, which gave players an opportunity to win their way into various events. In 1987 the WSOP series attracted 2,100 entrants. Participation in the Main Event peaked in 2006, with 8,773 players competing and Jamie Gold winning the Main Event prize of $12 million.

1970: The International Hotel was sold to the Hilton Hotels Corporation and in 1971 renamed the Las Vegas Hilton.

1971: THE UNION PLAZA OPENS DOWNTOWN

A group of businessmen, including J.K. Houssels Jr., Jackie Gaughan, owner of four Las Vegas casinos, opened the Plaza. In 1986, Jackie Gaughan became chairman of the board.

1972: Liberace began performing in the showroom of the Las Vegas Hilton, drawing sold-out crowds twice a night and earning a reported $300,000 a week—at that time a record amount for individual entertainers in Las Vegas.

1973: STEVE WYNN BECOMES THE GOLDEN NUGGET'S MAJORITY SHAREHOLDER

With helpful advice from banker E. Parry Thomas, Steve Wynn, along with several silent partners, purchased a stake in the Golden Nugget in 1972. He increased his share in 1973 and became controlling stockholder, the youngest casino proprietor in Las Vegas. In 1976 he opened the first hotel tower, and the resort earned its first four-star rating. In 1984 the new showroom opened along with an added second hotel tower.

Wynn spent $60 million converting the Nugget into the classiest downtown resort, a development which, in due course, became very profitable and propelled Wynn's rise to prominence in the gaming industry.

1974: New Year's Eve, Sam and Bill Boyd opened the 781-room California Hotel and Casino one block north of Fremont Street at 12 Ogden Avenue. The resort offered a true island atmosphere throughout, including the tropical motif of its guest rooms, which borrowed a page from the Hawaiian home of many of its frequent visitors. To date, it remains as one of the Boyd Group's several properties.

1975: Nevada's gaming revenues topped the $1 billion mark for the first time.

1977: The Maxim Hotel and Casino opened in July and thrived into the late 1980s, then began to decline as flashier, newer resorts opened on the nearby Strip. In 1999 the casino closed but the hotel remained open without gaming. In 2001, the resort closed in its entirety. It stood vacant until re-opening in 2003 as the Westin Casuarina, using the name of its successful resort in the Cayman Islands. The Maxim was the location of the shooting death of rapper Tupac Shakur.

Clark County gaming revenues surpassed the $1 billion mark in 1977. The state legislature passed a foreign gaming law allowing Nevada-based casino owners to operate casinos outside Nevada's borders.

1978: The Las Vegas Hilton was the site where Leon Spinks defeated Muhammad Ali for the World Heavyweight Boxing Championship.

1979: The Barbary Coast opened in March at a cost of $11.5 million. The 198-room casino hotel on the northeast corner of Flamingo road and the Strip was built by Michael Gaughan and became part of Coast Casinos Inc. Later it was sold to the Boyd Group and renamed Bill's Gamblin Hall & Saloon. The first entity built on this site was the Times Square Motel.

1979: The Las Vegas Hilton, previously the International, expanded to the largest resort complex in the world, with 3,174 rooms and more than 3,600 employees. From its original Y-shaped configuration, the mega resort added the East Tower in 1975, the North Tower in 1978, and a North Tower Annex in 1979. When Baron Hilton reportedly was offered $400 million for the 30-story behemoth, his answer was, "it's not enough."

1979: The original Sam's Town Hotel & Casino opened on the Boulder Highway.

1980: THE FIRE AT THE MGM GRAND

Faulty wiring behind the wall of a first-floor restaurant was reportedly the cause of the worst disaster in the city's history, killing 87 people.

Author's Note: I hold fond memories of the original MGM. After the tragic fire, the refurbished MGM opened with a great poker room next to an escalator. While playing poker there, I saw comedian/actor Dudley Moore amusing onlookers by trying to walk down the "Up" escalator. All of us in the poker room were laughing. Another celebrity at the MGM was comedian/television star Redd Foxx, who frequently played $1 to $5 seven-card stud there.

1980: THE SUNDANCE HOTEL OPENS DOWNTOWN

Moe Dalitz's Sundance Hotel & Casino opened as the tallest building downtown. Eight years later it was sold and renamed Fitzgeralds, and is currently owned by Jerry Turk and Phil Griffith.

1981: Almost three months after the fire at the MGM Grand, a fire broke out in the top floors of the Las Vegas Hilton. Eight people died.

1981: The new El Rancho was built by Ed Torres but soon fell on hard times. The property sat unused for eight years before its implosion, which made room for Turnberry Condominiums.

Las Vegas celebrated its Golden Anniversary of gaming.

1981: THE CAESARS PALACE GRAND PRIX

Caesars Palace spent nearly $7 million converting one of its parking lots into a Grand Prix race track and promoting upcoming Formula 1 races. Unfortunately, the races lasted only four events, ending in 1984. Due to the extreme desert heat, the Grand Prix races turned out to be unpopular among the drivers.

1983: CASHMAN FIELD OPENS

Owned and operated by the Las Vegas Convention and Visitors Authority, the 9,334-seat stadium is the home field of the Las Vegas 51s minor league, the AAA affiliate of the Toronto Blue Jays baseball team.

THE LAS VEGAS CHRONICLES

1985: NATIONAL FINALS RODEO (NFR) COMES TO LAS VEGAS

Originating in Dallas, Texas, in 1959, and known popularly as the "super bowl of rodeo," the NFR was established to determine the world champion in each of rodeo's seven main events: calf roping, steer wrestling, bull riding, and saddle-bronc riding. Nowadays, the 10-day NFR is every December at the Thomas & Mack Center in Las Vegas, bringing in more than 170,000 fans.

1987: JAPANESE BILLIONAIRE BUYS THE DUNES

Investor Masao Nangaku purchased the Dunes for a reported $155 million. He was unable to make it a financial success, primarily because of competition from the newer and more exciting mega-resorts being built, such as the Mirage. The Dunes was sold for the last time in November 1992 to Steve Wynn for $75 million. Then, after its historic implosion in 1993, Wynn built the $1.6-billion mega-resort Bellagio in its place, which opened to glowing reviews in October 1998.

1987: The Castaways closed and was later purchased by Steve Wynn. It was eventually demolished to make land available for the Mirage, and later for Treasure Island adjacent to it.

The land that the Mirage and Treasure Island stand on today has a storied past. Back in 1931 the Red Rooster Nite Club was the first business built on the site. That structure was destroyed by fire in 1933, later rebuilt. In 1942 the San Souci Auto Court was erected adjacent to the Red Rooster. In time, the Rooster merged with Sans Souci Hotel, Inc., which in October 1957 opened as the Sans Souci Hotel. In 1963, the Castaways Hotel-Casino was built on the site but did not succeed financially. Eventually it was sold and renamed Oliver's New Castaways Casino. During the 1960s, in an attempt to drum up business, the owners built a 15,000-gallon aquarium behind the hotel's front desk and staged a show three times a day with three naked women swimming in the aquarium.

In February 1970, as part of his historic spending spree to acquire Nevada real estate, billionaire Howard Hughes purchased the Castaways for $3 million. The troubled resort operated until July 1987, when it and the surrounding property were purchased by Steve Wynn.

1988: Arizona Charlies opened in April on Decatur between Charleston Boulevard and what was formerly West Fremont Street (presently US 95.) The popular resort is the result of the Becker family, long-established developers in Las Vegas. The casino's namesake was a distant Becker relative, "Arizona" Charlie Meadows, a sharpshooter in Buffalo Bill's Wild West Show.

1988: THE PEPCON EXPLOSION

Located on the Boulder Highway, PEPCON was one of two American manufacturers of the product ammonium perchlorate, an oxidant used in the Space Shuttle's solid fuel rockets. With the space shuttle program frozen as a result of the 1986 Challenger loss, large quantities of the product had to be stored on-site.

On May 4, 1988, employees making repairs with a welding torch inadvertently ignited a chemical fire, causing subsequent explosions at the Pacific Engineering Production Company of Nevada (PEPCON) plant. The disaster claimed two lives, injured 372 people, and caused over $100 million in damages. Of the seven total explosions, the two largest produced seismic waves measuring 3.0 and 3.5 on the Richter scale. More than 8 million tons of ammonium perchlorate exploded, leaving a crater 15 feet deep and 200 feet wide.

1988: Binion's Horseshoe acquired the adjacent Mint Hotel from the Del Webb Corp. for $27 million, more than doubling the size of the Horseshoe's casino by adding a 24-story 296-room high-rise tower.

1989: STEVE WYNN'S MIRAGE USHERS IN A "NEW LAS VEGAS"

With the opening of the luxurious new mega-resort the Mirage, resort operators in Las Vegas were virtually catapulted into an entirely new way of thinking that set the trend for future Strip resorts. The Mirage pioneered new standards for design, ambiance, and entertainment, thereby precipitating the development of a class of super-resorts in Las Vegas felt for years after.

Wynn hired Siegfried and Roy in 1990 to perform as headliners at the Mirage for an annual guarantee of $57.5 million, and in 2001 they signed a lifetime contract with the resort for an undisclosed amount.

Over the years the Mirage proved to be very successful, and it, along with the Golden Nugget downtown, would ultimately be the foundation for Wynn's Billionaire status. He would also build Treasure Island adjacent to the Mirage, then the Bellagio on the old Dune's site, and the Beau Rivage in Biloxi, Mississippi. Later he would create the Wynn Las Vegas, and Encore, on the site of the old Desert Inn. Then in 2010, Wynn Macau would open on the island of Macau, China.

1990: THE EXCALIBUR OPENS

At the time of its opening, The Excalibur was the world's largest hotel, with 4,032 rooms.

1990: Clark County reached a population of 741,459 residents; Las Vegas, 258,295.

1990: The victors of "March Madness," NCAA basketball champions the UNLV "Runnin Rebels," were honored with a victory motorcade by thousands of Las Vegans who lined the streets of downtown.

1990s: The Stratosphere Tower was erected, conceived by casino owner Bob Stupak. The Stratosphere stood on the site of his Vegas World casino on Las Vegas Boulevard just north of Sahara Avenue.

1990: The Sante Fe Casino opened with a warm southwestern atmosphere, quickly becoming a local favorite. The property expanded in 1994, then in June 2000 Station Casinos purchased it for $205 million and renamed it Sante Fe Station.

1992: Downtown's infamous Block 16 came to an end as the demolition of old buildings on the site made way for a covered parking lot.

1992: The first Las Vegas Bowl was held at the Silver Bowl.

1992: Main Street Station opened between Ogden and Stewart Avenues in downtown Las Vegas, originally intended as a paid-admission nighttime entertainment complex with a casino on the side. Owned and operated by an Orlando, Florida, businessman lacking experience in running casinos, Main Street Station went belly up less than a year after its opening. In 1997, the Boyd Group reopened the property, adding a brewpub in the process. The casino is said to be the most unusual in town, thanks largely to the concept by the original owner of a gentlemen's 20th century pub. Today the casino contains enough antiques, original art, and oddities to furnish a museum.

1993: The five-acre amusement park named Grand Slam Canyon Adventuredome at Circus Circus opened in August. The facility featured 25 rides and attractions, including the Canyon Blaster roller coaster, a rock-climbing wall, an 18-hole miniature golf course, an arcade, and clown shows.

1993: The Luxor opened in October with 2,526 rooms. The gross win by Nevada casinos surpassed the $6 billion mark for the first time.

1993: TREASURE ISLAND (TI) OPENS ADJACENT TO THE MIRAGE

Originally conceived by innovative developer Steve Wynn, the $450-million TI celebrated its grand opening with 2,664 rooms and 220 suites. Some of its many features included a modern tram connecting it to the nearby Mirage, a large video arcade, and icons such as its skull-and-crossbones Strip marquee. a pedestrian bridge to the adjacent Fashion Show Mall shopping center. Another attraction in front of the casino was Buccaneer Bay, where onlookers viewed staged pirate battles nightly.

In 2003 the resort largely abandoned its original pirate theme, which was intended to attract families with its whimsical pirate features. Instead, TI became a more contemporary resort focused on adult interests.

In March 2009, real estate investor Phil Ruffin became TI's owner of record.

1993: KERKORIAN OPENS THE SECOND MGM GRAND

Opening in December, the massive MGM Grand was built on the old Marina site at the northeast corner of the Strip and Tropicana Avenue. Originally designed as a "family-friendly" destination resort, with the Adventure Theme Park built behind the casino, however all that changed in 2002 when Kerkorian announced the resort would have a more contemporary adult theme. Ultimately, the former theme park was developed into a condominium complex, and parts of the casino were renovated to attract more adults.

1993: IMPLOSION OF THE DUNES

On October 22, with television cameras rolling and 250,000 people in attendance, Steve Wynn orchestrated a simulated cannon shot from the pirate ship at Treasure Island a mile away that a few seconds later made the Dunes collapse from the planned explosive demolition.

Author's Note: Prior to the implosion of the Dunes, I had the opportunity to play blackjack there at the same table with Telly Savalas. I remember it well, because it was a $25 minimum table, which at the time was more than I really wanted to play. Also, I recall that during the few hands I did play, Telly flirted with at least three cocktails waitresses and kissed the right hand of every one of them. Afterward, he graciously charmed each girl with that wonderful smile of his, along with a comment about how beautiful she was.

In another anecdote, Johnny Moss, the renowned three-time WSOP champion and poker room manager at the Dunes and

Horseshoe, had a habit of firing his poker dealers when they dealt him a bad beat. A fellow I know nicknamed "Trapper," told me the story of what had happened one time when he worked as a poker dealer at the Horseshoe.

As the story goes, Moss often played in the high stakes games, and during his later years if he experienced a bad beat at a particular table he was known to take it out on the dealer. Moss would typically call over the floor man and tell him he wanted the dealer fired. This was usually just a temporary situation, because most often Moss would rethink his actions and the next day the fired dealer would be unfired. One night, though, things got out of hand when Moss fell into a horrible losing streak. By the end of the night he had fired several dealers. Then when he took another bad beat, he again called the floor man over and told him to fire this particular dealer.

The floor man looked around the poker room, peered down at Moss, and said with a look of total bewilderment, "Johnny, if you fire this poker dealer, we will have to close down the poker room."

"Why is that?" asked Moss.

"Well, except for this dealer, you have already fired every poker dealer in the room."

The Dunes somehow endured 38 years until its famous implosion, razing old buildings to make land available for its replacement by the world's costliest hotel; the $1.6 billion Bellagio opened its doors in 1998. On its 11-acre site, the Bellagio had among its many features such as a 22-million-gallon lake with synchronized dancing fountains, the Bellagio Gallery of Fine Art, and a spectacular show called *Cirque du Soleil*.

1993: The Flamingo Hilton announced plans to raze Bugsy Siegel's suite and office.

1994: The off-Strip Boomtown Casino opened with a 300-room hotel on Blue Diamond at I-15. Later it was renamed Silverton Casino Lodge.

1994: The local favorite Sam's Town on Boulder Highway which opened in 1979, expanded with the opening of a 650-room tower and lush plant-filled atrium.

1994: Two major construction projects were completed: four skywalks were built over the intersection of the Strip with Tropicana Avenue, and the opening of the McCarran Interstate 15-airport connector road system, that tunneled under the east-west runways, was opened.

1994: A clone of Palace Station, Boulder Station opened in August along the Boulder Highway, with five restaurants and 300 rooms and suites.

1994: The 100-room Fiesta Rancho, the first hotel-casino in North Las Vegas, opened.

1994: The last Helldorado Days parade, a tradition for 60 years, was celebrated on Fremont Street. Later in the year, the street was permanently closed to vehicular traffic to make way for construction of the Fremont Street Experience.

Of historical interest, Fremont Street was named after John Charles Fremont, a 19th century U.S. Army general and explorer, who made camp near the headwaters of the Las Vegas Springs in 1844, 150 years earlier.

1995: CREATION OF
THE FREMONT STREET EXPERIENCE (FSE)

The FSE is a downtown attraction encompassing the westernmost five blocks of Fremont Street, including the area nicknamed "Glitter Gulch" and portions of other adjacent streets. Essentially, it's an urban theater under a 10-story four-block-long space-frame canopy, and it features a dazzling light show choreographed to booming state-of-the-art sound, street performers such as Carl "Safe Sax" Ferris, and live bands. It has the biggest video screen in the world, with a 550,000- watt sound system and over 12-million LED lights. Remarkably, Las Vegas is renowned for never turning off its outside casino lights—with one exception. Each FSE show begins by turning off the lights on all of the buildings, including the casinos under the canopy.

1995: The world's first Hard Rock Casino opened in Las Vegas, and Phase I of the Monorail began operation between the MGM Grand and Bally's. Las Vegas visitor volume was reported at a record 29 million for the year, and gross gaming revenue statewide surpassed $7.3 billion total, of which Clark County produced $5.7 billion.

1995: Owned by Station Casinos, Texas Station opened on Rancho Drive in North Las Vegas with 200 rooms and a 91,000-square-foot casino.

1995: LANDMARK IMPLOSION

Opening the Fourth of July weekend, the futuristic-themed resort showcased Danny Thomas performing in the Landmark's showroom. Its explosive demolition 26 years later was immortalized by a cinematic portrayal of Martians destroying

Galaxy Hotel in Tim Burton's *Mars Attacks!* The property gained notoriety when Howard Hughes purchased it in 1968, and prior to the hotel's demolition starred in a few other films, notably *Diamonds Are Forever,* and *Casino.* The purpose of the Landmark's destruction was to make room for 2,000 parking spaces for the neighboring Las Vegas Convention Center.

1996: SANDS IMPLOSION

When we think of classic Las Vegas, most of us visualize Frank Sinatra performing on stage in the Sands' Copa Room with his Rat Pack cronies Dean, Sammy, Peter, and Joey. Today the Pack can be seen in the 1960 film *Ocean's Eleven* performing together on stage in the Copa Room. The renowned showroom was the setting for other great performers, including Judy Garland, Lena Horne—nicknamed "The Satin Doll"—and Shirley MacLaine.

Demolition of the Sands cleared land for Sheldon Adelson's Venetian mega-resort, a $1.8 billion picturesque reproduction of Venice canals and streets. Later, in 2007, Adelson added a second property to the site, the Palazzo.

1996: The Stratosphere Tower, the tallest free-standing observation tower in the U.S. and the tallest structure west of the Mississippi River, opened in April.

1996: The Monte Carlo opened in June, a joint venture of Circus Circus Enterprises and Mirage Resorts Inc.

1996: The $72 million, 1,100-acre Las Vegas Motor Speedway opened featuring tracks for drag, stock car, and formula car races.

1996: The $13 million Strip beautification project was completed, with 76,000 palms, shrubs, flowering foliage, and ground covers planted along the Strip.

1996: Work was completed on the Desert Inn Road arterial that established the first tunnel under the Las Vegas Strip.

1997: NEW YORK-NEW YORK OPENS

Opening in January, more than 100,000 people a day visited the new Las Vegas resort during its first days in operation. To date it is the only Strip resort built without a marquee.

1996: The Orleans opened along West Tropicana Avenue, but at first did not perform up to expectations. In 2003 several amenities were added, including the 9,000-seat Orleans Arena that converts to an ice rink. A second hotel tower was added in 2004. The property ultimately became successful, a testament to the value of renovations in the latter years. The final performance of famed stand-up comedian George Carlin took place at The Orleans in 2008.

1997: THE DESERT INN BECOMES THE WYNN LAS VEGAS

The DI resort underwent major renovations, giving it a fresh, upscale appearance, more in line with the cosmopolitan direction of newer mega-resorts. After Howard Hughes purchased the Desert Inn in 1967, along with its prized 18-hole golf course, the DI changed owners several times, owned in the late 1980s by MGM Grand Inc., then by Starwood Hotels & Resorts Worldwide, under whose ownership it became known as the Sheraton Desert Inn. In 1997 its new owner was none other than Steve Wynn, who had a vision of what he wanted. That vision resulted in the leveling of the resort's Augusta Tower in 2001. The DI's remaining smaller towers were used as offices for Wynn Resorts and housed Wynn's art collection until an early autumn morning in 2004 when, with little fanfare, it was physically demolished.

From his revelation emerged the un-themed Wynn Las Vegas, a $2.7 billion mega-resort centered around a gleaming amber-colored, 60-story tower, which opened in April 2005. Later, the Encore was built adjacent to the Wynn opening in late 2008.

1997: Sunset Station Hotel-Casino opened in June. In August of the same year, the Forum Shops at Caesars Palace greeted tourists with 35 new shops, stores, and restaurants in a 276,000-square-foot expansion that doubled the size of the existing upscale shopping mall. Later the same year Caesars opened a new hotel tower.

1997: HACIENDA IMPLOSION

On New Years' Day, the Hacienda was demolished, having opened originally in 1967 on the southern outskirts of town as a 256-room resort, featuring family-friendly recreation that included miniature golf and a go-kart track. Over time the resort grew to 1,200 rooms, but the aging facility succumbed to both obsolescence and to visitor traffic lost to the new themed mega resorts being built farther north on the Strip.

The Hacienda was replaced by the successful Mandalay Bay Resort.

1997: Continuing the craze of themed restaurants, a Harley Davidson Café opened on the South Strip in September. It features an oversized replica of a Sportster motorcycle, measuring 32 feet in length and weighing 1,200 pounds and, which cost over

$750,000 to manufacture. The replica appears to burst through the front façade of the café. The view from the street was so dynamic that it was said to halt traffic on Las Vegas Boulevard.

1997: Harrah's Entertainment purchased Showboat Inc. in a $1.154 billion deal.

1998: THE DEBBIE REYNOLD'S HOTEL-CASINO AUCTIONED

Originally the Paddlewheel, the property is situated east of the Strip on Convention Center Drive. It became the Greek Isles Hotel & Casino, and in the mid-1980s was purchased by Reynolds and her husband at the time, Richard Hammett. They renovated the property, furnished it with Reynolds' movie memorabilia, and renamed it after her. The property, unfortunately, was never a success, and in 1997 Reynolds was forced to declare bankruptcy. A year later the troubled hotel-casino was sold at public auction to the World Wrestling Federation for $9.7 million. They, too, failed with the property. In 2010, the property became the Clarion Hotel and Casino.

1998: Originally the King 8 Hotel on West Tropicana, in July Starwood Hotels & Resorts Worldwide sold its partial ownership and the property was renamed the Wild Wild West.

1998: CONTROVERSIAL DEATH OF TED BINION

In September, Benny Binion's youngest son, Ted, the casino manager of Binion's Horseshoe and personally worth an estimated $73 million, was found dead in his Las Vegas home. Ted's live-in girlfriend, Sandra Murphy, and her alleged lover,

Rick Tabish, were both initially charged and convicted in Binion's death, but later granted a new trial and acquitted on the murder charges. However, the pair was convicted of attempted burglary of Ted Binion's $7 million in silver, which was buried in a desert vault in Pahrump, Nevada.

1998: ALADDIN IMPLOSION

The only part of the Aladdin Hotel and Casino to remain standing after its implosion was the Aladdin Theatre for the Performing Arts, which became the showpiece of the new Aladdin. The resort opened in 1966, eventually encompassing 36 acres with a 17-story tower, 1,100 rooms, and a checkered past full of financial troubles and mob involvement. Worst of all, it had a terrible location, isolated at the time too far south of all the prime Strip locations. A one-liner in the *Review-Journal* said poignantly, "Not even Wayne Newton's early-1980s co-ownership could fully save this seemingly cursed resort."

The first hotel originally built on the site was the Tally-Ho in 1963. A year later it was renamed the King's Crown, and failed after six months when it was denied a gaming license.

The new Aladdin opened in August 2000 at a cost of $1.4 billion. The "1001 Arabian Nights"-themed resort featured 2,600 rooms, 21 restaurants, a 500,000 square-foot shopping mall called Desert Passage, and 75,000 square feet of convention area. The resort eventually became Planet Hollywood in April 2007.

1998: In November a 66-year-old Las Vegas resident scored a $27.58 million Progressive Megabucks jackpot at the Palace Station Hotel Casino.

1998: Annual gross gaming revenue in Clark County reached the $8.1 billion mark. The annual number of visitors to Las Vegas reached a record of 30.6 million people.

1998: In December the Las Vegas Motor Speedway was sold by founders Bill Bennett and Ralph Engelstad for $215 million to North Carolina-based Speedway Motorsports Inc.

1999: PHASE 1 OF THE VENETIAN OPENS

Situated on the old Sands Hotel site, conventioneer-turned-developer Sheldon Adelson created the beautiful Venetian Hotel & Casino, a marvelous replica of Venice, Italy, with its own picturesque canals, singing gondoliers, Grand Canal Shoppes, and a huge poker room. Together with the adjacent Sands Expo Convention Center and the Palazzo Hotel, upon its completion the Venetian comprised the largest five-diamond hotel and resort complex in the world, featuring a grand total of 4,049 suites, 4,059 hotel rooms, and a 120,000 square foot casino.

1999: THE 100-YEAR FLOOD

In the morning hours of July 8, a rain dumped three inches of water over Las Vegas, triggering a flash flood that inundated hundreds of homes and businesses and took the lives of two people. Traffic came to a standstill on Interstate 15, and parts of Boulder Highway were closed for a week while clean-up crews cleared debris. The local paper reported that "Two weeks after the 100-year flood, President Clinton declared Clark County a federal disaster area, providing relief to 363 local residences that suffered an estimated $1.5 million in damage. County officials predicted it would cost more than $20 million to repair damage to roads and other public property."

1999: Later in July, the master-planned community at Summerlin opened on the 22,500-acre Husite parcel Howard Hughes had acquired in the 1940s. Named for Hughes' grandmother, Jean Amelia Summerlin, the community is situated near the Spring Mountains and Red Rock National Conservation Area. It is ranked as one of the country's best-selling and popular master-planned developments.

1999: In September, the $500 million, 2,900-room Paris Casino-Resort opened on the Strip. Three additional events occurred: Harrah's Entertainment purchased the Rio Hotel-Casino for $888 million; Mandalay Bay Resort opened its doors with 3,300 rooms; and the Four Seasons Hotel opened with 424 rooms.

1999: As a fitting conclusion to the twentieth century, among the many great entertainers booked by Las Vegas resorts to ring in the new millenium were Barbra Streisand, Bette Midler, Rod Stewart, Elton John, Tina Turner, Wayne Newton, and Don Rickles.

2000: KERKORIAN'S MGM HOLDINGS MERGE WITH WYNN'S MIRAGE CASINO GROUP

Kirk Kerkorian's MGM Grand bought out Wynn's Mirage casino group, although Steve Wynn still maintained his casino holdings in Macau and at the old DI site. Eventually even that became the Wynn and Encore. Four years later Kerkorian acquired Bill Bennett's Mandalay Resort Group.

2000: Harrah's Entertainment of William Harrah fame, who was noted for creating the first authentic publicly traded gaming stock, acquired the glitzy Caesars Entertainment, becoming the largest casino conglomerate with over 50 properties worldwide.

2000: EL RANCHO IMPLOSION

Not to be confused with the original El Rancho Vegas that was the first casino resort built on the Strip, the new El Rancho never seemed to find its place or real identity in the ever-changing Las Vegas. Situated on the Strip just north of the Riviera, the El Rancho started out in 1948 as the Thunderbird, was sold, and in 1976 given the name Silverbird. Then in 1982 new owner Ed Torres gave the property a Western theme and named it the El Rancho. Because the resort never really caught on, after 10 years of losing money it was closed and sat empty for eight years, before being destroyed. Its new owners, Turnberry Associates, planned to make use of the site in conjunction with their adjacent high-rise condominium project, Turnberry Place.

2000: THE NEW ALADDIN OPENS, THEN RE-OPENS

Unlike Aladdin's magical lamp from which a supernatural genie popped out to grant its master's wishes, the Aladdin resort seemed cursed from its inception. Beleaguered by a poor location and constant financial difficulties, the owners realized that no matter what they did with the property, it ended in failure.

The New Aladdin seemed no different: it was scheduled to open at 6:00 p.m. on August 17, 2000, with fireworks at 10:00 p.m. But the opening was delayed while the building inspector completed its fire safety testing. Further delay occurred for last-minute repairs on the surveillance system. These postponements caused thousands of disappointed Aladdin visitors to leave the property for other entertainment, as well as many irate opening night hotel guests to wonder where they'd spend the night. Many high rollers had waited for hours on the sidewalk. Even worse, several guests were unable to claim their already stowed luggage, because the hotel had been locked down for testing.

In the interim, the Desert Passage mall, part of the Aladdin complex, opened with *I Dream of Jeannie* star Barbara Eden greeting the large crowd. At 7:45 a.m. the next day both the Aladdin's hotel and casino finally opened its doors, but to the resort owners' dismay 100 members of the Culinary Workers Union Local 26, as well as more than 1,000 other workers, appeared along the Strip to protest the Aladdin's opening without a union contract. As a result Eden's words, as well as other opening festivities, were drowned out by the bullhorns of the protesting workers.

The New Aladdin faced financial trouble from the start, exacerbated by the economic downturn that affected all Las Vegas casinos. The property was sold in June 2003 to a partnership of Planet Hollywood and Starwood Hotels & Resorts Worldwide.

2000: The Clark County Department of Aviation unveiled a $1 billion plan to expand and renovate McCarran International Airport.

2000: PCL Construction Services was awarded a $113 million contract to expand the Las Vegas Convention Center.

2000: In September the Boyd Group opened the Sun Coast Hotel and Casino.

2000: In December, after extensive renovations costing $65 million to the old Continental Hotel, Terrible's Hotel and Casino opened in its place.

2001: IMPLOSION OF THE DESERT INN

To make room for the $2.7 billion Wynn Las Vegas, the first Desert Inn implosion razed the Augusta Tower in October, of 2001.

For nostalgic readers and film and television buffs, the Desert Inn has a very colorful past. As said earlier, the classic film *Ocean's Eleven* starring Sinatra's Rat Pack was shot there in 1960. The 1985 film *Lost in America* starring Julie Hagerty, was filmed there, too. The 1993 film *Sister Act 2: Back in the Habit* took place in the Grand Ballroom of the DI Hotel.

The hotel served as a primary backdrop in the television show *Vega$*, which aired on ABC from 1978 to 1981 and starred the late Robert Urich, who portrayed lead character Dan Tana.

In 1960, Louis Prima and Keely Smith recorded, live at the Desert Inn, their DOT Records LP *"Louis Prima and Keely Smith: On Stage"*. In 1971, Bobby Darin's famous album *"Bobby Darin —Live! At the Desert Inn,"* was recorded there.

NBC's 1980s hit television show *Remington Steele* filmed its Las Vegas episode at the DI, showing throughout the episode both interior and exterior views.

The DI saw its last commercial use in the film *Rush Hour 2,* released in 2001. In time, the film was converted into the *Red Dragon*, which had an Asian-themed casino set.

2001: In November, the Palms opened on West Flamingo across from the Rio. A prime hangout for well-heeled youth, the property offered two high-rise hotel towers and a 50-story luxury hotel-condo featuring floor-to-ceiling windows with amazing views of the Strip.

2001: In December the upscale Green Valley Ranch Resort and Spa opened in nearby Henderson. It's a joint venture of Station Casinos and the Greenspun Corporation, with 490 guest rooms, eight restaurants, and a 50,000-square-foot casino.

2002: THE RAMPART CASINO AT SUMMERLIN OPENS

Over the years the resort has had four names. It was first named the Resort at Summerlin, then the Regent Las Vegas, then JW Marriott Las Vegas.

2003: CASINO MONTELAGO
AT LAKE LAS VEGAS OPENS

Originally owned by Cook Inlet Region, Inc., a corporation owned by members of an Alaskan American Indian tribe, the property was also affiliated with the Ritz Carlton Hotel. The 3,600-acre development located about 20 miles southeast of Las Vegas, had more than 1,700 residential units in addition to the hotel, restaurant, shops, and casino.

2003: The Cannery, a $105 million, 1940s themed resort, opened on Craig Road four miles north of downtown. Las Vegas Premium Outlets also opened in downtown Las Vegas.

2003: In November the Westin Casuarina opened on the site of the old Maxim Hotel and Casino. Owners paid $38 million for the Maxim, then spent an additional $90 million renovating it into a high-end boutique hotel.

2004: The completed phases of the Las Vegas Monorail, a $654 million mass transit system, opened to the public.

2004: In June the Strip dimmed its lights in reverence to President Ronald Reagan's passing. Other dignitaries to receive such a remembrance upon their passing include President John F. Kennedy, George Burns, Rat Pack members Sammy Davis Jr., Dean Martin, and Frank Sinatra.

2004: In August, the Palms and St. Andrews Towers were imploded on the old DI site to make room for Encore, which completed construction in December 2008.

2005: WYNN LAS VEGAS OPENS

After clearing away the old Desert Inn structures, the site was made ready for the luxurious Wynn Las Vegas, which opened in April. Together with the Encore, which opened its doors in 2008, the two resorts occupy 215 acres on the Strip directly across from the Fashion Show Mall. The complex also has an 111,000 square-foot casino, a huge convention center, an 18-hole golf course, and 76,000 square feet of retail space. The Wynn and Encore combined offer a total of 4,750 rooms, ranging from 640 square feet to luxurious villas at 7,000 square feet.

The Wynn Las Vegas and its sister property Encore collectively hold more *Forbes* five-star awards than any other resort and casino. It is considered to be one of the finest hotels in the world.

2005: THE ATOMIC TESTING MUSEUM OPENS

This unique facility documents the history of nuclear testing at the Nevada Test Site (NTS), located 60 miles northwest of

Las Vegas. The museum covers the period from the first test at NTS, originally named the Nevada Proving Ground founded in January 1951 to the present. Among its many exhibits that portray American nuclear history, the Ground Zero Theater simulates the experience of observing an atmospheric nuclear test.

2005: In October the Cosmopolitan of Las Vegas, a resort-casino featuring a hotel and condo project, broke ground south of the Bellagio. The $4 billion multi-purpose resort was, unfortunately, foreclosed on by Deutsche Bank, which completed the development and opened to the public in December 2010.

2005: "Condo-mania" hit Las Vegas, with numerous developers from Donald Trump to Kirk Kerkorian announcing plans for high-rise condominium projects. Other condominium projects already underway along the Strip included CityCenter, Echelon Place, the Fontainebleau, and Turnberry.

2005: Visitor volume surpassed the record-breaking level of 37.4 million set in 2004.

2005: Houston-based Landry's restaurants purchased downtown's largest casino, the Golden Nugget.

2005: Two notable mega-mergers occurred. In June, MGM Mirage and Mandalay Resort Group completed their $7.9 billion union. A month later, Harrah's Entertainment purchased Caesars Entertainment for $9.4 billion, making it the planet's largest gaming company with over 50 casinos.

2005: The South Coast opened, and the following year Michael Gaughan purchased it from Coast Casinos, and renamed it South Point. It became the first mega-resort built south of McCarran International Airport and the Las Vegas Strip.

2006: BOURBON STREET IMPLOSION

As of this writing no plans have been announced for the Bourbon Street, imploded in January after its casino was closed the preceding October. The off-Strip property, first known as the Shenandoah, opened at 120 E. Flamingo Road in 1980 with several owners, including Wayne Newton. It unfortunately, was never approved for a gaming license, and after four years in operation filed for bankruptcy. Keeping the name Bourbon Street, a Canadian based company reopened the New Orleans-themed property in 1985, becoming the first non-U.S. company to obtain a gaming license in Nevada.

In 2005 Harrah's purchased the property, and along with several surrounding properties assembled an eight-acre parcel just off the Strip adjacent to the Las Vegas Monorail.

2006: POPULARITY OF
THE WORLD SERIES OF POKER PEAKED

Inaugurated by Benny Binion in 1970, the phase of the tournament called the "Main Event" reached its peak in player participation in 2006 with 8,773 poker players competing. Since its inauguration, ESPN has greatly expanded coverage of the WSOP to include many of its preliminary events, especially No-Limit Texas Hold'em.

2006: SHOWBOAT/CASTAWAYS IMPLOSION

Built originally in 1954 with a Mississippi riverboat theme as the Showboat, this property received numerous upgrades over the years, including bowling lanes in 1959. The addition of several hotel towers gave the resort 500 rooms. The bowling center expanded to 106 lanes, and in its heyday held several televised professional events. The resort also featured a sports pavilion, and gained notoriety by showcasing boxing, wrestling, and roller derby.

In 1998, Harrah's purchased the property and went on to open other Showboat-themed resorts in New Orleans, Atlantic City, Illinois, and Australia. Harrah's sold the Las Vegas Showboat in 2000 to a group of investors who gave it a tropical island theme and renamed it the Castaways. Three years later the property fell on hard times, and after going into bankruptcy, it finally closed in January 2004. To date, Station Casinos are the owner of record.

2006: BOARDWALK IMPLOSION

The Strip anomaly called the Boardwalk, with its faux-ferris wheel façade complete with dummy passengers, surrounded by such picturesque resorts as New York New York, the MGM Grand, and Monte Carlo, was looking more out of place every day. The *Review-Journal* wrote: "The aging and inefficient Boardwalk provided more entertainment value in its explosion than perhaps at any point during its operation." Its demolition cleared the land for the MGM Mirage's $11 billion CityCenter project, a mixed-use resort and entertainment complex that combined gaming, shopping, state-of-the-art architecture, upscale hotels, and highrise condominiums.

2006: HOOTERS HOTEL AND CASINO OPENS

Located just east of the Strip next to the Tropicana, and across the street from the MGM Grand, the Hooters resort opened with 696 hotel rooms and a 35,000-square-foot casino. Originally the hotel was built in 1973, opening as a Howard Johnson Motel. After several changes in ownership, it became the Hotel San Rémo in 1989.

2006: Opening in April as the newest development of Station Casinos, Red Rock Casino Spa was the first billion dollar property built off the Las Vegas Strip.

2006: Nevada celebrated 75 years of legalized gaming.

2006: Boyd Gaming Group announced plans to build Echelon Place, a $4 billion resort development with 5,300 hotel rooms, on the old 63-acre Stardust site. Later, because of the economic downturn, construction on the project was halted.

2007: In September, O.J. Simpson was arrested for armed robbery at the Palace Station casino and sentenced to 33 years imprisonment, with a minimum of nine years without parole.

STARDUST IMPLOSION

2007: On March 13, engineers imploded the notorious 48-year-old Stardust Casino, which Boyd Gaming closed the doors on the previous November. This put to rest the storied life of the iconic resort. Its demolition made room for a multi-purpose complex of shopping and condominiums called Echelon Place.

Over the years, the Stardust's clandestine history of money skimming and related mob ties made it the focus of several federal investigations, yet it gained even more fame when moviegoers realized it was the inspiration for the acclaimed film *Casino*.

2007: THE ALADDIN IS TRANSFORMED INTO PLANET HOLLYWOOD

Under the auspices of Harrah's Entertainment, Planet Hollywood emerged from the troubled Aladdin in April.

2007: NEW FRONTIER IMPLOSION

With a momentous crash on November 13, the New Frontier came tumbling down, ending the reign of the second oldest hotel on the Las Vegas Strip. Although the Frontier was not quite as rich in romantic nostalgia as some of the other demolished resorts such as the Sands and Desert Inn, it did share in the archives of Las Vegas history. This was the resort where Elvis Presley made his disastrous Las Vegas debut in April 1956. Siegfried & Roy headlined there for the first time in their own show called *Beyond Belief*.

Until its implosion, the Frontier was the last operating casino-resort owned by Howard Hughes and the site of the longest-running labor strike in U.S. history—six years and four months.

Because of the economic downturn, plans for the cleared site where the New Frontier once stood are currently on hold.

2007: THE LAS VEGAS SPRINGS PRESERVE OPENS

Considered the birthplace of Las Vegas, the 180-acre cultural and historic attraction that features museums, galleries, and the future Nevada State Museum, opened to the public.

2007: Town Square Las Vegas, a new retail, dining, and entertainment project, opened on South Las Vegas Boulevard at the junction of I-15 and the 215 Beltway.

2007: CAESARS PALACE RAISES ITS TABLE LIMITS

In December, Caesars Palace increased its table game limit to the highest in Las Vegas. Their latest policy change confirms that Caesars wants the high-roller action. Prior to the increase, blackjack players could play three hands with a maximum bet of $10,000 per hand. The new limits allow players to either bet $50,000 on a single hand or play three hands at $25,000 per hand. For the craps table the maximum line bet was raised from the previous $5,000 to the new limit of $50,000. At the roulette table the inside betting limit was raised from the previous $500 to $3,000. These newly raised limits are available only in the high-limit gaming area, whereas table limits in the other areas of the casino were not changed.

2007: The NBA All-Star game came to Las Vegas, marking for the first time in history that the game was played in a city without a resident NBA team. Also of note, Wayne Newton sang "Viva Las Vegas" during player introductions.

2008: STEVE WYNN'S ENCORE OPENS

The Encore opened in December, joining its sister property next door, Wynn Las Vegas. The $2.3 billion, 2,034-room hotel was built on the footage remaining along Las Vegas Boulevard where the Desert Inn once stood.

2008: The Palazzo, built adjacent to the Venetian, celebrated its grand opening.

2008: The downtown Golden Nugget completed a $60 million expansion project, adding convention space and a new nightclub.

2008: In August the Eastside Cannery opened on Boulder Highway near Sam's Town, replacing the Nevada Palace, which had opened in 1977.

2008: In November Station Casinos new Aliante Station opened in North Las Vegas.

2008: Bette Midler became the new resident headliner at Caesars Palace Colosseum, replacing Celine Dion after her successful five-year run.

2009: THE 90-ACRE M RESORT OPENS

March 1 saw the opening of M Resort, located on Las Vegas Boulevard 8.3 miles south of Mandalay Bay in Henderson. The $1 billion resort featured a 400-room luxury boutique hotel, receiving in the same year the prestigious *Forbes* Four-Star Award, adding to the MGM's list of lavish international hotels.

2009: The Hard Rock Las Vegas introduced a 490-room Paradise Tower.

2009: In October, "Mr. Las Vegas," Wayne Newton celebrated his 50th year of entertaining audiences at the Tropicana with a farewell of "Once Before I Go."

2009: Developers of the $3 billion Fontainebleau Las Vegas filed suit against a group of banks for terminating an $800 million loan when construction was already 70 percent complete. The 63-story, 3,815-room development, located on the site of the old El Rancho and Algiers Hotel, was scheduled to open in October 2009. Financier Carl Icahn purchased the property and announced he will not resume the venture until the Vegas economy rallies.

2009: Another property weathering the stormy recession is the Cosmopolitan, which was under construction next to CityCenter. Deutsche Bank foreclosed on the $3.9 billion development, and finished out the resort in December 2010. Projects that never got off the ground because of the weak economy include an Elvis-themed property adjacent to the MGM Grand, a second Trump Tower, and an upscale version of New York City's famed Plaza Hotel.

2009: CITYCENTER PHASE ONE OPENS

Considered the single most expensive, privately funded project in the western hemisphere, the first phase of the gargantuan $11-billion project named Aria Resort & Casino, opened in December on the Strip between the Bellagio and Monte Carlo resorts. By the time it is completed, the massive 16.8 million-square-foot mixed-use complex will combine gaming, shopping, state-of-the-art architecture, luxurious hotels, and upscale high-rise condominiums.

2010: CASINO MONTELAGO
AT LAKE LAS VEGAS CLOSES

Burdened with $728 million in liabilities, the troubled economy, and now in bankruptcy, and with the nearby Ritz Carlton having closed on March 7, operators of Casino MonteLago said they would shutter the resort March 14. The casino opened in May 2003 at a time when Lake Las Vegas and all of southern Nevada was booming, but the oncoming recession and the worst real estate downturn in memory stripped away all desire for locals and tourists to visit luxury properties built on the man-made lake. Since its opening the property never had sufficient visitors to sustain it financially. Meanwhile, debts piled up, and an ominous sign of trouble appeared in 2009 when the resort's famous golf courses closed.

A Las Vegas resident commented on the closing of Casino Montelago in the *Review-Journal* about the closing of Casino MonteLago: "It is about time that Las Vegas return to its roots of being a decent priced place where you can come and enjoy yourself. Somewhere along the way, everyone started to think that we were some French Riviera where we could have outlandish priced restaurants, $400 a night rooms, and $300 for a show. I enjoy seeing the moderate priced Vegas starting to re-emerge from this mess."

2010: Las Vegas reached the top of the foreclosure and unemployment rankings during the summer of 2010. Despite these gloomy facts, Clark County continues to grow and remains the 15th largest county in the nation, according to data released by the U.S. Census Bureau. It also remains the 30th largest metropolitan area in the United States.

2010: On October 17, due to the economic downturn and poor visitor attendance, the Liberace Museum closed its doors to the public. Liberace himself opened the museum in April 1979, with his brother George becoming its director. Two buildings comprise the museum: The Jewelry and Costume Gallery, and the building where the pianos and cars are showcased.

To conclude this Las Vegas Timeline, we quote from an interview of some 30 years ago with the MGM's Kirk Kerkorian. About the economic outlook of the Las Vegas gaming and resort industry, he said, "there will be a leveling-out time, and the best hotels and the best operators are going to suffer less than the others."

Chapter 9
LAS VEGAS FACTS, TRIVIA, AND ATTRACTIONS

*W*ho in 1931 would have ever thought that when Humboldt County Assemblyman Phil Tobin introduced his gambling bill, that it would have such a tremendous impact on Las Vegas or for that matter the entire state of Nevada? At the time, it didn't seem that big of a deal. The intent of Tobin and the state legislature had been to somehow help Nevada businessmen afflicted by the Great Depression. Even after gambling was legalized, Reno Mayor E. E. Roberts didn't think the new bill would increase revenues much.

Mayor Roberts would be amazed to know that in 2009, the City of Reno collected $3.8 million in taxes from gross gaming revenue of $759 million.

In Southern Nevada revenues were more than ten times those generated in Reno. In Clark County alone, 76 casinos generated $8.8 billion in gaming revenue in 2009. The average blackjack table on the Las Vegas Strip that year won about $523,062, while a craps table had an average win of $762,000. For the entire year of 2009, the Las Vegas Strip casinos took in the largest portion, with gross gaming revenues of $5.5 billion.

WHAT CASINOS WIN?

Any gambler should feel discouraged to learn that not one game of chance in Las Vegas shows anything but a profit. A Strip baccarat table, for instance, produces a whopping annual win of almost $4.7 million. At the lowest end of the gaming spectrum, penny slots show a meager win of $6,444 per machine.

If you wonder how the state of Nevada makes its money on gaming, here's some insight: In addition to levying a gross revenue tax of about five percent, each casino game is levied, on average, a tax of $324 a year. There are also licensing fees. For example, casinos paid fees of about $80 a year for each slot machine, and for each table game, about $625. If a casino has live entertainment, it pays a tax of 5 percent to 10 percent on gross revenue, depending on the number of seats available.

NUMBER OF SLOTS AND TABLE GAMES

All told, the Las Vegas metropolitan area has roughly 2,316 blackjack tables, 324 craps tables, 394 roulette tables, and 208 baccarat tables, along with a total of 197,806 slot machines. Every machine in 2009 produced an average annual profit of almost $57,000, according to the Nevada Gaming Control Board.

WHAT IT TAKES

To generate these billions in gaming revenue takes people, millions of people, who come to Las Vegas with, on average, $587 to gamble with over a stay that averages 4.3 days and 3.7 nights. Over the course of their stay, visitors in 2009 spent an average of $250 for food and drink, down from $274 the previous year, and $53 per person for local transportation, down significantly from 2005-2008 figures. Visitors spent an average of $102 for shopping, also down significantly from $137 in 2005, $141 in 2006, and $122 in 2008. Each visitor spent $40 on shows, down significantly from past years.

These statistics are courtesy of the Las Vegas Convention and Visitors Authority, which has assimilated every piece of tourist data one could possibly imagine. For instance, in 2009:

- ι A little more than 36 million visitors came to Las Vegas, down almost 4 million visitors from its peak in 2007.
- ι Fifty-eight percent of visitors to Las Vegas arrived by ground, 42 percent by air.
- ι The average visitor's age was 50.
- ι Fourteen percent of visitors were international, 26 percent came from California.
- ι Visitor spending was $35.2 billion, down $6.4 billion from the year before.

ı 19,394 conventions were held in Las Vegas, with attendance about 4.5 million, down 1.7 million from a peak of 6.2 million in 2007.

Visitors who gambled on their current trip to Las Vegas were asked which casino game they played most often. Seventy percent said they played the slot machines most frequently, followed by blackjack (11 percent), video poker (7 percent), and live poker (4 percent).

Being one of the largest convention facilities in the world with 3.2 million square feet of space, the Las Vegas Convention Center, hosts events with an estimated 200,000 participants per event.

The Las Vegas metropolitan area boasts about 350 hotels, motels, and inns, which add up to a total of 148,941 rooms—remarkably more hotel rooms than any other city on earth. Seventeen of the world's 20 largest hotels are located on the Las Vegas Strip, all within a five-mile radius of each other.

LAS VEGAS ATTRACTIONS

In 2009, the 76 Las Vegas area casinos that comprise downtown, the Strip, and Boulder Highway took in $8.8 billion in gross gaming revenue. Add to that another whopping $35.2 billion in visitor spending on food, entertainment, hotels, and transportation. Such an extraordinary amount of money heads for Las Vegas with more than three million visitors a month prepared to spend it, that one has to ask the question, what's the big attraction?

Visitors to Las Vegas can freely wager their money on casino games such as blackjack, craps, roulette, Texas Hold'em, three-

Welcome to Las Vegas

card poker, baccarat, slot machines, sports books, and a couple of Asian games called Sic-Bow and Pai-gow. When they tire of gambling they can see, in person, famous entertainers such as Cher, Celine Deion, or Elton John perform on the stages of the entertainment capital of the world.

Las Vegas casino resorts seem to know no boundaries in their creativity for developing grandiose projects. The resort owners' imaginations appear limitless. Every year it seems a new world's largest casino-hotel appears on the Las Vegas landscape.

The city itself is already the gambling and entertainment capital for the world. Las Vegas is also fast becoming the world's convention headquarters, with more than 10 million square feet of convention space available in 2010.

In case you've never been to Las Vegas, allow me to give you a written tour of this high-desert oasis with the constantly changing skyline. "Las Vegas has something to please everyone, and it's usually available 24 hours a day. There's a saying in Las Vegas: If you don't find what you're looking for, please wait one moment, it is probably already under construction."

A STROLL ALONG THE LAS VEGAS STRIP

Although Las Vegas is a bustling town active 24 hours every day, 365 days a year, the best time to view its awe-inspiring sights is at night. That's when all the themed resorts are doing their thing to attract your attention: the fountains are dancing, the Coney Island coaster is rolling, King Arthur's knights are jousting, the pirates are dueling—and the entire Strip is aglow in multi-colored neon. Daytime is different—the temperature is much warmer and the Strip is not as active—but you do have a picturesque view of the surrounding mountains in the background.

Your tour of Las Vegas begins where it all started some 65 years ago, at the intersection of Las Vegas Boulevard South and Flamingo road. This particular intersection is famous for at least three reasons. First, it encompasses some of the most valuable real estate in the world. Second, if you recall the story earlier, this is where Steve Wynn sold his narrow parcel of real estate to Caesars Palace, earning him the seed money to buy controlling interest in the Golden Nugget. The 1.5-acre parcel runs westerly along Flamingo road from the Strip, the parcel that started Wynn on his way to being a Las Vegas billionaire. And third, many of the city's most famous casino-resorts are situated on or near this historical intersection, including Caesars Palace, the Flamingo, Bellagio, and Bally's.

THE STRIP AND FLAMINGO ROAD

When you stand in front of Caesars Palace and look east across the boulevard to the Flamingo Hotel, imagine what it was like in the mid-1940s when Billy Wilkerson first viewed the then-barren 33-acre site the Flamingo stands on today. Picture too, circa 1947 after Wilkerson was muscled out of the Flamingo, how Ben Siegel and Virginia Hill struggled to make the troubled resort a success.

Near the Flamingo's pool area you can visit the Wildlife Habitat, home to more than 300 exotic birds, featuring among them the Chilean flamingos. As you stroll north along the boulevard visit the Imperial Palace. It has the auto enthusiast's dream—the world's largest classic car showroom featuring 250 antique cars that span more than a century of innovation.

Cross over Las Vegas Boulevard and explore the Mirage, which features a simulated erupting volcano, a dolphin habitat, exotic tigers behind glass, and a miniature rain forest. Next door at the TI, every night sexy sirens battle a band of renegade male pirates in Siren's Cove.

VENETIAN, WYNN, AND ENCORE

Across the Strip from the Mirage and the TI is the picturesque Venetian, a replica of Venice, Italy, where a gondola will take you along winding canals. Inside the Venetian enjoy the Grand Canal Shoppes where you can meander along the center's cobbled streets.

Next door on the site of the old Desert Inn stand the Wynn and Encore resorts. There you can enjoy mountain waterfalls, a Ferrari dealership, and a great 18-table poker room. Across the Strip and heading towards downtown, free circus acts at Circus Circus and the five-acre Adventure Canyon entertain you. Farther north where the Strip and Sahara intersect stands the Stratosphere Tower, and south of it across Sahara Avenue is the vacant lot where the original El Rancho Vegas once stood.

Now stroll back to the spectacular 93-acre Caesars Palace, with its marvelous array of Forum Shops, including 150 boutiques and 15 restaurants. From Caesars Palace head south across Flamingo road to the Bellagio, the site where the Dunes once stood. There in an 8.5-acre lake, 1,200 synchronized fountains nightly dance to music from Pavarotti to Sinatra. Next to the Bellagio stands the new $11.3 billion CityCenter with its featured Aria Casino and adjacent multi-purpose facilities.

Across the boulevard is the beautiful Paris Resort, with its outdoor Parisian café and replicated Eiffel Tower. From atop the 460-foot tower you can enjoy a panoramic bird's-eye view of the entire Las Vegas Strip. North of it is Bally's, once the site of the original MGM Grand. Across Flamingo road is Bill's Gamblin Hall & Saloon, once the Barbary Coast and before that the Times Square Motel.

STRIP AND TROPICANA AVENUE

Another grouping of magnificent themed resorts is situated where the Strip intersects Tropicana Avenue. We begin this picturesque tour at a replica of King Arthur's Castle named after the much sought-after sword, the Excalibur, complete with a moat, a drawbridge, and nightly jousting matches. North of it stands New York New York, a resort that resembles Manhattan's famous skyline, complete with replicas of the Statue of Liberty in the foreground, the Empire State Building in the background, and a Coney Island roller coaster looping high above the entire site. Notice too, that it's the only Strip casino without a marquee.

Directly across the Strip from New York New York stands the huge MGM Grand. There you can see the Lion Habitat, and—from the rear of the property—take the Monorail north to other casinos. Across Tropicana Avenue stands the Tropicana resort, where you can swim in the pool and play poolside blackjack too.

At Blue Diamond Road on the southern end of the Las Vegas Strip stands the Silverton Hotel and Casino, that features a massive 117,000-gallon saltwater aquarium. It's also home to free shows in which a marine biologist, equipped with full face communication mask, interacts with guests while feeding the fish, made up of a huge array of tropical fish, stingrays, eels, and sharks. Heading north along the boulevard there's Mandalay Bay's Wave pool, and next to it, the Luxor Pyramid Hotel. Cross over the boulevard and visit Planet Hollywood, which used to be the Aladdin and before that the Tally-Ho.

TAKE THE "DEUCE"

From anywhere on the Las Vegas Strip 24 hours a day, take a ride downtown on the red double-decker bus called "the Deuce" and enjoy the Fremont Street Experience (FSE). The FSE is a wondrous display of free nightly shows, ablaze with 12.5 million lights and pulsing with 550,000 watts of amazing sound. Enjoy special events and free nightly concerts throughout the year, including 10-year veteran Carl "Safe Sax" Ferris performing on his saxophones.

Adjacent to the FSE is the Fremont East District, which offers comedy clubs, blues and jazz nightclubs, and with other musical entertainment venues.

In North Las Vegas visit the CSN Planetarium and Observatory, which offer educational and entertaining programs year-round.

OTHER ATTRACTIONS

Among its many themed resorts, Las Vegas has other attractions too, such as 37 golf courses. It has the University of Nevada Las Vegas (UNLV), the nation's third largest campus complex with 335 acres and 20,000 enrolled students. It features the 18,500-seat Thomas and Mack stadium where the Runnin' Rebels play. They're a perennial favorite, noted as the 1990 NCAA Champions and usually one of the country's top 20 collegiate basketball teams. In November of every year the Thomas and Mack features the Superbowl of rodeo when the National Finals Rodeo comes to town.

For another sports venue there's Cashman Field, home to the Las Vegas 51s, the AAA affiliate of major league baseball's Toronto Blue Jays. Vegas also has a sports stadium called Sam Boyd Stadium, once the Silver Bowl, which seats 36,800 spectators and is the official site of the UNLV football team.

The city has a huge 1500-acre multi-purpose facility called the Las Vegas Motor Speedway, with a 1.5 mile superspeedway, a 2.5-

mile Grand Prix road course, a half-mile dirt oval track, and a drag strip. While you're there, try your hand at the Las Vegas race car driving school, which allows visitors to satisfy a higher need for speed whether they're riding shotgun or driving solo. The school offers two types of racing options: stock car and open wheel.

For the more daring visitor, there's Stratosphere Roller Coaster and Insanity Ride atop the 900-foot tall Stratosphere Tower.

If you're into nuclear fission, visit the Atomic Testing Museum. It documents the history of nuclear testing at the remote Nevada Test Site located 60 miles northwest of Las Vegas.

Other nearby attractions within a short driving distance to Las Vegas include Hoover Dam, Lake Mead, the Valley of Fire, and Red Rock Canyon. Within a 50-mile radius to Las Vegas is picturesque Mount Charleston with adjoining Lee Canyon, which at 8,000 feet features snow skiing during the winter months. You can also enjoy helicopter tours of the Las Vegas Strip as well as the Grand Canyon, located about 280 miles from Las Vegas.

Yet the most popular attractions are the free or inexpensive things to do in the Las Vegas area. Here's a sampling of those attractions, in a nutshell:

- Adventure Canyon at Circus Circus
- Bellagio Fountains and Conservatory
- CSI Experience and Lion Habitat at MGM Grand
- Eiffel Tower replica at the Parisian
- Excalibur Tournament of Kings
- Flamingo Wildlife Habitat
- Exotic Car Rental

- *ι* Fremont Street Experience
- *ι* Gondola Ride at the Venetian
- *ι* Hoover Dam
- *ι* Imperial Palace Auto Collection
- *ι* Insanity Ride and "Big Shot" at Stratosphere Tower
- *ι* Mirage Dolphin Habitat, exotic tigers, and Erupting Volcano
- *ι* New York New York Roller Coaster
- *ι* Sirens at Battleship Bay at the TI.

Many people, including retirees, find Las Vegas an attractive place to live, not only for its great attractions, but also because of special economic benefits. These include no state income tax, reasonable home prices, and inexpensive hydroelectric power generated by nearby Hoover Dam.

A leisurely stroll or a sightseeing bus ride along the hallowed Las Vegas Strip, especially at night, is an exhilarating experience. This playground is simply the most exciting place on earth, entrenched in history, beautiful people, and non-stop fun!

Did I miss anything? If I did, they're probably building it as I write this.

LAS VEGAS TRIVIA

Have you ever wondered what people earn who are employed in Las Vegas casinos? Generally, all casino dealers earn about the same small salary based on minimum wage, augmented by tips or tokes. In Las Vegas, the amount of tokes earned varies substantially depending on whether one works downtown or out on the Strip. For instance, craps dealers, at the Wynn in 2009 earned about $100,000 in tokes, which at the time was the pinnacle in dealer tip earnings. Earnings are all downhill from there, because all depends on the class of clientele and the amount of tokes dealers receive from those clients. Many downtown dealers earn minimum wage plus tokes and a meal, which varies between about $20,000 to $40,000 annually. The top dealing job downtown in 2010 was at the Golden Nugget.

You may wonder how Steve Wynn manages to pay his floor people about half what most dealers earn, yet avoid dissention and quibbling among them? It's the perks. Back in 1989 when Steve Wynn opened the Mirage, the managerial positions of box man and on up received free golf at his private golf course.

In the early 1980s before dealer tokes were pooled, the best jobs were dealing baccarat at the top Strip casinos. The next best dealing jobs were craps when tokes were table for table, which means the table does not share tokes with the other table game dealers, or "go for themselves." Last were the blackjack dealers. Today Las Vegas poker dealers usually go for themselves and often earn $50,000 to $60,000 or more annually.

Bartenders and waitresses usually belong to the culinary union and do pretty well in tips, especially in the higher-class

Strip casinos. Showroom captains in the top Strip resorts make great money.

The greatest jobs until the mid-1980s were cocktail servers, valets, showroom captains, baccarat dealers, and dice dealers at the Dunes, Caesars Palace, the DI, Tropicana, and the Sands. Pooling tips ended that, taking away the incentive for individuals to provide exceptional service. Today, except for a few prime Strip casinos, service roles are just another job.

REMEMBER WHEN . . .

Can you remember when complimentary cigarettes were available in plastic containers on most Las Vegas table games? If you do, you were in Las Vegas in the 1960s and 1970s when it was polishing its image as the "playground of the stars." Every so often in the late afternoon of many Strip casinos you could hear operators over the loud speaker system announce, "Telephone call for Mister Howard Hughes. Mister Hughes, please call the hotel operator." Or, "Paging Mister Spencer Tracy. Mister Spencer Tracy, please call the hotel operator."

"Harriet, did you hear that? They just paged Spencer Tracy."

"Wait a minute: didn't he die in 1967, or something?"

VALUABLE OLD TOKENS

Remember when the Castaways was once the Sans Souci or the Palace Station was the Bingo Palace? Or can you remember when the Cannery on Boulder Highway was the Nevada Palace and when the Thunderbird transformed into the Silverbird, then into the El Rancho, and today the new Fontainebleau?

Then there's the notorious Stardust Hotel, originally going to be called the Starlite Hotel—the name owner Tony Cornero dreamed up for it in 1954. Cornero, if you recall from Chapter 2, was a colorful bootlegger and casino operator who ran two gambling ships off California's coast.

Incidentally, every time a casino changes its name, or changes cheques, the old cheques are required under Nevada law to be destroyed. Those cheques still in circulation kept by visitors as souvenirs, eventually become worth more than their face value. For instance, a $25 cheque from the original El Rancho Vegas reportedly sold for $125 in 1985.

With the proliferation of casinos throughout America, many people became collectors of casino tokens (cheques), in the same way as others engage in stamp collecting and coin collecting. Casinos often have special commemorative editions with the photo image of someone special printed on the token, such as an entertainer who performed at the resort. Casinos love collectors because their $5 token costs them less than one dollar to produce, earning a profit every time a collector takes a token home instead of redeeming it for five dollars.

When Caesars Palace opened, it issued a special 50-cent token for playing the Big Six wheel. One day co-owner Nate Jacobsen happened to be walking through the casino and when he noticed the token in play he screamed bloody murder. He is reported to have bellowed, "Our image will be ruined!" The idea of even $1 tokens in the casino bothered him. He settled down once someone explained to Jacobsen that he himself had ordered the tokens and signed the purchase order. In time the 50-cent tokens were destroyed, but the few that eluded his rants are said to be worth more than 24 times their original value.

Bill Borland, founder of the World Wide Casino Exchange, believes the most valuable casino token in circulation is from Tony Cornero's gambling ship the SS Rex. A $1 token would bring $375 or more today. Tokens from the original MGM Grand have increased in value too, because after the casino was acquired by Bally's the logo was changed and the old inventory destroyed.

BAD IDEA FOR THE TALLY-HO

Ed Lowe made a fortune popularizing the game of bingo, and he invented the dice game Yahtzee. In Las Vegas, however, he had the distinction of taking a horrible idea and making it worse by building it in a terrible location. In 1963 Lowe built the only hotel on the Las Vegas Strip without a casino, the Tally-Ho, an English Tudor-style resort. Lowe reasoned that the time had come to cater to people who wanted to get away from the big gambling hotels. Thus, it was his idea to provide an environment better suited to upper echelon people of "taste and distinction" who visited Las Vegas. The Tally-Ho had no casino, and no showroom. What it did have were good restaurants with lots of ambiance, derived from great-looking furniture, high wood-beamed ceilings, and plush carpeting. In *Las Vegas: Behind the Tables,* Barney Vinson wrote, Lowe considered his hotel "an extension of his home, and this gave him the right to lay down a few rules to his guests— watch the cigarette ashes, and no gambling!"[72]

Mister Lowe obviously was bright when it came to marketing games, yet he was naïve when it came to gaming and Las Vegas. He never quite grasped why the Tally-Ho failed so miserably.

Vinson described Lowe's failure with the Tally-Ho in this way: "He didn't realize that 'class' and 'distinction' are just words in a dictionary when it comes to Las Vegas. Once he 'caught' four men playing cards out by the swimming pool. 'Gentlemen,' the very proper Lowe began, 'I must ask you to cease your loutish behavior instantly.' The players, in no kind terms whatsoever, told Lowe where he could put it. He sold the hotel shortly after that."[73]

Since Ed Lowe's Tally-Ho, the troubled property has undergone numerous changes in ownership and extensive renovations, which include the following:

- 1965: The property opened under a new name called the "Kings Crown Tally-Ho," but failed after it was denied a gaming license.
- 1966: Sold to Milton Prell for $19 million and renamed the Aladdin Hotel and Casino.
- 1968: Parvin Dohrmann Corp. took over ownership.
- 1972: Sold to Sam Diamond, Peter Webbe, and Richard Daly for $5 million.
- 1976: Theater for Performing Arts opened.
- 1979: Several casino executives convicted of conspiring to allow "hidden" owners to exert control over the resort.
- 1980: Sold to Wayne Newton and Ed Torres for $85 million.
- 1982: Wayne Newton sold his interest in the Aladdin for $8.5 million.

- 1984: Placed under bankruptcy protection.
- 1985: Sold to Ginji Yasuda for $54 million.
- 1989: Placed under bankruptcy protection.
- 1991: Federal judge gave Bell Atlantic Tricon the deed to hotel, and it emerged from bankruptcy with Joe Burt of JMJ Management as owner.
- 1993: Joe Burt killed in motorcycle accident.
- 1994: Sold to Jack Sommer of the Sigman Sommer Family Trust for $80 million.
- 1998: Site imploded except for the Theater of the Performing Arts.
- 2000: Opened New Aladdin at a cost of $1.3 billion.
- 2003: Financial problems caused the sale of the Aladdin to a partnership of Planet Hollywood and Starwood Hotels & Resorts Worldwide.
- 2009: Westgate opened the PH Towers, a timeshare and hotel linked with the casino and main hotel.

These days the property is owned by Harrah's Entertainment under the brand Planet Hollywood Resort and Casino.

PAY ADMISSION TO A CASINO?

Jay Sarno tried something similar to Ed Lowe's idea, but in reverse—building a casino without a hotel. When Sarno opened Circus Circus in 1968, he originally charged $1 admission to enter his casino, supposedly to see the Circus acts. The problem was that people didn't like paying admission to gamble. Bill

Bennett took over Circus Circus, got rid of the admission fee, built a hotel, and the resort became very successful.

MORE LAS VEGAS TRIVIA

The state's name Nevada means "snow capped" in Spanish. It was shortened from "Sierra Nevada," the name originally given to the nearby mountains. The elevation of Las Vegas is 2,028 feet above sea level.

Besides the honor of being the capital of conventions, gambling, and entertainment, Las Vegas is also the marriage capital of the United States, with 50 wedding chapels in the metropolitan area. An average of 315 weddings take place every day. Cost of a wedding varies upwards from $45 about ten times as much to untie the knot: a divorce in Las Vegas averages $450, cheap compared to other states.

There are 30 casinos on the Las Vegas Strip: 76 overall in the Las Vegas metro area. On any given night the casino vaults at the Strip's larger mega-resort hold from $30 to $60 million in cash. That amount doubles on holiday weekends.

The first slot machine was invented in 1899 by Charles Fey of San Francisco. It was named the Liberty Bell. The world's largest slot machine jackpot was won in Las Vegas by a woman at the Excalibur. The amount won was $39.7 million and the event occurred in March 2003.

The game of blackjack is believed to have its origins about 1910 at an underground gaming parlor along the Ohio River in Evansville, Indiana.

Trivial Contempt: Back in 1995 when I worked at Harrah's New Orleans Casino, a woman was playing a slot machine with her young son by her side. The woman went to the bathroom, after instructing her son not to play the machine. But he did, and remarkably hit a $250,000 jackpot. Harrah's wouldn't pay because the player was underage. The woman sued to get the jackpot, which she figured was owed to her, but lost her suit. Harrah's had the entire episode on surveillance film, proving that the underage boy, and not the woman, hit the jackpot.

Elvis Presley performed 837 consecutive sold-out performances at the International (later renamed the Las Vegas Hilton).

"The all-time single concert box-office record occurred in Las Vegas. The show took place on New Year's Eve 1999 for the Barbra Streisand concert production at the MGM Grand. It grossed $14,694,750 from 12,477 tickets sold."[74]

The first topless showgirls debuted in "Minsky's Follies" at the Dunes in 1957.

The year 1959 marked the beginning of the longest running show in Las Vegas, the *Follies Bergere* at the Tropicana Hotel.

In 1993 the MGM Grand Las Vegas was the largest hotel in the world. Today, with its 6,852 rooms, the MGM Grand is the second largest, after the Venetian. Average number of pillow cases washed daily at the MGM—15,000.

In Las Vegas, the Rio and the Wynn casino-resort do not have any elevator floors that start with the number "four." According to feng shui, the ancient Chinese belief in aesthetics, the number four is unlucky. Also due to superstitions, 13 is considered an "unlucky" number. Thus most hotels skip the floor or do other things to avoid using the number 13.

REMEMBER LAS VEGAS JUNKETS?

Once upon a time junket operators assembled groups of 50 or more avid gamblers, crammed them into a chartered airplane and flew them to Las Vegas. When they arrived, limousines and buses would hurry them to the sponsoring casino-hotel, where the players were wined and dined, then flown home three days later—a lot lighter in cash, of course.

One of the great junketeers was "Big Julie" Weintraub of the Dunes. A New York City diamond dealer, he ended up owing the Dunes a gambling tab of $100,000. The Dunes offered him a deal to pay it off if he would bring other diamond dealers to play at the Dunes. Supposedly, during his reign as "Junket King," he brought more than 12,000 players to the Dunes out of New York City—and that's how junkets originated.

Many of the stories I relate to evolved during my 12 years of working in Las Vegas. Perhaps the best advice I ever got came from a gravelly old gentleman I met playing poker at the Sahara Casino in 1981. His name was Al, and he sat next to me at a $1-$5-limit seven-card stud game. Earlier, I had learned that Al was a very wealthy man and had made his money investing in Vegas real estate. At the time, I was interested in real estate, but had just moved to Las Vegas and was broke.

After a few hours of getting acquainted with Al, I asked him a pertinent question. "Al, what kind of advice would you offer an up-and-coming real estate investor who wanted to buy their first property in Las Vegas?"

Al thought for a moment, then simply replied, "Buy land on the Strip." That's all I ever got out of him. Later I was told by someone who knew Al well that he held several ground leases on huge parcels of land on the Vegas Strip where a number of large casinos were built. Notably, Al usually arrived at the Sahara in a chauffeur-driven limousine, and his driver typically sat nearby while Al played $1-$5 stud poker.

GLAMOUR AND GLITZ

Las Vegas has a myriad of titles, and no one is more proud of that than the Las Vegas Convention and Visitors Authority. They'll tell you that Las Vegas is the convention capital, the sign capital, and the gambling capital, and ever since the city captured the National Finals Rodeo in 1985 it's the rodeo capital. Yet its grandest title, one, according to the *Review-Journal,* "it clings to with sheer two-fisted tenacity, is 'The Entertainment Capital of the World.'"

Over the years, the world's greatest entertainers and most beloved stars graced the stages of Vegas venues. Jimmy Durante opened the Flamingo in 1947. Elvis Presley debuted at the New Frontier in 1956. In the early 1960s, Frank Sinatra's legendary Rat Pack brought fans to Las Vegas from all over the country. Over the years many great performers made Las Vegas their home, including such greats as Johnny Carson, Redd Foxx, Paul Anka, Wayne Newton, Robert Goulet, Alan King, and Jerry Lewis.

Although not all these celebrities lived in Vegas, the city served them in other important ways. For instance, Natalie Wood and Robert Wagner honeymooned here. Elvis married Priscilla here, and he made his comeback at the International in 1969. Ronald Reagan attempted a nightclub show here, and Wally Cox bombed as a stand-up comedian here.

In Las Vegas you could see the great Hollywood stars, Cary Grant and Gregory Peck sitting ringside at Caesars Palace or the MGM Grand arena. Some of the most famous prize fights were fought here, including Sugar Ray Leonard versus Tommy Hearns in September 1981, Marvin Hagler versus Tommy Hearns in April 1985, and the trilogy of bouts between Evander Holyfield and Riddick Bowe between 1992 and 1995.

Jerry Lewis hosts his Muscular Dystrophy Telethon in Las Vegas, and the PGA hosts the pro-celebrity golf tournament here. From the best of times to the worst of times, entertainment's finest stars still shine in Las Vegas. You can see these real-life legends in person everywhere you look on the fabulous Strip. Nowadays it's Cher, Elton John, or Celine Dion performing at Caesars Palace. You can see Garth Brooks at the Wynn, or Penn and Teller doing their magic at the Rio. And performing at Harrah's is comedian mainstay Rita Rudner.

MOVIES SET IN LAS VEGAS

Over the passage of time, film makers discovered that scenic Las Vegas helps augment the production of vivid photography, hence the city has become popular among both film and television producers. Following are the release dates of films set in Las Vegas:

1957; *The Amazing Colossal Man.* 1960; *Ocean's Eleven.* 1964; *Viva Las Vegas.* 1971; *Diamonds Are Forever.* 1978; *Corvette Summer.* 1987; *Over the Top.* 1988; *Rain Man,* and *Midnight Run.* 1991: *Harley Davidson and the Marlboro Man,* and *Bugsy.* 1992; *Honeymoon in Vegas.* 1993; *Indecent Proposal.* 1994; *The Stand.* 1995; *Casino, Showgirls, Leaving Las Vegas,* and *Leprechaun 3.* 1996; *Swingers.* 1997; *Austin Powers: International Man of Mystery, Con Air,* and *Vegas Vacation.* 1998; *Fear and Loathing in Las Vegas, Speedway Junky,* and *Very Bad Things.* 1999; *Go,* and *Jack of Hearts.* 2000; *Pay It Forward.* 2001; *3000 Miles to Graceland, Rush Hour 2,* and *Ocean's Eleven.* 2003; *The Cooler.* 2005; *Miss Congeniality 2: Armed and Fabulous.* 2007; *Lucky You.* 2008; *The Grand, 21, What Happens in Vegas,* and *Crazy Girls Undercover.* 2009; *The Hangover.*

TELEVISION SHOWS
PRODUCED IN LAS VEGAS

The list of TV shows produced in Las Vegas includes such old-time favorites as *Vega$* starring Robert Urich as private detective Dan Tana, to today's popular *Las Vegas,* starring James Caan as president of the storied Montecito Casino. Other TV series include *Pawn Stars, Poker After Dark, High Stakes Poker,* and *CSI: Crime Scene Investigation.*

ECONOMIC OUTLOOK FOR LAS VEGAS

"It was the best of times. It was the worst of times," wrote Charles Dickens.

Economically 2007 was the best year ever for Las Vegas. More than 40 million visitors came to our city, and remarkably they gambled and spent record amounts of money. Unfortunately, that same year saw the start of a terrible economic downturn and the beginning of a housing devaluation. In time, it crippled the Las Vegas economy and adversely affected the overall real estate market, hurting many middle-class homeowners by sending realty values tumbling. Las Vegas eventually acquired a new unwanted title—the foreclosure capital of America.

Adding to the city's woes, gaming revenues and overall spending, along with visitor traffic, were off nearly 20 percent from their peak in 2007. By July of 2010, residential realty values had fallen an average of 53 percent. Convention activity in Las Vegas was also off by 1.5 million visitors in 2009.

Since late in 2007, "Southern Nevada's economy is submerged in the deepest recession the United States has seen since the Great Depression, and not even the most extravagant megaresort opening in the history of Las Vegas is going to pull it out," said UNLV economist Mary Riddel in December 2008.

The *Review-Journal* noted, "Virtually every sector of the local economy, particularly tourism and construction, shed jobs this year, pushing the unemployment rate to 13 percent. Home prices have yet to find their bottom and foreclosures continue to mount."

Another economist made an interesting observation—Prior to this horrible recession, people used the increase in home values as an ATM machine, and that's not happening anymore!

Evidence of the economic downturn can be seen along Las Vegas Boulevard. Projects such as Fontainebleau, the Echelon, and the St. Regis condo tower at Palazzo stopped construction, costing the local economy $1.16 billion in lost construction in 2008, and almost $2 billion in 2009.

Nevertheless, given sufficient time Las Vegas will rebound as it always has, continuing to be America's top tourist attraction, reigning entertainment showplace of the nation, rodeo capital, and a generally a great place to live.

On the more positive side, if Billy Wilkerson were alive today, he would be astounded to know that Las Vegas casinos have generated over $200 billion in gaming revenue and visitor spending since the Flamingo opened in 1947.

WYNN LAS VEGAS
SETS A NEW DESIGN STANDARD

When the Wynn Las Vegas opened in May 2005, thousands of tourists streamed into the lavish $2.7 billion casino-resort to ogle its Ferrari dealership, 22 restaurants, 18-hole golf course with a waterfall, and man-made mountain.

"But even in over-the-top Las Vegas, bigger is not necessarily better. For all its hype, Wynn Las Vegas was built with intimacy in mind," said Ron Kramer, president of Wynn Resorts from 2002 to March 2008, in a *Review-Journal* interview. "The scale of things became too big, Las Vegas started to lose its appeal."

Legendary casino entrepreneur Steve Wynn set a standard for luxurious mega-resorts when he built the Mirage in 1989. His casino-resorts are known for their eye-catching attractions, such as the erupting volcano at the Mirage, pirates battling the British in a lagoon at Treasure Island, and 1,200 synchronized fountains that dance to music in a 8.5-acre lake at the Bellagio.

He decided to redesign the prototype of the Las Vegas casino-resort with his latest creation. "That's why it took him two years just to design it," explained Kramer. "He re-examined all components because Las Vegas has evolved."

Wynn Las Vegas is huge, with 2,700 hotel rooms. But it shows another departure from traditional casino design. The concept was to do away with the seemingly endless corridors that have become the norm in the city's big casino-hotels. Instead, Wynn designed several elevator banks along the resort's curved length. "People don't want to walk 15 minutes just to get to the elevator," says Kramer.

Kramer explained, "Before, the entertainment or attraction was on the outside. But here we're not giving away entertainment on the street level." Actually, the 50-story bronze-colored structure is the attraction itself. The Wynn Las Vegas has windows in every conference room, and restaurants overlook the lush landscape outside. Picturesque views are a significant shift from the traditional ploys of eliminating clocks and windows in hopes of enticing gamblers to stay on the casino floor by keeping them from noticing the passage of time—a ploy introduced by Billy Wilkerson in his original Flamingo design.

Both casino operators and their guests have matured. The new-age casino operators realize that visitors to Las Vegas don't have to be tricked into gambling, as there are plenty of other ways to get them to part with their money. Much like other big casino resorts in the city, the Wynn Las Vegas developed substantial non-gaming enterprises, such as theaters, spas, bars, and restaurants, thereby establishing comprehensive entertainment centers under one roof.

The benefits are clear: Las Vegas generated $35.2 billion in non-gaming revenue in 2009, which was four times the amount of gaming revenue, according to the Las Vegas Convention and Visitors Authority. "Las Vegas was about gambling. Now it has evolved into an entertainment center. There's the ability to mix the two," said Kramer.

"Wynn Las Vegas is just the beginning of a new 'fourth generation' of casino development in Las Vegas," says David Schwartz, head of the Gaming Research Studies Center at the University of Nevada Las Vegas, which released this report in 2008. "The first generation was that of 'glorified clubs with casinos,' such as gangster Bugsy Siegel's infamous Flamingo Hotel of the 1940s. Next came casinos with large-scale hotels with as many as 1,500 rooms in the late 1960s," Schwartz added. The third generation of the 1990s had a much bigger emphasis on non-gaming revenue and attractions."

The up-and-coming $11.3-billion CityCenter project is another example of fourth-generation casino development. Its stronger residential component is exemplified by its luxury condo towers, in addition to casinos, hotels, and shopping arcades.

Wynn Las Vegas set a new standard for design and luxury, but the company knew it must also have its base of mass market consumers. "Its Ferrari dealership, for example, serves as much to create buzz as to sell cars. 'There will be the person who decides to spend $300,000 on a new Ferrari,' said Kramer. 'But then there's the larger market who can afford a $16 T-shirt and gets to take his picture next to the car.'

Kramer concluded, "As we grow the top end of the market, we also grow the bottom end. It's not just about high-roller business but also about slot machines and growing the masses."

Something else as an added perspective about designing the casino as an inducement to gamble, and displaying extreme luxury to make guests feel welcome. According to author, Chris Roerden, today's shrewd casino developers use "an aura of wealth and opulence as psychological strategies to immerse guests in such wealth and comfort for timeless days that they enjoy living the lifestyle to which they aspire: that they want more of it; that they actually deserve more of it; and that the easiest and quickest path for reaching the lifestyle that they've a right to have is to gamble and win it."

IS THE MOB STILL IN LAS VEGAS?

Most don't think so. Back in the old days, most lenders wouldn't finance Las Vegas casinos. It was Teamster money that ultimately financed Las Vegas casinos. In 1967 new legislation made it easier to finance Nevada casinos, and made it less complicated for corporations to own casinos. Some believe the mob may have their fingers in the restaurants, but not in the casinos.

Steve Wynn financed his Mirage with junk bonds, and Bill Bennett financed his Circus Circus empire with a public stock offering.

The years of Howard Hughes are in the past, but his influence will be forever felt. All together, 14 publicly owned conglomerates bought into Nevada in the 1960s and 1970s. The Nevada Legislature passed in 1967 and amended in 1969, several Gaming Acts allowing corporations to own casinos, which forever changed Las Vegas. It allowed publicly traded corporations to be registered as holders of gaming licenses, providing a broader base for investment in the gaming industry and giving Nevada that long-sought respectability.

Who would ever imagine that the legitimization of a seductive vice would be responsible for creating some 76 Las Vegas casinos. Or that those casinos would ultimately generate over $200 billion in combined gaming revenue and visitor spending by the end of 2009?

This author contends that it was the acclaimed Hollywood publisher and nightclub owner Billy Wilkerson who truly invented Las Vegas. It was solely his idea to design and build a desert oasis that would house all his passions under one roof, so nothing could interfere with the true gambling experience. His Flamingo resort would become the inspiration for modern Las Vegas and would alter the landscape of the city and casino gaming forever.

Bugsy Siegel and the boys back East merely muscled in on the partially constructed Flamingo, and wrongly got credit for its creation. Siegel, of course, because of his connection to the Flamingo in the final phases of its development, was also erroneously credited with creating the Fabulous Las Vegas Strip. But you and I know differently, regardless of what was said in the film *Bugsy*, that credit really has to go to Billy Wilkerson.

Best of luck in your own Las Vegas adventure.
—Andrew James McLean

ENDNOTES

1. A compilation of quotes by Warren Beatty from the 1991 film *Bugsy*.

2. Wilkerson, W.R. III. *The Man Who Invented Las Vegas.* Beverly Hills, CA: Ciro Books, 2000.

3. Ibid.

4. Balboni, Alan. *Beyond the Mafia: Italian Americans and the Development of Las Vegas.* University of Nevada Press. 2006.

5. Kelley, Kitty. *His Way: The Unauthorized Biography of Frank Sinatra.* Bantam Books, 1986. P.159.

6.	Hopkins, A.D. *Las Vegas Review-Journal* article. The First 100 Persons: Robbins Cahill.

7.	Smith, John L. *Sharks in the Desert*. Barricade books, 2005. P. 62.

8.	Ibid. P. 64

9.	Smith, John L. *Sharks in the Desert*. Barricade Books, 2005.

10.	Roemer, William F. Jr., *The Enforcer: Spilotro, Chicago's Man Over Las Vegas*. New York: Donald I Fine, 1995. P. 9.

11.	Holdorf, Bob. *Las Vegas Review-Journal* article.

12.	Smith, John L. *Las Vegas Review-Journal* article: The First 100 Persons. Part II; Resorts Rising. Moe Dalitz.

13.	Ibid.

14.	Ibid.

15.	Ibid.

16.	Bruno, Anthony. Crime Library online.

17.	*Las Vegas Review-Journal* article: The First 100 Persons; Ben Siegel.

18.	Smith, John L. *Las Vegas Review-Journal* article September 10, 2003. Marshall Caifano.

19. Maas, Peter. *The Valachi Papers.* 2003. Harper Paperbacks.

20. Smith, John L. *Las Vegas Review-Journal* article September 10, 2003. Marshall Caifano.

21. Rappleye, Charles, and Ed Becker. *All American Mafioso—The Johnny Rosselli Story.* New York: Doubleday, 1991.

22. Ibid.

23. Pileggi, Nicholas Casino: *Love and Honor in Las Vegas.* 1995. P. 24–25.

24. Roemer, William F. Jr. *The Enforcer: Spilotro, Chicago's Man Over Las Vegas.* New York: Donald I. Fine, 1995.

25. O'Connor, Matt. *Chicago Tribune* article May 21, 2005. P. 4.

26. Hopkins, A.D. *Las Vegas Review-Journal* article, The First 100 Persons. Benny Binion.

27. Knapp, George. Newsnow.com. Street Talk.

28. "A History of the WSOP: The Champions." PokerRoom.com. On game Network Ltd.

29. Maheu, Robert, and Richard Hack. *Next to Hughes: Behind the Power and Tragic Downfall of Howard Hughes,* New York: Harper Collins, 1992.

30. *Life* magazine article, April 6, 1951.

31. Maheu, Robert, and Richard Hack. *Next to Hughes: Behind the Power and Tragic Downfall of Howard Hughes*, New York: Harper Collins, 1992.

32. Evans, K.J. *Las Vegas Review-Journal* article. The First 100 Persons. Howard Hughes.

33. *Las Vegas Review-Journal* article. The First 100 Persons. Kirk Kerkorian.

34. Ibid.

35. Torgenson, Dial. *Kerkorian: An American Success Story.* 1974.

36. *Las Vegas Review-Journal* article. The First 100 Persons. Kirk Kerkorian.

37. Ibid.

38. Ibid.

39. Torgerson, Dial. *Kerkorian: American Success Story.* 1974.

40. *Las Vegas Review-Journal* article. The First 100 Persons. Parry Thomas.

41. Hopkins, A.D. *Las Vegas Review-Journal* article. The First 100 Persons. Steve Wynn.

42. Vinson, Barney. *Las Vegas: Behind the Tables.* Gollehon Press. 1988. P. 46.

43. Ibid. P. 120.

44. Weatherford, Mike. *Las Vegas Review-Journal* article. The First 100 Persons. Frank Sinatra.

45. Kelley, Kitty. *My Way: The Unauthorized Biography of Frank Sinatra.* Bantam Books, 1986.

46. Fischer, Steve. *When the Mob Ran Vegas.* Berkline Press. 2006. P. 166.

47. Kelley, Kitty. *My Way: The Unauthorized Biography of Frank Sinatra.* Bantam Books, 1986.

48. Ibid.

49. Ibid.

50. Mckuen, Rod. www.mckuen.com/flights/

51. Guralnick, Peter. *Last Train to Memphis: Rise of Elvis Presley.* Abacus. 1995. P. 168.

52. Ibid.

53. *Newsweek* magazine, unknown author and date. Compiled from *Review-Journal* article: The First 100 Persons; Elvis Presley.

54. Guralnick, Peter. *Last Train to Memphis: Rise of Elvis Presley.* Abacus. 1995.

55. Hollywood Five-O, online site.

56. Tosches, Nick. *Dino: Living High in the Dirty Business of Dreams.* Vintage, London, 1999, P. 57.

57. *Las Vegas Review-Journal* article. The First 100 Persons. Dean Martin.

58. Ibid.

59. Wikipedia online. Dean Martin.

60. Smith, John L. *The Animal in Hollywood.* Barricade Books, 2004.

61. Freedland, Michael. *Dean Martin: King of the Road.* Robson Books Ltd, 2004.

62. Ibid.

63. Ibid.

64. Davis, Sammy Jr., *Yes, I Can: The Story of Sammy Davis Jr.,* Farrar, Straus & Giroux Inc., 1965, 1990.

65. Ibid.

66. *Las Vegas Review-Journal* article. The First 100 Persons. Wayne Newton.

67. Online. Gamblers handbook.net. Kerry Packer.

68. *New York Magazine* article, May 7, 1984.

69. *Sydney Morning Herald* article. Kerry Packer, December 28, 2005.

70. Frey, James H., and William Eadinton. *Gambling Views From the Social Sciences. The Annals of the American Academy of Political and Social Science.* Beverly Hills, CA.: Sage Publications, 1984. Compiled from *Las Vegas: Behind the Tables,* P. 43-44

71. Fremont Street Historical Facts, on-line site.

72. Ibid.

73. Ibid. P. 194-195.

74. earlyvegas.com. History of MGM Las Vegas Hotel.

BIBLIOGRAPHY

Bacall, Lauren. *By Myself.* New York: Alfred A. Knopf, 1979.

Balboni, Alan. *Beyond the Mafia: Italian Americans and the Development of Las Vegas.* University of Nevada Press, 2006.

Chung, Su Kim. *Las Vegas Then and Now.* Thunder Bay Press, 2007.

Davis, Sammy Jr., *Yes, I Can: The Story of Sammy Davis Jr.* Farrar, Straus & Giroux Inc., 1965, 1990.

Davis, Sammy Jr., *Sammy: The Autobiography of Sammy Davis, Jr.,* 2000.

Davis, Sammy Jr., *Why Me? The Sammy Davis Jr., Story,* Warner Books, 1990.

Demaris, Ovid and Ed Reid. *Green Felt Jungle.* Buccaneer Books, 1963.

Denton, Sally and Roger Morris, *The Money and Power: The Making of Las Vegas and Its Hold on America.* Vintage, 2002.

Dietrich, Noah. *Howard: The Amazing Mr. Hughes.* Coronet, 1972.

Edmonds, Andy. *Bugsy's Baby: The Secret Life of Mob Queen Virginia Hill.* Secaucus, New Jersey. Carol Publishing, 1993.

Fischer, Steve. *When the Mob Ran Vegas.* Berkline Press. 2006.

Flamini. Roland. *Ava.* New York: Coward, McCann and Geoghegan, 1983.

Freedland, Michael. *Dean Martin: King of the Road.* Robson Books Ltd, 2004.

Frey, James H., and William Eadinton. *Gambling Views From the Social Sciences.* The Annals of the American Academy of Political and Social Science. Beverly Hills, CA. Sage Publications, 1984.

Guralnick, Peter. *Last Train to Memphis: The Rise of Elvis Presley.* Little Brown, 1994.

Hammer, Richard. *Playboy's Illustrated History of Organized Crime.* Playboy Press, 1975.

Higham. Charles. *Ava.* New York: Delacorte Press, 1974.

Hopkins, A.D., and K. J. Evans, editors. *The First 100: Portraits of the Men and Women Who Shaped Las Vegas.* Las Vegas, Nevada. Huntington Press, 1999.

Johnston, David. *Temples of Chance; How America Inc. Bought Out Murder Inc. to Win Control of the Casino Business.* Doubleday, 1992.

Kelley, Kitty. *His Way: The Unauthorized Biography of Frank Sinatra.* Bantam Books, 1986.

Lacey, Robert. *Little Man: Meyer Lansky and the Gangster Life.* Little Brown, 1991.

Lewis, Jerry. *Dean & Me: A Love Story.* Doubleday Books, 2005.

Linn, Edward. *Big Julie of Vegas.* Greenwich, Connecticut: Fawcett Publications, 1974.

Maheu, Robert, and Richard Hack. *Next to Hughes: Behind the Power and Tragic Downfall of Howard Hughes.* New York: Harper Collins, 1992.

Neff, James. *Mobbed Up: Jackie Presser's High-Wire Life in the Teamsters, the Mafia, and the FBI.* New York: Dell, 1989.

Niven, David. *The Moon's a Balloon.* Penguin, 2005.

Pileggi, Nicholas. *Casino: Love and Honor in Las Vegas.* New York: Simon & Shuster, 1995.

Presley, Priscilla. *Elvis and Me.* Putnam Pub Group (T); 4th Edition. 1985.

Rappleye, Charles, and Ed Becker. *All American Mafioso—The Johnny Rosselli Story.* New York: Doubleday, 1991.

Roemer, William F. Jr., *The Enforcer: Spilotro, Chicago's Man Over Las Vegas.* New York: Donald I. Fine, 1995.

Smith, John L. *Sharks in the Desert.* Barricade Books, 2005.

Smith, John L. *The Animal in Hollywood.* Barricade Books, 1998.

Torgenson, Dial. *Kerkorian: An American Success Story.* New York. The Dial Press, 1974.

Turner, Wallace. *Gambler's Money.* Houghton Mifflin; 1965.

Victor, Adam. *The Elvis Encyclopedia.* Overlook Hardcover, 2008.

Vinson, Barney. *Las Vegas: Behind the Tables.* Gollehon Press, 1988.

Wilkerson, W.R. III. *The Man Who Invented Las Vegas.* Beverly Hills, CA: Ciro Books, 2000.

MAGAZINES AND NEWSPAPERS

Chicago Tribune	*Look*
Daily News	*Los Angeles Times*
Esquire	*Newsweek*
Las Vegas Business Press	*New York Magazine*
Las Vegas Review-Journal	*Photoplay*
Las Vegas Sun	*Sydney Morning Herald*

INTERNET

City of Las Vegas History, LasVegasNevada.gov.

Fremont Street Historical Facts, on-line site.

History of MGM Las Vegas Hotel. earlyvegas.com.

PokerRoom.com.

RECOMMENDED READING

*R*egarding Las Vegas statistics, the author read articles by the Las Vegas Convention and Visitors Authority, State of Nevada Gaming Control Board, and McCarran International Airport.

Havers, Richard. *Sinatra*. DK Publishing. 2004.

Las Vegas Review-Journal article about Siegfried & Roy by the Humane Society of the United States (HSUS).

Tapert, Annette. *Siegfried & Roy: Mastering the Impossible*.

PORTRAITS
AND PHOTO CREDITS

PORTRAITS BY DAVID TOMASOVSKY,
GULFPORT, MISSISSIPPI

pp. 3, 15, 36, 66, 78, 85, 98, 107, 111, 141, 144, 178, 180, 181, 193, 206, 211, 221, 228, 236, 243, 253, 263, 269

PHOTO CREDITS

Personal Collection of the Author, pp. 7, 183, 188, 211, 300, 320, 324, 369
FBI Files; Freedom of Information Act, pp. 56, 87
Private collections; pp. 7, 183, 188, 211, 300, 322, 326, 373

ABOUT THE AUTHOR

a former casino executive and 12-year resident of Las Vegas, Andrew McLean was a table games employee at the Flamingo, the Dunes, and Circus Circus. He's a graduate of Michigan State University, 1972, and along with his partner and soul mate, Liz Rouse, resides along the Gulf Coast of Mississippi.

McLean is the bestselling lead author of *Investing in Real Estate* (6th Edition) and co-author with George H. Ross, Donald Trump's right-hand man in *Trump Strategies For Real Estate; Billionaire Lessons For the Small Investor*, published in four languages by John Wiley & Sons. McLean is also the author of several other books listed on the following page.

Investing in Real Estate with Gary Eldred, 6th edition, John Wiley & Sons. 2009. Other translated versions available in Russian, Chinese, and Vietnamese.

Casino Player's Handbook: The Ultimate Guide to Where and How to Play in America's Casinos. 1998.

The RV Book: The Ultimate Guide to Selecting and Operating a Recreational Vehicle. 2000.

The Complete Guide to Real Estate Loans. John Wiley & Sons, 1983.

Making Money in Foreclosures: How to Invest Profitably in Distressed Real Estate. McGraw-Hill, 2007.

Invite Andrew to your next event for a lively and entertaining look at Las Vegas history, celebrities, gamblers, and gangsters! Visit www.AndrewJamesMcLean.com for more details.

INDEX

C

D

T

X

Xanadu Princess Resort, 125

Y

Yasuda, Ginji, 169, 382
Young, Brigham, 302
Yuman, Bernie, 225

Z

Zech, Oscar, 186
Zwillman, Longy, 50

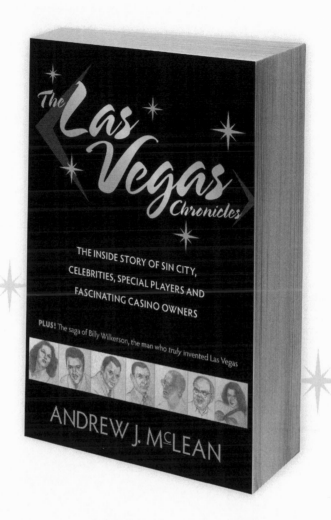

Visit www.AndrewJamesMcLean.com to order extra copies of *The Las Vegas Chronicles: The Inside Story of Sin City, Celebrities, Special Players and Fascinating Casino Owners* and discover additional photos of Vegas past and present!

Bulk Discounts Available for Dealers!

www.AndrewJamesMcLean.com